The Work of Disaster

The Work of Disaster

Crisis and Care Along a Himalayan Fault Line

AIDAN SEALE-FELDMAN

The University of Chicago Press
Chicago and London

The University of Chicago Press, Chicago 60637
The University of Chicago Press, Ltd., London
© 2025 by The University of Chicago
Published 2025

34 33 32 31 30 29 28 27 26 25   1 2 3 4 5

ISBN-13: 978-0-226-84386-5 (cloth)
ISBN-13: 978-0-226-84539-5 (paper)
ISBN-13: 978-0-226-84538-8 (ebook)
DOI: https://doi.org/10.7208/chicago/9780226845388.001.0001

Library of Congress Cataloging-in-Publication Data

Names: Seale-Feldman, Aidan, author
Title: The work of disaster : crisis and care along a Himalayan fault line /
    Aidan Seale-Feldman.
Description: Chicago : The University of Chicago Press, 2025. |
    Includes bibliographical references and index.
Identifiers: LCCN 2025022960 | ISBN 9780226843865 (cloth) |
    ISBN 9780226845395 (paperback) | ISBN 9780226845388 (ebook)
Subjects: LCSH: Nepal Earthquake, 2015 (April 25). | Crisis intervention (Mental
    health services)—Nepal. | Crisis intervention (Mental health services)—Moral
    and ethical aspects—Nepal. | Mental health counseling—Nepal. | Disaster
    medicine—Nepal. | Non-governmental organizations—Nepal.
Classification: LCC HV600 2015.N35 N43 2025 | DDC 362.2/04251095496—
    dc23/eng/20250724
LC record available at https://lccn.loc.gov/2025022960

Authorized Representative for EU General Product Safety
Regulation (GPSR) queries: **Easy Access System Europe**—Mustamäe tee 50, 10621
Tallinn, Estonia, gpsr.requests@easproject.com
Any other queries: https://press.uchicago.edu/press/contact.html

How could there be destruction
Without becoming?
How could there be death without birth?
There is no destruction without becoming.

NAGARJUNA, "Examination of
Becoming and Destruction"

Contents

Map viii
Abbreviations ix
Transliteration xi
Prologue: Notes on Disaster xiii

Introduction: Rupture 1

1: Crisis 23

2: Loss 46

3: Solidarity 64

4: Efficacy 86

5: Care 109

Conclusion: Repair 131

Acknowledgments 141
Notes 145
Bibliography 163
Index 181

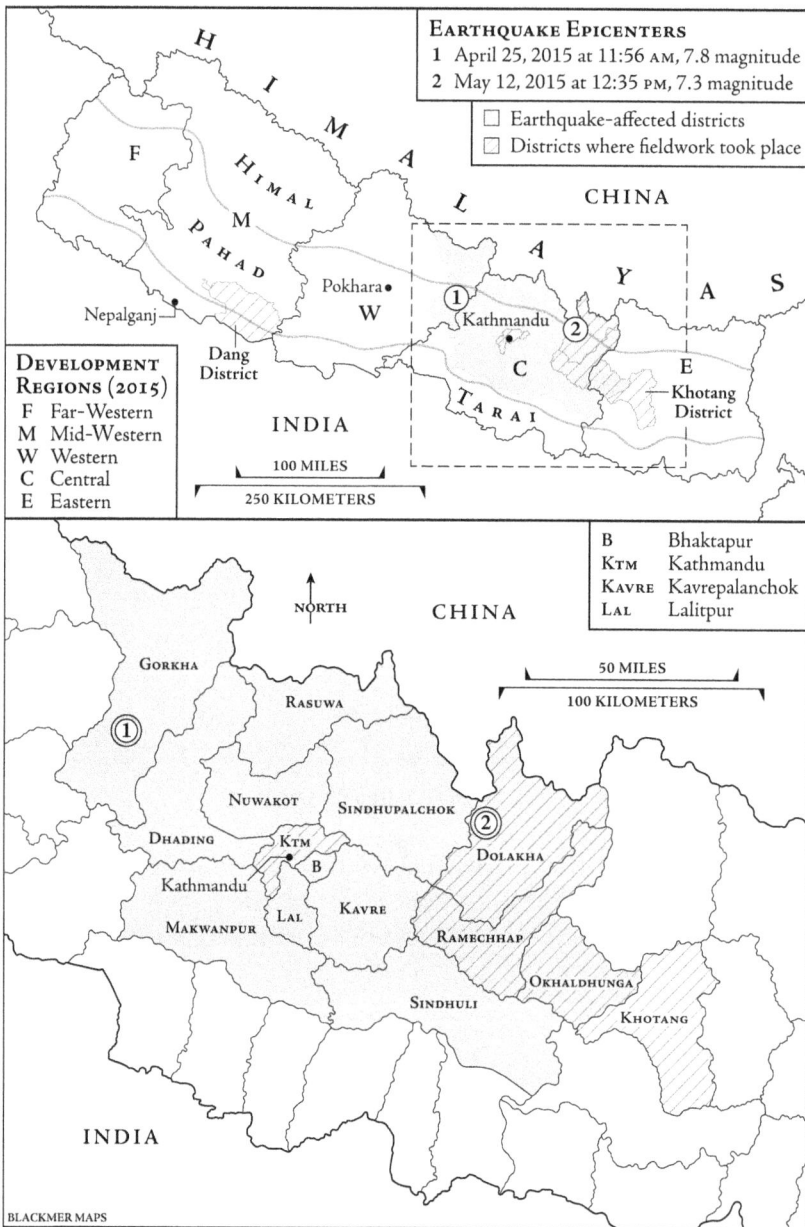

Map of earthquake-affected districts in Nepal (2015). Created by Kate Blackmer.

Abbreviations

c p s w : community psychosocial worker
f c h v : female community health volunteer
i a s c : Inter-Agency Standing Committee (a forum to promote humanitarian coordination)
i n g o : international nongovernmental organization
m g m h : Movement for Global Mental Health
m h p s s : mental health and psychosocial support
n g o : nongovernmental organization
r c t : randomized control trial
u m n : United Mission to Nepal
v d c : Village Development Committee
w f m h : World Federation for Mental Health
w h o : World Health Organization

Transliteration

Nepali is an Indo-Aryan language that is written in the Devanagari script. When translating Nepali words into English, I have chosen to remove diacritic marks and represent words phonetically in order to make the sounds of the Nepali language more accessible for a broad audience. For example, āmā (mother) is spelled as ama, and cāmal (uncooked rice) is spelled as chamal.

Prologue

Notes on Disaster

1.

Radha said that on the night before the earthquake, the moon was upside down.[1] I was in the forest herding goats with two sisters when the earth started shaking. We crouched down and held on to each other. We saw people standing outside their homes, and then we heard them screaming. We watched from the forest above. A strange fog descended. The shaking stopped. Some boys lit a fire of dry pine needles, and it ignited. We were cold, and it was warm. We gathered around the fire and listened to the news about the earthquake on the cell phone radio of a man dressed in white, the Hindu color of mourning.

2.

I didn't see the images until two days later. Radha, her husband (Chandra), and I were watching one of the only televisions in the village. There were images of people lining up for water in Kathmandu, holding buckets and bottles, images of people being loaded into helicopters, images of stone houses flattened into piles of rubble and tin roofs collapsed like a scattered deck of cards. An old man stands in the rubble of his home and is interviewed by a newscaster. "What can you tell us about your suffering?" the newscaster asks. "We've received a little bit of *chamal* [uncooked rice] from the government, that's all," he says. A child is shown with bandages on her hands and feet. She is sucking on a partially inflated balloon.

3.

Chandra talks about the evils of *tension*. He says "tension is a disease" and that I can't worry about the earthquake or about death. Others agree that tension is an illness. They say sheep die from tension. Chandra says he's not afraid of death because it will just happen, like fainting. I ask, "What if it is a slow process?" He replies that there is one world, and even though I was born in America, now I have family and friends here. He says, "We are all human, your heart is the same." He says, "You have no reason to feel *tension*. You are our *mit chhori*, adopted daughter, you have food, a place to stay, you can stay ten years and there wouldn't be a problem."

4.

When the earthquake happened, everything seemed silent.

5.

All I can think about is my friend M's two-year-old sister being buried by the stones of her house. Of the voice on the phone—"M's sister has died."

6.

Hira and Gauri, the neighbor's daughters, come into my room to visit me. They stay and chat. Gauri brushes my hair and braids it. She puts lipstick on me and *gajal* (eyeliner). She gives me a *bindi* (a dot placed between the eyebrows). Everything is calm and quiet. Outside the sun has come out, and there is a gentle breeze.

7.

I heard that during the earthquake the ground moved one meter into the air and then fell.

8.

On the radio: A story of a man wearing a wig running around Kathmandu screaming that the biggest earthquake would come tonight. The man was arrested but the rumors spread. Even Chandra asks me, "Will it come tonight?"

9.

While walking with Chandra from the bazaar to the village, I ask, "Why is it that people from my country rush to help Nepal, when they ignore those suffering close by?" "Prestige," he replies, in English.

10.

Last night, sleepless sleep. Sweating and the sensation of insect bites. Dreams also, but of what? The other night, dreams of someone breaking my microphone, and there was a scramble to put belongings into bags.

11.

On the radio they say: One hundred thousand cartons of instant noodles have been donated for the victims.

12.

I am attending a *bastu puja* at a friend's house in the village. The puja is for the health of the house and the animals. A priest is there to administer the ritual. The floor is covered in plates of leaves overflowing with offerings to the gods—rice, flowers, money, and rings of sweet fried dough (*sel roti*). The men bring in an uncastrated goat and sacrifice him behind a screen in a corner. Life offered for life. The priest lights the ritual fire. A pile of rope made of grass lies nearby, later to be tied around the exterior of the house for protection. The ground is decorated with a mandala drawn in flour. The smoke is thick inside the room. My eyes are burning. I step outside. Suddenly a deep rumbling comes from the earth—we are running. I have someone else's child in my arms. Everything is crooked.

13.

People say that the next earthquake will come between 12:00 and 2:00 p.m. every day. People go around talking about the earthquake; everyone feels like they could die at any moment. "We will all be killed," a man says, wandering drunkenly out of Didi's house. My village friend Pratima says this all happened because Nepalis are *papi*, sinful. "They take only for themselves while they let others suffer, they don't believe in God." She says only 50 percent believe in God and are good, dharmic people, while 50 percent are sinful. Grandmother, narrowing her eyes, corrects her. "No, only 1 in 3 people is dharmic, the rest are *papi*."

14.

Can't write, difficult to think.

15.

Last night the wholesale suppliers for the store came. They are young, around my age, and they drove by motorcycle from the district headquarters. The younger one drank a lot of beer and started talking about how, since the earthquake, they sleep inside because their "fate is written." If he is going to die, he is going to die, he said. He could die at any moment, on the road on the motorcycle, in his sleep in his bed. He's not afraid because his destiny is already determined. I want to say that where I'm from we believe in individual human agency, but instead, I stay quiet. Chandra talks about how strong his house is, after which even the man whose fate is already written says, "Yes, but if you see the houses that fell in Sindhupalchok, they were mud and stone just like yours."

16.

Dizziness, as if every minute another earthquake has come. Chandra keeps saying you can't let your heart-mind, *man*, dwell on the earthquake because you'll feel dizzy all day, *ringata lagne*. You could faint, and then when the earthquake comes, you won't be able to escape. Everyone's mind is on the earthquake. Wherever people go they are scanning the surroundings, thinking about where and how they will escape, *bhagne*. In the village everyone around is saying, "If we die, it's our fate."

17.

I say I am scared. Radha says, "We haven't left you."

18.

The man drinking *jar* (rice liquor) inside the shop says he can sleep well at night because "if you're going to die, you will die."

19.

We listen to Radio Nepal at high volume all day, every day, on the solar-powered system that is roped to the top-floor balcony. A melancholy recording from an older time plays over and over again. The song is called "Which Temple Will You Go To, Pilgrim?" ("Kun Mandirma Janchhau Yatri") and has been adapted from the famous poem by Laxshmi Prasad Devkota. In the song, the popular performer Robin Sharma sings about a pilgrim's journey to a sacred temple. "What temple are you going to, pilgrim? What ritual objects will you use, and how will you take them with you?" As the poem continues the pilgrim reaches not a physical temple but a corporeal one in which the body has become a holy structure; bones become pillars, flesh becomes walls, the brain a golden roof, "of the senses all the doors." The poem ends with the reassurance that "in songs of grief, Indra, god of the heavens, sings human-kind's afflictions" and summons the pilgrim to return home to "rub balm on all the sorrow and the smarting wounds" of human life.[2] The song fades out. A radio broadcast comes on the air:

> The catastrophic earthquakes have caused so much damage—we are with our listeners. We have been conducting programs related to rescue, relief, recovery, and psychosocial counseling. To be safe and to help others is the main work of this time. . . . The physical damage can be reconstructed, but do not cause suffering to others. Be a friend to others. The more you love, the more love is generated. The country is looking for love along with rescue, relief, and reconstruction. Citizens are sharing love and seeking love. . . . You are with Radio Nepal, the station that is with your shared happiness and sorrows.

20.

Listeners call in to the radio station from all over the country's earthquake-affected regions. They speak of the lack of tents provided by the government, political infighting among local leaders, and the inequality in distribution of aid between the rich and the poor. They make requests to the government to prioritize the elderly, the sick, and the disabled when providing resources. They reflect on the suffering of others and the fear that contemporary life has become increasingly subject to destruction. They philosophize about the meaning of loss and the uncertainty of life.

21.

Chandra is listening to a small handheld radio, his cigarette glowing in the darkness. Through the sounds of the night the crackling voice of a man could be made out as he describes the concept of depression and the benefits of counseling and sharing, spoken in a *Nepali bhasa* peppered with these English terms. The voice explains that there is medicine for depression but that it is better to begin with counseling. That people have many kinds of *tension*,

xviiiPROLOGUE

but when you share your tension, when you no longer make your tension hide, you can improve on your own; that your *man*, your heart-mind, will become light. "This is the meaning of counseling: listening to people's problems," says the voice. A caller calls into the show, his voice is barely audible. He says that he feels as if the earth won't stop shaking. Chandra switches off the radio.

Rupture

In the spring of 2015, suffering in Nepal was global news. For a brief period, it was immediate and pressing. Yet soon the world was flooded with other disasters, and Nepal faded from sight. From within Nepal, the disaster went on, seemingly without end. One disaster, the earthquake and its major aftershock, bled into another, a blockade at the Indian border, leading to fuel, gas, and medicine shortages. Many people who lost their homes on April 25 and on May 12, 2015, were still living in transitional shelters years later. By that time, most aid programs had already left or were phasing out because people were no longer perceived by humanitarians to be earthquake "victims" and there were other problems to tackle elsewhere. In this book, I raise the question: What are the consequences of transient care in a world of cascading disasters?

When the first earthquake struck on April 25, I was in a rural *pahadi* (hill) village in Khotang, a district in the eastern foothills of the Himalayas. I had been following a case of collective affliction among teenage girls, variously referred to in Nepal as "mass hysteria," "conversion disorder," and *chhopne* (being taken over by ghosts and spirits).[1] The district had been spared from total decimation, but the shaking was felt, heard, and feared. For the following month, my adoptive family and I slept outside, together, in cowsheds and on verandas, avoiding the inside of the mud-and-stone house as much as possible. The solar-powered radio was kept on at all times, and this was our main source of information. At night we listened to Radio Nepal, as we lay under blankets in the open air. On the broadcast voices spoke about mental illness (*manasik rog*); they explained the concept of depression, listing its symptoms. A psychosocial program called *Bhandai-Sundai* ("talking-listening," funded by UNICEF) aired on the national radio station every day.[2] Listeners called in to explain their symptoms and received live, on-air advice from a psychosocial counselor or psychiatrist.

One afternoon a man called in, describing a sensation of constant dizziness, *ringata lagne*. He said it was as if at each moment another earthquake had come. His heart was racing, and he was worried that he might have a heart attack. "*Atinu pardaina*," a calm voice replied. "Don't worry. Don't drink and stay with your family. Meet with a doctor or a psychologist." The broadcaster explained anxiety disorder (*atini rog*, or "worry illness"), describing its symptoms as "a heart that races when fear is on the mind." "This is not a physical illness," said the broadcaster. "It's nothing. Just stay in a safe place." As a new world of psychosocial care was carried over from Kathmandu by the radio waves that reached the village, I began to hear this unexpected transmission of psychological discourse as an indication that something else was shifting in Nepal. The disaster had brought a new and forceful focus on mental health that had not been present before. Mental health had suddenly become, to use Bruno Latour's phrase, a "matter of concern."[3]

When I began working in Nepal in 2012, mental health was considered a minor issue. But the visibility of affliction waxes and wanes in different times and places and is also tied to a politics of attention in which certain events enable particular forms of suffering to become momentarily visible while others recede into the background. I saw this happen when the massive 7.8-magnitude earthquake and 7.3-magnitude "aftershock" struck the central region. The earthquakes claimed over nine thousand lives, destroyed half a million homes, and inspired a sudden rush of humanitarian care for the mental health of Nepali people.

In response to the seismic rupture of the Indian and Eurasian plates, humanitarian organizations arrived flush with funding for psychiatric and psychosocial support to heal trauma in a country where mental health had not been incorporated into the public health care system. As an unprecedented flood of humanitarian aid projects suddenly placed mental health into the center of public discourse, humanitarians used the disaster as an opportunity to increase mental health governance in Nepal.[4] Over three hundred thousand "beneficiaries" received psychiatric and psychosocial support, many for the first time in their lives.[5] As one Nepali psychiatrist exclaimed during a UN cluster meeting for the coordination of humanitarian mental health and psychosocial support, "the earthquake was a boon for mental health in Nepal!" What does it mean for a disaster to become a boon—a godsend, a blessing, a bonus?

In May 2015, international journalists declared that the earthquakes had "unleashed a mental health disaster."[6] Journalists and foreign humanitarian organizations assumed that people living in the earthquake-affected areas would suffer from post-traumatic stress disorder (PTSD), a diagnosis requir-

ing emergency mental health treatment and psychosocial interventions.[7] As
one organization and international expert after another arrived, the sense
that mental health was in crisis became tangible. In the aftermath of the
earthquakes, Kathmandu's mental health nongovernmental organizations
(NGOs) buzzed with activity as they negotiated contracts, hired counselors,
and held training workshops. Yet the idea that something called "mental
health" (*manasik swastha*) should be managed with pharmaceutical drugs
and psychosocial counseling was relatively new in Nepal. In the Himalayas,
a region of ethnic, linguistic, and religious diversity, people had long treated
psychic and spiritual affliction with Ayurvedic and Tibetan medicine as well
as other forms of ritual and shamanic healing.[8]

In the village, in the days after the second earthquake, my friend Kanchi
became possessed by the ghost of her mother-in-law's sister, a woman who
wasn't able to have children. I arrived in medias res, joining the group of people who had gathered around her. When Kanchi was possessed, she began to
speak differently. "*Ai maree . . . maree* [I'm dyyying . . . dyyying]," she said, in
a voice I had never heard before. When the ghost spoke through her it cried
out: "I am all alone. Why did you leave me all alone?"

Kanchi writhed on the wooden cot outside her house under an old faded
Chinese blanket. Someone called the *dhami*, the shaman. Everyone was
watching. The neighbors kept their baby away from the scene, as ghosts were
known to cause illness in young children. That night the *dhami* sat at Kanchi's
house and performed a ritual puja called *chinta basne*.[9] Kanchi, he said, was
possessed by a *pisat*, the ghost of someone who died a bad death and had
transferred their affliction to the living. During the puja, the *dhami* made
offerings of alcohol, cigarettes, rice, and fruit to the ghost to appease her suffering and encourage her to leave the living in peace.

When Kanchi returned to herself, she asked for water and slept. The next
day she stayed in bed in the cot outside. "*Taha paunu bhaena* [I didn't know
what happened]," Kanchi said as I sat with her that morning. She had no
memory of the event. When the *dhami* came by again, he did *phuk-phak*,
blowing spells and incantations, and gave Kanchi a mixture of medicinal
plants, *jari-buti*, to rub on her body. Her daughters stayed nearby and took
care of her, massaging their mother's head with the wild mountain herbs.

Into the village in the hills of eastern Nepal, where few people spoke about
"mental health" or conceptualized affliction in psychological terms, the radio's
sudden discourse on depression, anxiety, and counseling brought a new perspective.[10] When a man called in to *Bhandai-Sundai* and described his wife's
fainting episodes after giving birth to their daughter, the host explained that

it was a "psychological process," perhaps "postpartum depression," and that the new mother's behavior could be a way to achieve "primary and secondary gains," such as attention and care from friends and family. From a psychiatric perspective, Kanchi's possession would be similarly seen as an "idiom of distress" or form of "conversion disorder," in which repressed emotions were "converted" from the mind and expressed through the body.[11] As a Nepali staff member of a global mental health NGO in Kathmandu said to me a few months later, there had been reports of ghosts among the earthquake survivors, and she hoped to create appropriate guidelines for "behavior change" in the psychoeducation section of her organization's training manual. She said these "misguided beliefs" should be corrected because ghosts and spirits don't exist.[12]

Bhandai-Sundai was crafted for a public that was used to listening to discussions of intimate life on the FM radio but was not yet familiar with psychiatry and counseling, their ontologies of affliction, or their modalities of care.[13] Although Nepali doctors had established the country's first psychiatric services in the early 1960s, decades later there were still few psychiatrists among the population of thirty million people (approximately two hundred, as of 2020).[14] When psychiatric treatment was available, it remained largely concentrated in the capital of Kathmandu and other smaller cities, such as Pokhara and Nepalgunj. In the mid-1980s, the country's first rural community mental health program was launched by a British Christian missionary organization called United Mission to Nepal (UMN). Fourteen years later, UMN's programs concluded without having accomplished their goal of incorporating mental health into the public health care system.[15] A second round of rural mental health programs appeared in the wake of the decade-long People's War, the Maoist insurgency that stretched from 1996 to 2006, as Nepal became a popular site for donor-funded "postconflict" psychosocial support interventions. However, these programs attended to specific victim groups, such as ex–child soldiers, as opposed to the mental health of the population at large.[16] Since then, in the absence of state investment, local NGOs and global mental health projects have provided uneven access to psychiatric and counseling services in rural areas through various temporally finite donor-funded interventions. It was not until the earthquakes struck that the psychic life of the population became an urgent biopolitical problem requiring management, treatment, and intervention at a national scale.

An earthquake is an archetypal catastrophe. The imagery of flattened homes and mangled piles of rubble is paradigmatic of the spectacular suffering that inspires humanitarian sentiment and biopolitical intervention. If the logics of late liberal humanitarian reason require increasingly spectacular events of suffering in order to justify projects that foster life, then disasters are among the exemplary biopolitical events of our time.[17] As a form of power concerned with the management and regulation of the population, biopolitics seeks to monitor, control, optimize, and protect society from its internal and external "enemies" (disease, deviance, disaster, the Other).[18] Yet as Foucault observed, a biopolitics bent on "making live" is often accompanied by the proliferation of death, for every project of fostering life is also a determination regarding whose lives and ways of being are worth protecting and nourishing and whose are not.[19]

The scale of the seismic rupture of the Indo-Eurasian plates captured the world's attention, leading to a rush to aid Nepal with funding for psychosocial interventions to heal the trauma of earthquake victims and stop an imminent "mental health crisis" before it began. Supported by the surge of foreign donations, Nepali counselors were trained and dispatched into the unstable hills. After traveling for hours on crowded public buses, crossing over landslide-streaked mountains, and walking the steep network of paths connecting rural villages, the counselors arrived at the ruined homes and temporary shelters of those designated as earthquake victims. What they found was surprising.

In the immediate aftermath of the earthquakes, counselors met communities deeply shaken by the seismic rupture. However, six months later, most clients seen were those who suffered from afflictions that began far before the disaster occurred and who only happened to receive care because they lived in an earthquake-affected district. These were people who had been suffering all along from the slow disaster of poverty, from abuse in the family, from ghosts and spirits, from the risks of migration, or from severe, unrelenting psychic afflictions. Seen through the frame of crisis, such previously unexceptional forms of suffering had been temporarily transformed into problems worthy of care. This book explores what disaster generates and the limits and possibilities of transient care along a Himalayan fault line. Set in the time of the earthquakes, the ethnography moves between Kathmandu NGO offices, steep mountain trails, psychosocial interventions, and earthquake-affected villages as it tells the story of an emergent "mental health crisis" and the forms of care that followed in the disaster's wake.

The Work of Disaster

An earthquake is a sudden release of energy. When stress builds along a fault line, eventually it will rupture, generating seismic vibrations that travel through the earth's layers into the lithosphere. The seismic event and the shifting of tectonic plates occurs without respect to the network of lives above it. Yet the demands the event makes—the ethical response it elicits and the forms of work it requires—reflect the particular historical, social, and political conditions in which it occurs. A powerful earthquake is an extreme case of an unpredictable material intrusion that interrupts habitual modes of being-in-the-world and being-with-others, at least momentarily.[20] Approaching disaster, like the Nepal earthquakes, through the lens of critical phenomenology can help us follow collective processes of disorientation and reorientation and the ways a seismic rupture creates possibilities for care and for building the world back otherwise.[21]

To think about disaster phenomenologically is to track what I call the *work of disaster*—how the movements of the earth are perceived through historically situated processes of collective intentionality and the rippling aftereffects of these objectifications. The work of disaster encompasses what is generated by a disaster and what is destroyed, what is accomplished through claims of crisis and what is foreclosed, the processes by which suffering is made visible or rendered invisible, and the historical and material conditions that create the possibility for these formations. Such work is done by the earth itself, by transforming worlds, and by humans, who respond to the disruption of disaster with the concepts they have to guide them. The work of disaster thus explores how the destabilization of ground makes a demand that becomes embodied, producing varying responses across radically different ethical and philosophical traditions.[22]

It is often said that phenomenology is a philosophy of beginnings. This is because phenomenological description involves the purposeful *destabilization* of the taken-for-granted assumptions that organize our engagement with reality, a perennial return to experience *before* it is given meaning, and an awareness that there is always *more* to experience because perception is a function of intentionality. At its most basic level, phenomenology is the study of phenomena—things, problems, experiences, events—as they *appear* to a particular person or group of people.[23] In anthropology, phenomenology has long informed work on illness, healing, and morality, contributing careful studies of the way individual embodied experience is objectified and given meaning in interaction with others.[24] For example, you might perceive a vague sensation of heaviness in your body, but only later in consultation with a healer do you come to experience this heaviness *as* the presence of a spirit.[25] Phenomenologists call this intersubjective process of giving meaning to indeterminate experience "objectification." If normally one engages the world in an automatic way, then the method of phenomenological reduction, also known as "bracketing," is a practice of suspending these unreflective ways of perceiving so as to become aware of the concepts and frames that shape perception.[26] Alongside "bracketing," phenomenology also involves an awareness of "intentionality," the selective orientation of attention *toward* certain aspects of a phenomenon and not others. In this book, I use methods from phenomenology to not only explore embodied experiences of disaster but also track processes of collective intentionality, perception, and conceptualization. Like the sudden trembling of a body, the trembling of the earth also invites multiple interpretations, treatments, and therapeutics.

Since the groundbreaking work of Frantz Fanon, phenomenology has been used as a critical method for describing how historical, social, and political structures shape perception and embodiment in social worlds of vast inequality.[27] Such critical approaches offer an important corrective to accusations that phenomenology has been overly focused on subjective experience while ignoring the political, economic, and structural conditions that order social life.[28] As contemporary philosophers and anthropologists have demonstrated, if phenomenology is to become critical, it must be combined with critical and intersectional approaches to power, political economy, racism, patriarchy, colonialism, and biopolitics.[29] Applying this approach to the context of disaster, I bring together theories of biopolitics with critical phenomenology to describe how suffering in Nepal became visible *as* a crisis requiring particular forms of care and intervention, and the consequences that followed. In doing so, this book expands the scope of critical phenomenology out from the study of individual experience to the study of conceptualization and collective intentionality.

For example, when applied to problems in global health, such as the lack of resources for psychiatry and counseling in Nepal, we can use the methods of critical phenomenology to analyze how economies of attention operate in this field. In the field of global health, some diseases are highly visible as problems, while other issues remain invisible and garner little attention. The determination of priorities is an outcome of the organization of collective attention, often backed by shock-inducing metrics, that allows a particular issue to become visible as a problem in need of intervention.[30] As multiple anthropologists have shown, economies of attention in global health have led to the prioritization of treating HIV with "magic bullet" solutions over numerous other issues, from cancer to a collapsing public health care system.[31] In this book, I show how the work of disaster transformed mental health into an urgent problem in need of expert intervention and attention in Nepal. If the economy of attention in global health is an outcome of how the global health community perceives and turns its collective attention toward a particular issue, then critical phenomenology offers a generative tool through which to track the ethics, politics, and unintended consequences of this collective act of intentionality and turning toward.[32]

Contemporary work in phenomenological anthropology has not only become progressively more critical but has also sought to expand its application beyond individual experience to include the study of conceptualization.[33] Robert Desjarlais first defined "critical phenomenology" as the study of lived experience as it takes form within social, historical, and political-economic contexts of inequality.[34] More recently Cheryl Mattingly has offered a second definition of critical phenomenology as conceptual critique, a project similar to what Jarrett Zigon has called "critical hermeneutics."[35] As Zigon has argued, the tools of phenomenology may also be used to analyze and deconstruct "the politics of the a priori," how the concepts we use limit possibilities for imagination and becoming.[36] When I use critical phenomenology as a method for tracking how a disaster and its aftermath are perceived through pregiven frames, I am invested in illuminating the histories that have determined whose frames and concepts become dominant. This phenomenology is critical as it is concerned with describing the dynamics of power and historical conditions of emergence that shape the way a disaster is perceived as a problem requiring particular kinds of management. Critical phenomenology is a method of tracking such processes of collective objectification; a way of following phenomena, perceptions, orientations, experiences, and events as they emerge and crystalize by way of the unexamined concepts and frames through which we perceive the world. Once we begin to do this, we can seize possibilities for interrupting objectifications by thinking from elsewhere—thus opening up and amplifying different ways of being, perceiving, responding, and repairing in times of disaster.

Studies of disaster have rightly focused on the geopolitical and social histories of inequality that determine patterns of vulnerability and risk.[37] However, this book explores not only what disaster destroys but also what it *generates*. The experience of being in the midst of a series of major earthquakes in the Himalayas led me to ask questions about a disaster's generative force—such as the sudden shift of tectonic plates that jolts the earth and sets into motion a massive movement of money, people, politics, medicine, interventions, attention, and gestures of care. Anthropologists of disaster have long argued that catastrophes reveal hidden truths about society and act as catalysts for transformation.[38] Governments and corporations have frequently seized disasters as opportunities to transform society through increased nationalism, securitization, development, privatization, and "disaster capitalism."[39] In this literature, a key issue at stake is how certain transformations and visions for the future are prioritized while others are not.[40] As Roberto Barrios has argued, disasters are "contested arenas" where people dispute visions of societal advancement.[41] Similarly, scholars of science and technology such as Adriana

Petryna, Kim Fortun, Manuel Tironi, and David Bond have shown how disasters can lead to new forms of knowledge practices, "enunciatory communities," and experimentation for the management of life.[42] As the planet rapidly changes, scientists are increasingly faced with the challenge of how to interpret and respond to a climate future that no longer fits their preexisting models.[43] In a world where disasters have become omnipresent, it is imperative that we critically examine the concepts and frames that organize perception and guide response. As Anthony Oliver-Smith and Susanna Hoffman have argued, "disaster exposes the way in which people construct or 'frame' their peril (including the denial of it), the way they perceive their environment and their subsistence, and the ways they invent explanation, constitute their morality, and project their continuity and promise into the future."[44]

In his study of frames, Erving Goffman noted that wherever there is an event, there will be a primary framework through which it is interpreted.[45] These frames, in turn, allow its users to "locate, perceive, identify, and label a seemingly infinite number of concrete occurrences defined in its terms."[46] The analysis of the frames that organize perception is urgent in times of disaster, when the act of conceptualization is both morally and politically charged.[47] As Judith Butler notes, "the frame does not simply exhibit reality, but actively participates in a strategy of containment, selectively producing and enforcing what will count as reality."[48] Frames shape what is possible to perceive. Understood through the humanitarian frame of crisis, suffering in Nepal became a problem in need of immediate psychosocial intervention. However, this concern would last only as long as the frame of crisis could be sustained. As Elizabeth Povinelli has shown, the objectification of a situation as "eventful" or as "in crisis" determines who and what is worthy of care or subject to abandonment.[49] When care and attention depend on collective perceptions of crisis, the biopolitical management of life becomes a phenomenological question of framing and *seeing as*. When determinations of crisis are a requirement for care, perception is an operation of power.

Resilience

Amidst the sufferings, I also saw a bright spark of hope. Everywhere I went, despite the repeated aftershocks and the ongoing suffering caused by death, injury and displacement, I found the Nepali people to be full of hope and confidence amidst the despair and suffering, and a firm determination for recovery. This demonstration of resilience and display of unity by Nepali society in this tragic time makes me the proudest of Nepalis.

PRIME MINISTER SUSHIL KOIRALA[50]

The devastation wrought by disaster was unevenly distributed across the rural-urban divide of Nepali society and stratified along lines of class, gender, caste, and ethnicity. The rural epicenters of the earthquakes added to the unequal destruction due to the landslide-prone geography, weak infrastructure, and high rates of poverty in the hills. The traditional homes of mud and stone, no matter how well-constructed, could never withstand multiple earthquakes of this magnitude. In the remittance-driven economy of Nepal, the leading source of employment was labor migration to India, Malaysia, Qatar, the United Arab Emirates, and Saudi Arabia.[51] In order to work abroad, people commonly took out large loans to pay "manpower" agents who secured their contracts with foreign companies.[52] As a result, many families living in rural areas were burdened with crippling levels of debt long before the disaster. Because migration was highly gendered, with the majority of young, able-bodied men traveling abroad to work, it was those who remained in the villages— women, children, and the elderly—who absorbed the force of the rupture.

Following the earthquakes, in international and national Nepali news articles, in public speeches, and in publications of humanitarian organizations, talk of "resilience" was everywhere. The Nepali people were celebrated in the media as "resilient" for their ability to keep going in the aftermath of extreme hardship, and reports were published on the need to rebuild a "more resilient Nepal."[53] There was something strange about this discourse of resilience. What did this word mean, what did it mask, what did it do? The concept of "resilience" is a deeply ingrained part of the vocabulary of disaster management, where it refers to the ability of a community to recover from a disaster with minimal impact, and the capacities that make such recovery possible.[54] In English, the term is synonymous with toughness and the elasticity of a substance. *Resilience* is drawn from the Latin *resiliens*, which means "to rebound" or "recoil."[55] In 2005 "resilience" was officially incorporated by the United Nations Office for Disaster Risk Reduction in the "Hyogo Framework for Action," further solidifying its centrality to disaster management at a global scale. Here resilience is defined as "the capacity of a system, community or society potentially exposed to hazards to adapt, by resisting or changing in order to reach and maintain an *acceptable level* of functioning and structure."[56] However as anthropologists of disaster have pointed out, by focusing on the behavioral choices that enable communities to cope with shock, discourses of resilience in disaster risk management render invisible histories of oppression and dispossession that create conditions of uneven vulnerability, ultimately celebrating resilience as the capacity to survive with minimal external assistance.[57]

Almost two years after the disaster, the international news media reported that little progress in rebuilding had been made. Despite the $4 billion that was pledged to Nepal in foreign assistance during the televised "International Conference on Nepal's Reconstruction: Towards a Resilient Nepal 2015," by January 2017 only one payment of $500 had been distributed to qualifying families who lost their homes and had been inhabiting shelters of wood and corrugated metal since April 2015.[58] These families had been promised a total of NPR 300,000 (about USD 3,000) to rebuild their homes, an amount that many said was insufficient to cover the full costs of rebuilding.[59] As one woman shared in a counseling circle, "What can I say? My three-story house collapsed. I don't think I will be able to make a house like that again. Neither my husband nor my son has a job. We have small children who are studying. I can't find work. It feels like a dream when I think about what to do. I get scared while sleeping at night. I feel as if I will die; then I think it might be better if I would die." The woman's words rang in dissonance with Prime Minister Koirala's claim that everywhere he went he "found the Nepali people to be full of hope and confidence amidst the despair."

In casting Nepalis as "resilient" from the beginning, there began a depoliticization and normalization of the delay in government aid to more than five hundred thousand families who lost their homes in the disaster. As political scientist Siera Tamang argued in an op-ed in *The Kathmandu Post*, the inability of the government to provide aid was deflected into a celebration of the resilience of Nepali people, particularly those inhabiting the remote and rural hill and mountainous regions.[60] "It should not be up to citizens—however resilient—to fend for themselves in a time of national disaster of historic proportions," Tamang argued. "The government has duties and obligations that it must fulfill. That is one of the main distinctions between being a subject and citizen."[61] Tamang's invocation of the distinction between subject and citizen spoke to Nepal's long struggle for democracy after centuries of Hindu monarchy. Until the end of the People's War in 2006 and the establishment of multiparty democracy, the people of Nepal were subjects of the king. As citizens of the New Nepal—a secular, democratic republic—people expected a certain amount of government support as their right.[62]

The romanticization of the rural poor as tough and ever-smiling in the face of extreme hardship has long been part of the way Nepali people have been seen by both Western eyes as well as the Kathmandu elite.[63] But "smiling" faces can be deceiving. As I would learn in the years that followed the earthquakes, in Nepal there was a strong tendency to hide one's worries in the heart-mind (*man*) and to conceal expressions of pain and suffering. I still remember a jarring encounter early in my fieldwork when I met an elderly woman along a rural village path in Dang. "In Nepal people are poor and sad [*garibi ra dukhi*]," she said to me, laughing. In fact, the celebration of resilience among the rural poor erased a violent history of domination that was largely responsible for Nepal's economic precarity in the first place.

It is often said that while Nepal was never colonized, it colonized itself internally. During the Rana era (1846–1951), taxation policies were put in place that exploited the nation's resources for the benefit of the ruling family.[64] The vast majority of rural lands were controlled by a landowning elite composed of absentee landlords and civil employees who collected taxes from peasant sharecroppers and exercised authority over the inhabitants of the land. Despite land reform legislation in the 1960s, the legacies of nineteenth-century land policies can still be seen, with a large portion of the rural population left with insufficient landholdings to produce enough food for year-round subsistence. The People's War was a direct response to the long history of oppression and exploitation of rural farmers, a condition that Maoists described as "semi-feudal."[65] As a young, economically struggling village friend from Khotang put it simply, "Nepal is only hurtful to itself."

The use of the term *resilient* to describe rural Nepalis served to cover over an unpleasant truth: that the government was failing to respond with aid in a timely manner and that the people had no choice but to wait and endure. Public criticism of government inaction revealed new expectations regarding the rights of citizens and the role the state should play in the management of the population. In response to vast destruction, earthquake-affected communities expected help to arrive not only from the government of Nepal but also from the many foreign nations who had provided development aid since the country first opened its borders in the 1950s. Yet while earthquake-affected communities hoped for cash payments, food, and housing materials, psychosocial interventions constituted a radically new and unexpected form of assistance.

Mental Health Governance in Nepal

The last major earthquake to rupture in Nepal was in 1934. According to a report written by Major General Brahma Shumsher Jung Bahadur Rana, offers of foreign aid were not accepted. Volunteers from local civic society groups provided medical aid and distributed clothing, rice, money, and milk to the victims, but the provision of psychological support was not considered to be a mode of repair.[66] Today "psychosocial" interventions have become ubiquitous in humanitarian responses to war and disaster. While the concept of the psychosocial has been used since the turn of the twentieth century to refer to the confluence of social and psychological factors in the production of deviance, over time the term came to stand in for what Sharon Abramowitz has called the "'black box' relationship between individual psychology, social relations, and cultural norms."[67] "Mental health and psychosocial support" (MHPSS) in disaster- and conflict-affected settings aims to rebuild stability in societies from the ground up through the rehabilitation of individuals from specific victim groups.[68] What exactly a psychosocial approach entails, however, is often left undefined. Activities that take place under the label of the psychosocial can range from individual and group counseling sessions to psychoeducation programs and prescriber trainings. In Nepal, the psychotherapeutic modalities taught to counselors in NGO-led training workshops were similarly eclectic, including approaches derived from cognitive behavioral therapy, systemic family therapy, mindfulness exercises, and even constellation therapy.

I first learned about psychosocial interventions in 2012 when I accompanied a group of NGO staff to a district in the midwestern Tarai region near the Indian border where they were running a program to treat PTSD among victims of the Maoist insurgency. We flew from Kathmandu to Nepalganj on a small propeller plane and then drove for hours in a white jeep through lush valleys of yellow mustard fields to reach the district headquarters of Dang. During the visit, the NGO ran a mental health training for rural health-post workers focused on diagnosing and treating psychiatric disorders with medication. On off days, we delivered furniture to small health posts, each donation emblazoned with the logo of the organization. Mostly I remember the stifling monsoon heat and people herding water buffalo and goats along dirt roads, carrying big black umbrellas to shield them from the burning sun.

I returned to Dang again the next year and then once more the year after that. This time the NGO staff were conducting a final evaluation of the program, and they invited me to accompany them as they visited clients and health-post workers to gather feedback. In the villages I heard stories of worry, fear, tension, and insomnia (*chinta, dar, tension, nindra na lagne*). I met a woman whose one-month-old infant had died and another who had been abandoned by her husband after he returned from working abroad. At a rural health post, a group of female community health volunteers (FCHVs) reported that the most common problems they saw were fear, headaches, and *manma kura khelne* (things playing in the heart-mind). In Nepali, the heart-mind is the seat of emotion, mood, and intentionality; likes and dislikes; love and pain.[69] The heart-mind is the place where one keeps private thoughts, secrets, feelings, and desires. Through training in psychoeducation, the health volunteers had learned to attend to the heart-minds of their patients, identify mental health problems, and ask, "What makes it hurt?" (*Ke karanle dukhyo*?) when patients came in with complaints of headaches and *gyastric* (gastritis). They said this was the first time there had been this type of care in the area. "What will happen when the program ends?" asked the evaluators. "There will be suffering," the health volunteers replied.

As psychosocial interventions in conflict and disaster zones have proliferated over the past thirty years, the mental health of populations has become a global concern. Today, global mental health has emerged as the new terrain of biopolitics, that distinct form of power bent on *making live* (or *letting die*) that first emerged in eighteenth-century Europe alongside the fields of demography and social hygiene that made population thinking possible.[70] Global mental health, a subfield of global health established in the mid-2000s, focuses on improving mental well-being on a global scale by filling the "treatment gap," the lack of access to evidenced-based mental health services, in low- and middle-income countries primarily through "task-shifting," the training of laypeople to provide community-based psychosocial interventions.[71] In Nepal, the governance of mental health has been led largely by foreign development experts and applied anthropologists, who, since the 1980s, have drawn on various rationales and forms of scientific knowledge to manage the problem of mental health in a country with many shamans but few psychiatrists.

In Nepal, the expansion of psychosocial counseling has a unique history that is closely linked to the study of culture and mental health in North American anthropology. In the 1980s and '90s, there was a proliferation of anthropological scholarship on shamanic healing and the relation between culture, mind, and emotion in Nepal.[72] This body of work would serve as a foundation for the next generation of anthropologists, who sought to operationalize Nepali ethnopsychology into the applied domain of global mental health with the aim of developing culturally sensitive psychosocial interventions.[73] The uniquely Nepali translation of psychosocial counseling as one who "advises on matters of the heart-mind" (*manobimarshakarta*) is a direct outcome of the application of anthropology in global mental health that aimed to destigmatize mental illness and promote the use of counseling by emphasizing psychosocial care as concerned with the heart-mind, *man*, the seat of emotion, as opposed to the brain, *dimag*, the location of madness and pathological distress.[74] Over the past two decades, Nepal has served as an important site in the Movement for Global Mental Health (MGMH), providing data, case studies, and evidence and serving as a node through which leading experts within the network of global mental health have circulated.[75]

However, it was only in the aftermath of the earthquakes that mental health became a central point of government concern.[76]

Since its inception, the field of global mental health has been the site of a series of polarizing debates. Anthropologists and other critics have argued that global mental health is a form of neocolonialism that universalizes Western psychiatric diagnostic concepts, medicalizes social suffering, produces psychiatric subjects, opens new markets for pharmaceutical companies, and ignores or displaces local understandings of affliction and practices of care.[77] Global mental health practitioners have responded by arguing that depression and anxiety are leading causes of the global burden of disease and access to evidence-based mental health treatments is a human right.[78] Across five chapters, this book places debates on global mental health in dialogue with the questions and concerns of counselors, clients, humanitarians, and NGO staff as they surfaced on the ground in the postdisaster psychosocial response. Because of the absence of colonial psychiatry, the historical role of anthropologists in Nepali NGOs for mental health and counseling, the lack of reference to diagnostic categories in interventions, and counselors' avoidance of issues related to ghost and spirit possession (*bhut-pret lagyo*), postearthquake psychosocial interventions did not lead to medical imperialism or the "globalization of the American psyche" but, instead, introduced the option of psychiatric medication and a novel form of care based on listening without judgment.[79]

This book neither romanticizes traditional approaches to healing nor champions global mental health. Rather, it explores how the work of disaster led to the introduction of specific forms of therapeutics, and it examines the ethics of providing brief psychosocial and pharmaceutical interventions to people living in regions where such treatments are otherwise unavailable. The temporary prescription of psychiatric drugs in earthquake-affected districts remains one of the most troubling aspects of the story of disaster and mental health in Nepal. Such prescriptions are concerning because they risk both tranquilizing the suffering caused by poverty and social inequality and creating chemical dependencies on substances that cannot be easily obtained and that can have serious side effects that require close monitoring. As a result, this book focuses on the consequences of humanitarian mental health interventions that give care only to take it away.

Ethnography in/of Disaster

As the earth beneath Kathmandu was jolted ten feet to the south, it destabilized the material landscape and my understanding of anthropology. In the village, days after the second earthquake, a friend turned to me smiling and said, seemingly in jest, "You will leave us and go back to your country. You will leave us to die here." Was she really joking? Her words seemed to capture all of the anxiety and privilege of anthropological research. As anthropologists we often move through multiple worlds, but what are the ethics of leaving? In a life-threatening situation, the ability to be evacuated, to escape, to leave, makes visible the disquieting elements that continue to haunt the heart of the anthropological project.[80] After the disaster, everything became an ethical response—leaving, staying, doing something, doing nothing.

In the days following the first earthquake, I was offered the possibility of evacuation to the United States by my funding agency. I declined. In retrospect, I've come to realize that the decision to remain in the field was connected to what I thought "real" anthropology was supposed to be. Since Bronisław Malinowski's creation of the method of in-depth, long-term participant observation, this troubled vision of fieldwork as individual existential trial has become part of the discipline's mythology and rite of passage.[81] My fieldwork began to break down. The notebook became my transitional object; the ritual of writing field notes a way of holding myself together.[82] But was ethnographic research even possible, as I imagined it then?

Instead of abandoning anthropology, I searched for new methods. By the end of May, I returned to Kathmandu, seeking a way to put my expertise in medical and psychological anthropology to use in the postdisaster response. Prior to the disaster I had worked closely with Nepali NGOs for mental health and counseling. When I was invited to conduct collaborative ethnographic research alongside a leading Nepali NGO, I found myself situated in a position from which I could begin to translate anthropology into a form of immediate and engaged action. At the same time, the disaster was "there" for me to encounter, perceive, and interpret because of the historical conditions that made it possible for me to arrive as an anthropologist in Nepal in the first place.[83]

My fieldwork methodology was soon transformed from traditional ethnographic and qualitative research to a collaborative and engaged mode of ethnography in the service of mutually determined goals.[84] As an "ethnographic consultant" for the Centre for Mental Health and Counselling (CMC–Nepal), one of the main organizations providing mental health and psychosocial support in the earthquake-affected districts, the subject-object dichotomy of researcher and researched quickly dissolved. As I became part of their team, I attended trainings for supervisors, counselors, and community psychosocial workers. I participated in meetings; attended the UN cluster meetings for mental health and counseling; interviewed NGO staff members, foreign

psychologists and project managers, psychosocial counselors, and community psychosocial workers; analyzed gray literature and news articles; and,
over the course of a year, accompanied three psychosocial counselors into
the earthquake-affected districts to observe their interventions. I took my
observations back to the NGO, which used them in training workshops for
Nepali supervisors and counselors and discussed them in collective "intervi-
sion" meetings among the counselors' supervisors. My observations and field
notes served as a foundation from which we built more engaged practices of
support for counselors in the field. Given the extensive anthropological critiques of humanitarianism, I was uncertain if joining a humanitarian psychosocial project was a viable form of anthropological engagement. Ultimately, I
resolved to adopt a critical perspective on humanitarianism while constantly
asking what forms of care might still be possible within and in spite of it.

Six months after the earthquakes, I accompanied three psychosocial counselors into the earthquake-affected districts of Dolakha, Ramechhap, and
Okhaldhunga. The Kathmandu-based NGO supervisors and the foreign project
manager wanted to know what the counselors were doing on the ground and
to find out what was working. With only forty-eight days of training throughout the course of the project, the minimally trained counselors felt they had
little guidance and welcomed any kind of additional support they could get in
the field. Because of the complex logistics of travel and social norms of gendered relationships in Nepal, all of the counselors I worked with were women.
Each was a local resident of her working district, and while all had previous
experience working as field staff on development programs, they had little
to no prior training in psychosocial counseling. Indira, a high-caste Hindu
mother of two, had forged a career working as field staff in global health development projects. Bina, a young Tamang woman and self-described "student of gender," had previously worked as a school teacher and a "house
mother" in a donor-funded orphanage. Anjana, a Rai activist with prior experience working in Indigenous-language revitalization, also brought experience working in donor-funded health development projects.[85] Unlike foreign
humanitarian staff, Nepali fieldworkers used public modes of transportation
and stayed in temporary shelters with local people. A lack of motorable roads
in the hills often meant the counselors walked eight to ten hours to reach clients in remote villages. By sharing exposure to risks of aftershocks and landslides, walking with Indira, Bina, and Anjana became an embodied methodology through which I came to understand the gendered work of postdisaster
counseling.

In her writings on ethnography as politics, Faye Harrison has argued that
reflexivity about one's shifting identity and positionality in the field can serve

as an important research instrument.[86] My identity shifted across radically different contexts and field sites as I moved between Kathmandu NGO offices and earthquake-affected communities in the Himalayan foothills. My position as a young, white, able-bodied, female-coded American researcher shaped this research in many ways. It meant, first and foremost, that I had the possibility of entering and exiting the disaster zone. Yet it also meant that as a young woman in the village in the aftermath of the earthquakes, I was subject to decisions made by the patriarch and head of household, regarding safety and risk. It meant that I could only accompany female counselors in the earthquake-effected villages, due to the limited availability of lodgings and the gendered divisions of social life in rural Nepal. At the same time, it allowed me the opportunity to walk alongside counselors across rough terrain. When we reached the villages, I was welcomed into feminine worlds around the hearth and within the home. However, I was also sometimes accepted in masculine spaces restricted to my female peers. In a country with a sixty-year history of foreign-funded development, I was often placed in the category of "development worker" and was thus granted meetings with village leaders and other officials who associated me with the possibility of funding for future development projects. As a white foreigner I had no *jat* (caste, ethnicity), which allowed me to easily share food, water, and shelter with a range of people from different caste and ethnic groups in a region where caste discrimination remains deeply embedded despite its criminalization. At the same time, because of my skin color and nationality, I was sometimes able to gain access to elite spaces of power, such as UN cluster meetings, official conferences, and humanitarian hubs. As feminist thinkers have made clear, all knowledge, especially ethnographic knowledge, is situated in a particular body; it is from this starting point that my own orientation toward the disaster unfolds.[87]

Repair

While this book was generated by disaster, it is also a product of a moment when the field of North American anthropology began to shift from what Sherry Ortner has called "dark anthropology"—studies of the deadly effects of neoliberalism and increasing inequality worldwide—toward a set of concerns focused on alternative possible futures.[88] As Joel Robbins has provocatively argued, the focus on the "suffering subject" that dominated much of medical anthropology in the 1990s and 2000s has slowly been displaced by the "anthropology of the good."[89] This new phase of anthropology, which began to appear around the 2010s, inaugurated an area of inquiry focused on imagination, hope, care, ethics and morality and how people strive to live what they see as the good life. In many ways, this book is an artifact of this disciplinary transition—it strives to notice the boons of disaster while refusing to leave behind the problem of suffering.

Years ago, Eve Kosofsky Sedgwick, drawing on the psychoanalytic theories of Melanie Klein, argued for a shift from "paranoid" to "reparative" research.[90] This entailed a movement from an automatic, usually Foucauldian, "hermeneutics of suspicion" that sought to change the world by exposing hidden truths and forms of violence to a methodology concerned with attending to "reparative motives and positionalities" that might offer lessons in survival and sustenance in a deadly world.[91] While the anthropology of humanitarian reason has done much to reveal how care and compassion can become unintended forms of violence, it has operated largely from what Sedgwick would call the "paranoid" position, arguing, for example, that humanitarian care ultimately displaces possibilities for social change.[92] While this analysis is true, it does not easily allow for the simultaneous existence of any form of care that might persist within or in spite of the humanitarian endeavor. Throughout this book, I focus on revealing not only the violence of humanitarianism but also the moments of gentleness that surfaced between counselors and clients, paradoxically made possible because of the magnitude of the disaster and its humanitarian response.

Set in the aftermath of the seismic rupture, this book explores the intersubjective and ethical dimensions of therapeutic encounters in which chronic suffering was met with transient care.[93] Therapeutic encounters were stunted by a conception of crisis that operated under the assumption that affliction would be clearly linked to the event of the earthquakes, yet this was often not the case. By describing interactions between counselors and clients as they came face-to-face with the limitations of humanitarian care, I consider the violence of providing brief access to counseling and psychotropic medicines in places where they are otherwise unavailable. At the same time, I also describe gentle forms of being-with-others that were made possible by the seismic rupture and its troubled humanitarian assemblage.[94] To follow such intersubjective moments requires considering the limitations of transient care as well as its fleeting possibilities.

To do this, this ethnography tracks the work of disaster across various sites and scales: at the structural level of mental health governance, at the intersubjective level of care, at the existential level of embodied experience, and at the reflexive level of the ethnographic research itself. Each chapter uses the tools of critical phenomenology to show how humanitarian frames of "crisis," "loss," "solidarity," "efficacy," and "care" shaped and constrained the postdisaster response and its practices and imaginaries of repair. This perspective allows us to observe the historical contingency of the work of disaster that inaugurated the movement of particular forms of knowledge, therapeutics, pharmaceuticals, and care out of the infinite range of possible responses to the earth's destabilization and identify openings where things could become otherwise.

Chapter 1, "Crisis," describes how the seismic rupture created a brief opening to imagine what the future of Nepal's mental health system could become. While many organizations focused on providing short-term mental health and psychosocial support, some humanitarians, inspired by the World Health Organization's *Building Back Better* report framework, used declarations of crisis as an opportunity to expand mental health governance in Nepal.[95] Aligned with the Movement for Global Mental Health, visions of "the better" focused on increasing access to psychopharmaceuticals and training prescribers, as opposed to solving the problem of the abandonment of people with severe mental illness. While the disaster presented the opportunity to "build back better," ultimately "the better" was defined by foreign organizations, not local mental health activists. I draw on a combination of ethnographic and archival research to show how declarations of a "mental health crisis" and its imaginable solutions are rooted in a longer history of the biopolitics of mental health governance in Nepal and elsewhere. In doing so I demonstrate how a priori claims of "crisis" and "the better" created and foreclosed possibilities for building back otherwise.

Chapter 2, "Loss," takes us into the earthquake-affected villages of the central Himalayas to explore how different conceptualizations of loss delineate possibilities for repair after the destruction of a world. While the psychosocial approach operated under the assumption that facing loss and sharing suffering would lead to healing, this was in tension with strong cultural taboos against the outward expression of negative emotion. Traditional ways of working with loss assumed that speaking too much about those who have died a bad death strengthens attachments, causing the dead to become trapped in a liminal realm between death and rebirth. Yet people's struggles with the policing of personal expressions of grief also pointed toward a shadow side of culture. While anthropologists have long argued for the importance of incorporating the patient's cultural etiologies and approaches to healing into psychotherapeutic treatment, it is also possible that elements of one's cultural resources may not always be reparative or conducive to healing. Despite critiques that humanitarian psychosocial interventions are a form of therapeutic governance, in postdisaster Nepal, counseling sessions could not be solely reduced to a mode of governance. Assembled in the midst of ruins and rubble, counseling sessions were not conduits of "therapeutic citizenship" but unusual shelters where people grieved, hoped, and critically reflected on existence without censorship.[96]

As complex human and nonhuman entanglements, disasters compel us to address the relationship between earth and psyche in a way that privileges relationality and attends to embodiment. A critical phenomenology of disaster thus follows not only how a rupture and its repair are conceptualized in particular times and places but also how the materiality of a disaster becomes embodied, shaping ways of being, feeling, thinking, and caring for others.[97] An earthquake is a relational, embodied experience. Knocked off your feet, you are thrown, engulfed by waves of rumbling that emanate from deep beneath the earth's crust. In the Himalayas, earthquakes ripped through the landscape, causing bodies, hearts, and heart-minds to tremble. In psychosocial counseling circles, people spoke of ongoing blurred vision, dizziness, headaches, spinning sensations, loss of appetite, and the feeling of being physically "wobbly." As one Nepali man said in the early aftermath of the disaster, "my heart-mind shakes, my body trembles, my heart feels like it's moving [*manma hallinchha, jiu kamne, mutu hallieko jasto lagchha*]." Therapeutic encounters were also influenced by the unpredictable movements of the earth, as counselors set out on foot, crossing over unstable hills, valleys, and landslides in the midst of recurring aftershocks to listen to the worries people held in their heart-minds. In Nepal, care was shaped not only by personal, social, cultural, and structural forces but also by the geography of the Himalayas.

Chapter 3, "Solidarity," describes the embodied work of counseling to show how shared exposure to risk in the Himalayan disaster zone generated unexpected affordances for solidarity in an otherwise hierarchical model of humanitarian care. Within the humanitarian response, as in many forms of charity, hierarchies of power and inequality were deeply embedded at multiple levels. While foreign humanitarians were provided special protections in the disaster zone, Nepali counselors did not have access to these resources and traveled long distances by foot to reach local people. By moving between the material conditions of the therapeutic landscape and the internal psychic landscapes of counselors, this chapter describes how topography, personal history, physical exertion, and the cultural meanings of walking shaped care in the aftermath of disaster. Clients acknowledged that the counselors had struggled to reach them and that they too were staying in temporary shelters, traveling by foot and on packed buses. The counselors' walking, exertion, and exposure to risk were not peripheral aspects of counseling but a central element that lent meaning to the therapeutic work.

Chapter 4, "Efficacy," explores the limitations of humanitarian conceptualizations of efficacy that are bound to donor timelines and imaginaries of victimhood. While the humanitarian intervention was designed to heal the trauma of earthquake victims, many clients suffered from chronic problems that predated the earthquakes—such as interpersonal abuse and severe mental illness. For these clients, the emergence of the postearthquake "mental health crisis" did not map onto the temporalities of their suffering. Even when pain was clearly linked to the loss human life in the earthquakes, grief could not be contained by donor timelines. By comparing the concept of "effectiveness" as defined by donors with clients' and counselors' reflections on efficacy, I bring together the anthropological study of metrics in global health with phenomenological work on the articulation of experience to show how lived experiences of suffering and healing overflowed the boundaries of humanitarian frames.

Chapter 5, "Care," returns to scenes of therapeutic encounters to examine the ethics of transient humanitarian care—both its limitations and its fleeting possibilities. Approached through the frame of crisis, people suffering from ongoing problems of gender-based violence, poverty, migration, and chronic mental illness suddenly became worthy of humanitarian concern. However, the lack of access to sustained mental health services became a problem as counselors provided people with brief access to care and psychopharmaceuticals in regions that otherwise did not have such resources regularly available. While the temporality of humanitarianism enacted a form of violence when it met chronic suffering with transient care, the encounters between counselors and clients that were inaugurated by the work of disaster also created unexpected possibilities—to discover novel treatments, visualize different futures, and experience kindness, hope, and gentleness. Despite prevailing anthropological critiques of the violence of humanitarianism, I argue that such moments of gentleness constitute an *intersubjective otherwise* that can instill small changes in the present, no matter how precarious the conditions of their creation.

Many books are organized around a binary critique of biopolitics on the one hand and a celebration of ways of living and caring that resist and endure in the face of biopolitical control on the other.[98] This book does something different. Instead of locating the *otherwise* outside the frame of humanitarianism, it explores the possibilities and foreclosures that were generated by disaster and its management and the contingency of these formations.

Crisis

In the aftermath of the 2015 earthquakes in Nepal, the sense that mental health was in crisis was palpable in Kathmandu. The once-quiet mental health NGO offices were frenetic with activity as project managers from donor organizations arrived in jeeps to negotiate contracts. Prior to the earthquakes, I had been spending time with different NGOs for mental health and counseling in Kathmandu as well as shadowing Nepali psychiatrists in a Kathmandu hospital outpatient psychiatric clinic. Now many of these experts had become directly involved in the humanitarian effort. As I sat in NGO offices researching situation reports on the status of postdisaster mental health in Nepal, activity swirled around me. There was a sense of urgency in the air.

The postdisaster mental health response encompassed a range of humanitarian activities funded by international NGOs (INGOs) and aid organizations such as UNICEF, the Swiss Agency for Development and Cooperation, Médicos del Mundo, IsraAID, Handicap International, and International Medical Corps (IMC), a California-based humanitarian NGO that had been chosen by Facebook as "its featured partner in a worldwide campaign" to help Nepal.[1] Two days after Mark Zuckerberg, founder of Facebook, posted and endorsed the IMC relief campaign on his wall, Facebook received over $10 million in donations from more than 500,000 individual contributors. Ultimately, Facebook raised over $15 million for IMC's work on mental health in Nepal.

The program activities that humanitarian organizations initiated to treat psychic suffering after the earthquakes were wide-ranging. They included setting up crisis hotlines and providing counseling, psychoeducation, and psychiatric medication to individuals and communities in the fourteen districts of the earthquake-affected region. They also involved work focused on "capacity building," such as organizing prescriber trainings to teach local health workers to diagnose and treat mental illness, as well as training and supervising counselors and community psychosocial workers in basic methods of counseling and support. The aim of these latter activities was to create a workforce that could carry out the humanitarian response to Nepal's new crisis of mental health.

Crisis is a surprising concept. In classical Greece, the term referred to a moment requiring critical deliberation between right or wrong, life or death, salvation or damnation.[2] In Greek, the root of the word *crisis* is *krino*, which means "to separate," "to choose," "to judge," "to decide."[3] As Reinhard Koselleck has observed in his conceptual study, in ancient Greece *crisis* had juridical, medical, and theological meanings, but in each sphere, it designated a critical situation requiring an act of judgment about "what is just or unjust, what contributes to salvation or damnation, what furthers life or death."[4] In this way, according to the classical sense of the term, *crisis* and *critique* are inseparably intertwined.[5] However, today we no longer recognize crisis as a time of careful deliberation. As we live through a period saturated by ongoing crises, the very meaning of *crisis* has been turned on its head.[6] Crisis, a now-dominant trope of mainstream media, no longer inspires critical reflection but instead generates a "crisis-paralysis circuit."[7] Janet Roitman has argued that, because crisis is assumed to be self-evident, determinations of crisis are rarely questioned—crisis is a blind spot.[8] We can see this play out in news headlines, such as one published in *WIRED* magazine that read, "Let's Stop Nepal's Mental Health Crisis Before It Happens."[9] To stare into the blind spot requires questioning a priori claims, narratives, and objectifications of crisis and the actions they make possible.

In Nepal, although a mental health policy had been drafted and endorsed by the government in 1996, it had never been implemented.[10] Two decades later, mental health had not yet been incorporated into the public health care system. Psychiatric services remained concentrated in the capital of Kathmandu and in select district hospitals, and mental health system development had been largely dependent on the work of NGOs. Outside of these institutional resources, for the past decade temporally finite donor-funded community mental health programs provided uneven access to care in a handful of districts. From this perspective, "mental health care"—narrowly defined as access to psychiatric and counseling services—had been "in crisis" for a long time but had not been critiqued as such in public discourse.

Humanitarians are aware that crisis can be harnessed to generate care, at least momentarily. In 2013, the World Health Organization (WHO) published a report titled *Building Back Better: Sustainable Mental Health Care After*

Emergencies.[11] In this report, the authors argue that because international aid flows during times of crisis, a situation of disaster or emergency should be seen as an "important opportunity for mental health reform and development."[12] The report is accompanied by a series of exemplary case studies from countries, including Iraq, Sri Lanka, and Indonesia, where mental health systems were constructed in times of emergency. In the period of crisis following the 2015 earthquakes, many organizations focused on providing short-term mental health and psychosocial support, but some humanitarians, inspired by the WHO's *Building Back Better* framework, used claims of crisis as an opportunity to expand psychiatry and counseling services in Nepal. Following the *Building Back Better* report, humanitarian organizations turned to the task of building Nepal's mental health system, blurring the boundaries between development and humanitarianism. This boundary-blurring work speaks to the growing awareness among humanitarians that crisis and disaster open windows of opportunity for rapid investment, development, and social transformation.[13]

Drawing on a combination of ethnographic and archival research, in what follows I place postdisaster narratives of "crisis" and definitions of "the better" into the context of a longer history of the biopolitics of mental health governance in Nepal. This story begins in the archives of a community mental health project in the 1980s, travels through the rise and fall of psychosocial interventions for trauma and PTSD in the mid-2000s, and ends (tentatively) with the emergence of the global mental health movement.[14] Across each period, I discuss the shifting narratives and imagined figures that have served as justifications for donor-funded interventions into the psychic life of the population. With this history in mind, the chapter then turns with fresh eyes to the UN cluster meetings, where a heterogeneous group of experts gathered in the aftermath of the earthquakes to seize the opportunity of crisis to "build back better" and to imagine what the future of Nepal's mental health system might become.

In Nepal, humanitarian frames of "crisis" and definitions of "the better" shaped the postdisaster response and its imaginaries of repair. Claims of crisis were used to justify specific forms of intervention and visions of mental health governance, many of which radically departed from preexisting ways of conceptualizing and caring for psycho-spiritual affliction in Nepal. To approach the emergence of a mental health crisis in this way is not to deny the lived reality of postearthquake suffering but to explore how affliction comes to be objectified as a problem requiring certain techniques of intervention in different times and places.[15] Following Bruno Latour, to study the crystallization of "matters of fact"—such as the fact of a mental health crisis—is not to argue that crisis is a mirage but is instead to observe *"how many participants are gathered in a thing to make it exist and maintain its existence"* as well as who is invited to gather and make such determinations.[16] In Nepal, international declarations of a mental health crisis functioned as performative speech acts that inaugurated the arrival of humanitarian organizations, the funding of psychosocial programs, and the gathering of mental health experts in UN cluster meetings.[17] These words and actions served as a powerful force of collective intentionality that transformed the suffering of earthquake-affected communities into a crisis in need of psychosocial intervention and psychiatric treatment. From a critical phenomenological perspective, it becomes possible to observe the historical contingency of the work of disaster that inaugurated the assembly of particular forms of knowledge, therapeutics, pharmaceuticals, and care out of an infinite range of possible responses to the earth's destabilization.

Deculturation

Large-scale interventions into the psychic life of populations are not a new phenomenon. In 1948, the World Federation for Mental Health (WFMH) was founded in London with the explicit goal of promoting modernization in the postcolonial commonwealth by identifying its local psychological impediments.[18] A central theory during the post–World War II era identified "deculturation"—that is, loss of culture—as a cause of mental illness among supposedly nonmodern and uncivilized people faced with a rapidly modernizing world. This argument first gained prominence in the 1930s as an explanation for "African insanity," a pathology justified in the language of racial and cultural difference.[19] As Megan Vaughan writes, a guiding assumption of deculturation theory was that " 'the African' in the twentieth century, like the European woman in the nineteenth century, was simply not equipped to cope with 'civilization.' "[20] In the decades that followed, the theory of deculturation would spread far beyond colonial Africa, becoming a dominant explanation for mental illness in the developing world used by international organizations. As the anthropologist Margaret Mead argued in the highly influential technical assistance manual *Cultural Patterns and Technical Change*, which she prepared for UNESCO on behalf of the WFMH, changes introduced by development programs disrupt cultural systems and have cascading effects, including increased mental illness.[21]

Mead's report outlined a new biopolitics of psychic life at a global scale, a project described in the manual's introduction as being "concerned with two new developments, the purposive attempt to cultivate mental health, and the purposive attempt to introduce technical change" in countries around the world.[22] The report goes on to note that while people everywhere have always been concerned with their own well-being, the work of the WFMH constituted a radically new way of thinking about the problem of mental health. As Mead writes, "What is new is the assumption, on an international scale, of responsibility for introducing changes which are needed among peoples in areas of the world which can visibly benefit from the knowledge which the peoples of other areas have—of techniques which will increase production and conserve natural resources; of nutritional practices which will improve the well-being of a people; of public health practices which will lower the death rate, the incidence of epidemic and endemic diseases, and rescue individuals now doomed to physical and mental illness."[23] By the 1950s, the management of psychic life was seen as the key to successful development in the postcolonial world, and as indicated by the participation of Margaret Mead in the report, the tools of anthropology were to play an important role in realizing this cross-cultural "rescue" mission. While Nepal was never colonized, the logics and rationale of its first mental health development program are conceptually linked to the approach of the WFMH.

The next major development in the management of mental health at a global scale took place in the 1970s, when the WHO began to shift its focus from individual disease eradication programs toward investment in basic health care services. In 1975, in the context of this institutional transition, the WHO's Expert Committee on Mental Health published a galvanizing report on the "Organization of Mental Health Services in Developing Countries."[24] A meeting was convened in Geneva in October 1974, where Nigerian psychiatrist and then–WHO Deputy Director General Dr. T. A. Lambo opened the event. Dr. Lambo emphasized that new advancements in psychopharmacology and the availability of "effective treatment methods to modify and attenuate a wide range of psychiatric disorders" had created previously unimaginable possibilities for mental health treatment in developing countries.[25]

The urgent need to develop mental health services was justified with statistics, declaring that "in the developing countries, over 40 million men, women, and children are suffering from serious untreated mental disorders."[26] Threats to "citizens' wellbeing" included "rapid population growth, crises in food production, internal migration, and accelerated social change."[27] Closely echoing the earlier ideas of the WFMH, the report argued that "development itself produces problems of adjustment and adaptation that should be of general social concern, as well as having important implications for mental health."[28] However, a central constraint to mental health system development was the problem of "manpower," that is, the scarcity of psychiatrists in developing countries. The experts conjured disturbing visions of the extent of the crisis when they described "the rural masses" and urban "concentrations of deviants" who were unable to manage their mental afflictions because of lack of access to psychiatric services.[29]

In his opening remarks, Dr. Lambo called for innovations in mental health care. Above all, the report was highly critical of "costly, centralized, custodial, mental hospitals" and argued that the only way forward was to strengthen community-based care.[30] The experts recommended improving basic mental health services through the use of minimally trained "primary health workers" and by integrating mental health into primary health care services, reducing the cost of drugs, developing and evaluating pilot projects in community mental health, drafting national policies on mental health, and, above all, recognizing that mental health was a problem not only for individuals and communities but also national development.

By the 1980s, Norman Sartorius, director of the WHO Division of Mental Health, noted in an article on the state of the field that "concern about the social and psychological consequences of rapid economic growth," including rapid urbanization, poverty, hunger, and apathy in developing countries, had generated increasing support and desire for mental health programs and psychiatric services among government leaders.[31] The idea that rapid development and modernization were leading causes of mental illness galvanized support among donor countries for the expansion of mental health services in developing countries. Inspired by the WHO's 1975 report on mental health and the Alma-Ata Declaration of 1978, which proclaimed primary health care to be the key to attaining health for all, in 1984 an interdenominational Christian missionary organization called United Mission to Nepal (UMN) launched the first mental health development program in the Himalayan nation.[32] UMN had worked in the area of health development in Nepal since the country first opened its borders in 1951 and was well positioned to introduce a new modality of therapeutics.

UMN's "Mental Health Project" ran for fourteen years and focused on drug abuse, community mental health, training health workers, counseling expats, and providing services in the Dhulikhel jail, where the abandoned mentally ill were incarcerated. The design of the project was modeled after the approach developed in the Community Mental Health Unit of the Department of Psychiatry at NIMHANS Bangalore, one of India's most prominent neuropsychiatric hospitals.[33] Following this model, mental health services were integrated into already existing community health services at the health-post level. Archival documents from the 1980s indicate a priority placed on diagnosing "psychosis, epilepsy, depression, neurosis, [and] mental

H 030401/0027

FIGURE 1.1. The first card in a set of training cards that were used in UMN's Mental Health Project to aid health workers in the psychiatric diagnosis and treatment of mental disorders. Each image depicted here corresponds to a specific behavior that may indicate mental illness and training card with further information.

मानसिक रोगका विभिन्न लक्षण

अनेक स्वास्थ्य समस्या (रोग) मध्ये मानसिक रोगको कारण र उपचार सम्बन्धमा सर्वसाधारण जनतालाई ज्यादै थोरै मात्र थाहा छ । यसैकारण यसको उपचारको लागि मानिसहरू फाल्फुक, तन्त्र मन्त्र, धामी फोकी र देवी देवताको सहारामा जानुछन् । यस्ता उपचारका विशिष्ट अपनाउनाले विरामीको समुचित उपचार गर्न ढिलो भै विरामीको स्वास्थ्यमा हानि पर्न सक्छ । औषधि विज्ञान तथा आधुनिक उपचार पद्धतिको क्षेत्रमा भएका महत्वपूर्ण वैज्ञानिक प्रगतिको फलस्वरूप अब लगभग सबैनसो मानसिक रोगको सस्तो, सुलभ, सरल र प्रभावकारी उपचार उपलब्ध छ । हामी सबैलाई थाहा भएकै कुरो हो कि जुनसुकै रोगको पनि सुरुमै रोग निदान र उपचार अति महत्वपूर्ण हुन्छ ।

हाम्रो समाजमा धेरै अगाडि देखि पर्दै आएका परम्परागत चलन र विश्वास भौ छन् । छोटो समयमा नै विस्तारै बदल्न संभव छैन । शिक्षित व्यक्तिहरू तथा समाजका अगुवाहरूको पनि यी परम्परामा गहिरो आस्था छ । सही जानकारी दिलाउने तपाईको निरन्तर प्रयासले यसमा परिवर्तन ल्याउन सक्छ ।

शायद तपाईलाई आफ्नो कार्यक्षेत्रमा पर्ने गाउँको मानसिक रोगीको बारेमा पहिले देखि नै जानकारी छ होला । भविष्यमा कमन्को शिलशिलामा अरू केही मानसिक रोगी संग पनि तपाईको भेट हुनेछ । साथै तपाईलाई थाहा नभएका रोगीहरूको बारेमा पनि सोधसोध गर्ने आवश्यक छ । यो शैक्षिक सामग्रीले मानसिक रोगबाट पीडित रोगीलाई चिन्न मद्दत गर्छ । त्यसको अतिरिक्त तपाईले बताउन चाहेका मानसिक रोगका लक्षणहरू दर्शकलाई चर्ल्लु पार्न यसले मद्दत गर्नेछ ।

यो शैक्षिक सामग्रीको उपयोग निम्न उद्देश्यको लागि गर्न सकिन्छ:–

१. समाजका मानसिक रोगी पत्ता लगाउन ।

२. मानसिक रोगीका परिवारलाई मानसिक रोगको बारेमा शिक्षा दिन ।

३. विशिष्ट व्यक्तिहरू जस्तै; शिक्षक, प्रध्यापक, सामाजिक कार्यकर्ता, स्थानीय अगुवा, गाउँ विकास समितिका पदाधिकारीहरू र अन्य शिक्षित युवाहरूमा मानसिक रोग प्रति सही दृष्टिकोण विकास गर्न ।

५. विभिन्न प्रशिक्षण शिविरको शिलशिलामा गाउँका अगुवा तथा सम्पूर्ण जनतालाई मानसिक रोगको बारेमा शिक्षित गराउन ।

FEATURES OF MENTAL DISORDERS

Of the many health problems (illness) the causes and treatment of mental illness are poorly understood by the general public. As a result people seek non-medical help from healers, priests, witch-doctor and often visit places of pilgrimage for help. People using these methods often can harm the patient by delaying proper treatment. Following major scientific development in the field of psychotropic drugs and modern techniques of treatment, simple, effective and inexpensive methods of treatment are now available for almost all the mental disorders. As you know, in all illnesses early recognition and treatment is most important.

The traditional beliefs and practices in our community have been there for many years. They can not be replaced in a short time. In addition, these are firmly held by the educated and the leaders of the community. Your repeated efforts to give the correct information would lead to change.

You may already know of some patients with mental illnesses in the villages where you are working. You are likely to see some of them in future during your work. In addition, you must actively enquire about similar patients who may not be known to you. This aid will help you in identifying people with mental illnesses. Moreover, the pictures would facilitate the viewers to visualize the features of mental disorders you are communicating.

This visual aid can be used for the following purposes:

1. to identify mentally ill persons in the community,
2. to educate the family members of the mentally ill,
3. to sensitize important people like local leaders, teachers, educated youth, and members of other service agencies on various mental disorders, and
4. to educate the general public and other village leaders during the Orientation Training Camps.

H 030401/0027

FIGURE 1.2. Back side of the first card in the set describing the possible uses of this visual aid. The card emphasizes the need to correct "traditional beliefs and practices" with "modern techniques of treatment."

भुतप्रेत वा आत्माको प्रभाव हुनु
BEHAVIOR ATTRIBUTED TO BLACK MAGIC
H 030401/0027

FIGURE 1.3. Front side of a UMN training card titled "Behavior Attributed to Black Magic." The card depicts a distressed a woman sitting in a ritual healing ceremony with a shaman (*dhami-jhakri*).

अनौठो व्यबहार गर्नु
BEHAVING IN A STRANGE MANNER
H 030401/0027

FIGURE 1.4. Front side of a UMN training card titled "Behaving in a Strange Manner," used to illustrate an example of behavior that may indicate mental illness.

retardation" and a particular concern with mental illness among women and urban drug users.[34] The program provided a small number of psychotropic medications to participating health posts and ran ten-day training workshops for health assistants, community medical auxiliaries, and a handful of nurses supervised by UMN psychiatrist Dr. Christine Wright and her senior health assistant. For training in the psychiatric diagnosis and treatment of mental illness, health workers drew on materials such as a Nepali-language "Mental Health Manual" developed by UMN as well as illustrated cards depicting "features of mental disorders" and hypothetical case descriptions.[35]

In the UMN project's training materials, Euro-American "scientific development in psychotropic drugs and modern techniques of treatment" was positioned against "non-medical help" from shamans, priests, healers, and visits to pilgrimage sites. Instead of translating diagnostic categories into "culturally appropriate" equivalents, UMN worked with a universal model of mental illness that was suspicious of Indigenous concepts of affliction. Health workers were encouraged to provide education to community leaders about psychiatry with the aim of correcting "traditional beliefs and practices." Underlined and in bold lettering the training card on "features of mental disorders" states: "The traditional beliefs and practices in our community have been there for many years. They cannot be replaced in a short time . . . **Your repeated efforts to give correct information would lead to change.**" In the early years of the WHO's turn to community mental health, traditional attitudes toward psychic affliction, which ranged from fear and stigma to what the WHO report described as "belief in the supernatural," were seen as a "major obstacle to the development of rational mental health services."[36] To the extent that the role of traditional healers was acknowledged, they were seen as either potential collaborators to be educated in the promotion of "rational" approaches to mental health or "unscrupulous" and "mercenary" figures who exploited their patients.[37] Similar attitudes toward Indigenous epistemologies of illness and healing, which involved witchcraft, spirit possession, and shamanic rituals, were replicated in the training materials of the early UMN program in Nepal.[38]

However, despite divergent epistemologies of affliction and its treatment, according to official internal reports, UMN's community mental health program was well received during its inaugural year. In a handwritten draft of a report assessing the Pilot Community Mental Health Program, Dr. David Hickingbotham, one of two UMN psychiatrists running the program, wrote, "The project staff have been greatly encouraged by many aspects of this pilot study. The level of interest of the H.P. [health-post] staff has been high, the community acceptance of the project has been widespread and the appreciation of the services provided, by the patients and their families has been heartfelt."[39] Dr. Wright summed up the overall project similarly in her annual report: "Has been steady and encouraging in most areas of the work, and I am often aware of the rightness of the timing for our project here in Nepal. There are many openings, and I feel, a real role at present for us in stimulating the development of services, and interest in alternative models of care. I am grateful to God for his guidance in so many new situations."[40]

Like the humanitarians that would arrive after the 2015 earthquakes, Dr. Wright emphasized that the *timing was right* to expand psychiatric services in Nepal. The need for mental health services in places like Nepal had been inspired by the WHO's sensationalizing presentation of statistics on rates of untreated mental illness in the developing world, which used metrics to make the problem of mental health visible at a global scale.[41] UMN's work itself was justified by a small study undertaken in Nepal in 1983, which concluded that over 10 percent of people in a village south of Kathmandu were suffering from mental illness.[42] Dr. Wright described the expansion of psychiatry, a secular form of therapeutics, as a project guided by God.

In the mid-1990s, UMN helped draft Nepal's first National Mental Health Policy, which called for the creation of a mental health department within the Ministry of Health and full integration of mental health into the health care system, with the aim of providing mental health services to the entire population of Nepal by the year 2000.[43] Yet Dr. Wright's sense of timing was not quite right, as ultimately the policy was never endorsed. While a description of UMN's project was included in the *World Mental Health Casebook* as an exemplary case study, the "Mental Health Project" officially ended in 2003 when the government of Nepal restricted the activities of foreign development organizations.[44] However, this restriction marked the transformation, not the end, of donor-funded mental health programs in Nepal.

The Empire of Trauma

When I first traveled to Nepal in the summer of 2012, the therapeutic landscape I encountered had been profoundly shaped by the Maoist insurgency and the victim-focused projects and programs it had attracted. I spent my days in an NGO that specialized in mental health services for victims of torture. Inside the converted bungalow, the office walls were decorated with paintings and cartoons of torture scenes alongside decorative sketches of the diverse faces of the people of Nepal.

In 2012, the country had just begun to emerge from a decade of protracted civil war that stretched from 1996 to 2006. Since the beginning of the

Panchayat era in the 1960s, pressure for democracy had been building, during which time King Mahendra had ruled the nation without allowing political representation. In 1990, a coalition of banned-political parties launched the First People's Movement (Jan Andolan), which drew widespread participation across Nepali society. Meanwhile, a new political party had been gathering strength in the villages of the midwestern hills. Inspired by the tactical strategies, rural focus, and anti-imperialist philosophy of Mao Zedong, they called themselves Maoists. At first the monarchy in Kathmandu paid little attention to the growing Maoist cells. In 1996 the Maoists submitted a letter to Nepal's prime minister. Listed in the document were forty demands and an ultimatum: if the demands were not met, the Maoists would launch an insurgency. The demands—which included restricting the role of foreign development organizations, interrupting India's political influence, redistributing land, and fighting caste, gender, and ethnic discrimination—were ignored. The Maoists declared a "People's War" against the state.[45]

The struggle between the state and the Maoist People's Liberation Army was long and violent. By the end of the decade-long war, over thirteen thousand people, including civilians, had lost their lives and two hundred thousand had been displaced.[46] Many had been raped and tortured at the hands of either the Nepal Police or the Maoists; thousands had been disappeared. The Maoists strategically used the hills to stage their battles, moving from village to village by night. By day the Nepal Police would follow, tracking the Maoists and brutally punishing, and often torturing and killing, anyone suspected of providing shelter to them.[47] Maoists soon became known for recruiting children into their ranks as they moved through different villages and gave ideological speeches in schools. The fragmentation of village life during this period created deep rents of distrust between people, particularly in close-knit rural communities. In the midst of the violence, human rights organizations began to pay close attention to the conflict, documenting cases of torture and disappearance and publishing them for national and international audiences.[48]

Occurring simultaneously with the People's War was the influx of one hundred thousand ethnically Nepali Bhutanese refugees, who were resettled in the eastern district of Jhapa by the United Nations High Commissioner for Refugees. Together the relocation of Bhutanese refugees and the violence of the People's War drew a new breed of international experts to Nepal. Peace and conflict programs funded by development and UN agencies proliferated. In the area of health, there was a new focus on psychosocial interventions in conflict-affected communities, with an emphasis on healing trauma and PTSD among victim groups, such as child soldiers. The psychosocial approach understood that individual psychological distress was embedded in social relations. By the late 2000s, psychosocial interventions had become a dominant component of many international development projects around the world, which operated under the assumption that healing individual trauma would repair the nation in the aftermath of war and conflict.[49] As the violence of the People's War escalated, mental health was framed by foreign development organizations as both a social and political problem.

One day at the NGO, I was given the file of a young woman who had received treatment for PTSD. The file offered a glimpse into the types of clients their projects focused on, such as victims of the People's War and specifically those that fell into the category of "Verified Minors and Late Recruits."[50] The NGO staff asked if I could write a case history of the young woman's story to highlight how the physical, psychiatric, and psychosocial care they provided had reduced her suffering, which they diagnosed as PTSD. After sitting with a staff member who helped me interpret the deeply disturbing and violent contents of the file, I dutifully wrote the report. But I did not yet understand how the focus on PTSD in Nepal was also part of the exponential rise of Euro-American-funded psychosocial interventions for victims of trauma.[51] By producing exemplary case studies about the successful treatment of PTSD such as these, the organization could secure continued funding from foreign donors.

In their analysis of the history and politics of trauma, Didier Fassin and Richard Rechtman have argued that as the concept of psychic wounding in the aftermath of violent events gained acceptance in the field of humanitarian psychiatry, trauma inaugurated a powerful new condition of victimhood.[52] Today those suffering from the traumas of war, violence, and disaster garner sympathy and gain access to compensation on the basis of their victim status, a process that is mediated by a vast network of international mental health and psychosocial support professionals who document their stories in detailed case write-ups. Fassin and Rechtman have called this phenomenon "the empire of trauma," describing how the language of trauma and PTSD became the dominant prerequisite for care, compensation, and even citizenship in the twenty-first century.

During that same summer of 2012, I traveled to the district of Dang to accompany NGO staff on a training workshop. The journey introduced me to the red earth and yellow mustard fields of the Dang-Deukari valley as well as the ongoing legacy of the People's War, which was referred to simply as "the conflict" (*dwandwa*). Dang had been an important site for psychosocial interventions as it was a major destination for internally displaced people during and after the war. As part of their work in the region, the NGO focused on not only psychosocial counseling for PTSD among victims of torture but also

basic psychiatric diagnostic training for health-post workers. In the swelter-
ing hotel training hall of a small town, the health workers assembled under
whirring fans, sipping hot tea to "cut iron with iron" (fight a force with a force
of the same nature, as the local saying goes) in the heavy monsoon heat of the
Tarai summer. Over the course of a week, the health workers learned to diagnose and pharmaceutically treat depression, anxiety, PTSD, and conversion
disorder among their patients.

Two years later, I returned to Dang once again. During my stay with a local
counselor, I joined her on an external evaluation of a psychosocial project
that was finally concluding. In many ways it was a typical project evaluation,
focused on documenting "success stories" from patients and health workers
who had benefited from participation in the program. We traveled by jeep
from village to village, visiting ex-clients in their homes and asking them if
and how they had benefited from counseling and medication. The evaluators
were surprised to learn that the leading cause of mental distress among the
participants was not the *dwandwa* but "love tragedy" and migration.

Nepal is among the top remittance-driven economies in the world. As of
2021, 22.3 percent of the gross domestic product (GDP) was generated from
personal remittances, totaling $8.23 billion.[53] For millions of Nepalis, due to
the lack of employment opportunities, labor migration to Malaysia and the
Gulf States has been the only option to earn a salaried wage. While some
groups have established strong diasporic communities in the US and the UK,
the vast majority of the population does not have the resources or connections
to migrate to Europe or the US. Instead, Nepal's majority male migrant labor
force relies on manpower agents to negotiate work contracts in factories and
construction sites in Saudi Arabia, Qatar, and the United Arab Emirates. The
Nepali and international media regularly report on high rates of death among
migrant workers abroad, many of whom die of unknown causes while working in conditions of extreme desert heat.[54] Despite the risks, labor migration is
not only a primary source of livelihood but a social expectation for many men
in Nepal.[55] These migration patterns, which began in the 1990s, have radically
reshaped Nepali society down to the most intimate level of family relations.

While labor migration has reconfigured the family, with women and the
elderly remaining behind to manage homes and farms as husbands and sons
work abroad for years, changing attitudes toward love and marriage have also
transformed the organization of kinship.[56] Access to digital technologies and
the increasing popularity of love marriage have, alongside migration, created
new modes of intimacy as well as emotional dissolution.[57] Yet neither love
tragedy nor migration seemed to fit into the figure of the trauma victim that
the postconflict psychosocial programs expected.[58]

Back in Kathmandu, the NGO office was increasingly quiet. Trauma-focused projects were phasing out, funding was drying up, and victims of conflict seemed to recede into the background. The NGO staff began brainstorming new project proposal ideas focused on gender-based violence (GBV) to circulate to their donors. Meanwhile, a powerful new turn in the world of mental health development was quickly taking root in another NGO across town. I would soon discover that my fieldwork had stretched across two paradigms of mental health governance in Nepal and elsewhere: from the empire of trauma to the rise of the Movement for Global Mental Health (MGMH).

A Global Burden of Disease

In 1993 the World Bank published the *World Development Report*.[59] This report introduced the concept of "disability-adjusted life years" (DALYs)—that is, the sum of years of healthy life lost due to early death, ill health, and years lived with disability—arrayed by country and by type of illness, as a way to measure the "global burden of disease." The publication of the highly influential book *World Mental Health* soon followed, presenting the "first systematic attempt to survey the burden of suffering" related to mental, social, and behavioral problems at a global scale.[60] Here, mental well-being was framed both as a universal human right and as an economic concern, for, according to this logic, by reducing the "burden of disease" caused by mental illness, it would become possible to increase economic productivity.[61]

A decade later, the *Lancet* commissioned the agenda-setting "Global Mental Health" series. The first article in the series began with the rallying cry, "No health without mental health" and signaled a return to the Alma-Ata goals of supporting the development of primary health care systems, with the inclusion of mental health.[62] Based on the WHO's 2005 estimates, 14 percent of the global burden of disease was attributed to neuropsychiatric disorders, with the majority due to depression, substance-use disorders, and psychosis.[63] The WHO's Global Burden of Disease Report found neuropsychiatric disorders to be a significant cause of disability, accounting for 31.7 percent of the total years-lived-with-disability worldwide.[64] Drawing on these metrics, the authors of the global mental health series outlined urgent priorities for mental health development in "low- and middle-income countries": improve the quality of health services, develop and evaluate psychosocial interventions for effectiveness, strengthen health care systems to include mental health care, and raise awareness about mental health.[65] The justification for the need to intervene in mental health at a global scale was made through various rhetorical devices. The field of global mental health constructed a powerful argument through health metrics such as DALYs that enabled the measurement of the global burden of mental illness and new visualization of a global crisis.[66] Metrics were also linked to a moral discourse that framed the refusal to address the "treatment gap" as a human rights issue and "failure of humanity," claims often supported with reference to images of the mentally ill in chains as a result of stigma and lack of access to psychiatric services.[67] Based on these powerful arguments, over the next decade global mental health would become a rapidly expanding new area of focus in the field of global health.[68]

In 2016 the World Bank, in partnership with the WHO, held a high-profile event entitled "Out of the Shadows: Making Mental Health a Global Development Priority."[69] Here, during the inaugural panel, mental health was framed, once again, as a major constraint to development. Citing figures showing that mental illness is the leading cause of years lived with disability (YLDs), it was announced that "1 trillion dollars is lost every year due to lost productivity in the work place due to depression and anxiety," while every dollar invested in the treatment of depression and anxiety yields a four-dollar return in better health and the ability to work.[70] The role of the World Bank in this new global crisis would be to provide funding and technical support for the development of mental health systems in order to decrease the prevalence of mental illness in resource-poor countries, with the ultimate goal of increasing economic productivity. The neoliberal economic framing of the cost of mental distress galvanized donor support and transformed mental health into an economic problem worthy of investment. As the management of mental health in populations was justified in economic terms, the old link between biopolitics, capital, and the economization of life became clear.[71]

Since the birth of the new movement, Nepal has figured prominently in global mental health research, generating case studies and data and serving as a key node in multicountry projects.[72] With funding from the UK Department for International Development, the European Commission, Grand Challenges Canada, and the WHO, a handful of global mental health projects have focused on strengthening Nepal's mental health system and developing evidence-based psychosocial interventions. One irony of this history is that while Nepal may lack widespread access to psychiatric and counseling services, like the "experimental exuberance" of family planning projects in Bangladesh described by Michelle Murphy, the Himalayan nation has attracted a high concentration of international experts in the "psy" fields and cutting-edge experimentation in global mental health.[73]

Unlike UMN's earlier efforts to replace Nepali concepts of affliction with Euro-American diagnostic categories, the new generation of global mental health researchers in Nepal had anthropological training and placed cultural concerns at the core of their work. These researchers were well-versed in the field of psychological anthropology and its studies of ethnopsychology, shamanism, and the phenomenology of illness and healing in Nepal.[74] This corpus of anthropological literature on culture and emotion was used to design culturally sensitive psychosocial interventions informed by Nepali ethnopsychology.[75] By operationalizing culture, global mental health researchers created new languages for mental health. For example, efforts were made to decouple madness from its traditional association with dysfunction of the brain (*dimag*) and reassociate it to the heart-mind (*man*) the seat of emotion and desire. This semiotic intervention aimed to destigmatize mental health care by conceptualizing the psychosocial counselor as one who listens to worries held in the heart-mind.[76]

This was not the first conceptual intervention in the history of mental health development programs in Nepal. In the 1990s, UMN introduced the diagnosis of "nerve illness" (*nasako rog*) in a similar attempt to promote the use of psychiatric services. Through the concept of *nasako rog*, UMN psychiatrists encouraged Nepali people to reconceptualize ghost and spirit affliction as a biological disease caused by nerve problems so that they might seek psychopharmaceutical treatment instead of shamanic healing from a *dhami-jhakri*.[77] The invention of *nasako rog* in the 1990s promoted a strictly biological understanding of mental illness that resonated with Western psychiatry's turn to the biological model of mental illness. In contrast, the later introduction of the concept of the "psychosocial counselor" as *manobimarshakarta*, one who "advises on matters of the heart-mind," reflected the field of global mental health's promotion of simple therapeutic interventions that emphasized the role of listening to emotions over diagnostic categories.

Throughout the history of mental health governance in Nepal, the problematization of mental health has largely been determined by international experts—the WHO alongside foreign NGOs and public health researchers—and reflected the shifting trends of the field of global health. These actors have introduced both the framing of the problem of mental health and delineated its possible solutions, a project that has repeatedly involved the introduction of new concepts of affliction and care.[78] These are the historical a prioris that shaped the perception of a new mental crisis and determined the conditions of its emergence.[79] With this history in mind, we now return to the scene of humanitarian intervention in the aftermath of disaster, where a group of international experts gathered to define and solve the crisis of mental health at a scale never before seen in Nepal.

Gathering Around a Matter of Concern

On May 29, 2015, seventeen days after the second major earthquake, the UN Mental Health Sub-Cluster held its first coordination meeting in a small tent outside the Ministry of Health and Population after the National Health Cluster meeting had adjourned. At the National Health Cluster meeting, international humanitarian organizations were highly visible. Everywhere people wore vests emblazoned with logos and acronyms—UN, WHO, UNICEF, MSF, IOM, MDM—which served as both marker of their expert status and potent symbol of proximity to money and power.

The Mental Health Sub-Cluster was relatively small, an apt reflection of its minor status vis-à-vis "physical" health in the cluster system hierarchy. Yet it was precisely through such official spaces of gathering that the crisis of mental health began to emerge as fact. In the first meeting, the country directors of IsraAID, International Organization of Migration (IOM), Médicos del Mundo (MDM), Médecins Sans Frontières (MSF), and Handicap International were there, alongside representatives from Nepali mental health NGOs. After the meeting, I spoke with a humanitarian who mentioned it was her first time in Nepal. Prior to arriving in Kathmandu, she had worked with victims of domestic abuse in Israel, with survivors of the Sewol Ferry accident in South Korea, and with those impacted by the tsunami in Sri Lanka. Like many others, her organization was planning a six-month intervention in Nepal, with the possibility of extension.

The UN Cluster System is a bureaucratic mechanism organized by the UN Office for the Coordination of Humanitarian Affairs (OCHA) in order to manage the coordination of humanitarian activities across organizations, collect data on activities implemented, and avoid "duplication" of services. As Elizabeth Cullen Dunn writes reflecting on the humanitarian response to internally displaced people in the Republic of Georgia, "the cluster system rendered suffering technical by breaking human needs into nine categories managed at the level of population: shelter, food security, water and sanitation, health, logistics, early recovery, protection, security, and telecommunications."[80] Such coordination and categorization turned out to be a difficult task. Two parallel groups concerned with mental health were created: the Mental Health Sub-Cluster, part of the Health Cluster, held in the Ministry of Health and Population office, and the Psychosocial Working Group, part of the Protection Cluster, held across town in the Ministry for Women and Children. I attended both groups, as did many others. Activities were reported on a weekly basis by the cluster leaders to each group, documenting the who,

what, when, and where of humanitarian action. This information was gathered by OCHA for the purpose of tracking and preventing duplication, and
was shared in regular emailed minutes. Meetings proceeded by going around
the table, where each representative shared the number of "beneficiaries"
reached and described their organization's activities. I attended these groups
from their formation in May 2015 until their dissolution in November 2015
when an "unofficial" blockade at the Indian border made petrol so scarce that
members could no longer justify the cost of black-market fuel needed to attend the meetings.

The blockade made life in Kathmandu increasingly unbearable. As fuel
became scarce, my neighbors began cooking their food over scrap wood
fires outside. One day I observed a long line of bottles tied to a rope snaking
around the block as people waited their turn to buy kerosene. When possible,
petrol was procured in small plastic bottles and siphoned into motorcycle
tanks. The border blockade was an artifact of the country's turbulent postdisaster political transformation. In September 2015, the members of Nepal's
Constituent Assembly had voted in favor of a new constitution after years of
political deadlock following the end of the Maoist insurgency in 2006. The
2015 constitution officially marked the transformation of Nepal from a centralized Hindu nation to a secular republic based on federalism. In response
to the terms of the new constitution, Madhesi communities in the southern
Tarai region along the Indian border launched a series of protests, including
a six-month blockade at the Indian border. Because Nepal is a landlocked
country, by blocking the border with India, Madhesi activists were able to
halt the movement of goods into the country. Because Madhesi people are
culturally, linguistically, and ethnically tied to communities in India, official
narratives of the protests by the Nepali government accused India of supporting the border blockade.[81]

Over a seven-month period, from May to November, I watched as many
new faces came and went in the cluster meetings. In addition to INGOs and
multilateral organizations, there were representatives from multiple Nepali
mental health NGOs who had been subcontracted by INGOs and UN groups
to hire and train psychosocial counselors and do the work of mental health
and psychosocial support on the ground in the earthquake-affected districts.
The cluster meetings were thus split between Nepali NGO and INGO staff,
expatriate development workers, and new foreign humanitarians. In order to
facilitate the work, meetings were held in English.[82] In the case of the Psychosocial Working Group, the ministry official who attended the meetings would
arrive at the start of the meeting, give an update of government activities in
Nepali that was translated into English, and then leave the room. There was

no ministry official in attendance in the Mental Health subcluster, which was held in the Ministry of Health and Population building, reflecting the fact that there was no Department of Mental Health in the Ministry of Health and Population.

To address the quality of humanitarian MHPSS, in 2007 the Inter-Agency Standing Committee (IASC)—a UN-created forum focused on promoting humanitarian coordination, decision-making, and policy design—published the *Guidelines on Mental Health and Psychosocial Support in Emergency Settings*.[83] The guidelines aim to address "potential threats to populations who were receiving untried, untested, and unmonitored mental health and psychosocial support (MHPSS) in the aftermath of wars and disasters."[84] As Sharon Abramowitz and Arthur Kleinman point out, the IASC guidelines were a direct response to the fact that in many places, humanitarian mental health interventions had been conducted without coordination and had been employing staff with little training. In an extreme case, they cite the WHO as having documented over one hundred uncoordinated humanitarian mental health programs operating in Bosnia after the war.[85]

In Nepal, perhaps due to years of competition between Nepali NGOs for the donor-funded projects that kept their organizations afloat, communication and collaboration between local organizations was limited. Each organization implemented its own unique training of psychosocial counselors, even when some were subcontracted by the same INGO. Outside of established organizations, there was a constant flow of small, independent groups and individuals, both foreign and Nepali, who had decided to provide trauma support in whatever ways they deemed appropriate. One day a European couple appeared in the meeting of the Mental Health Sub-Cluster. When it was their turn to speak to the group, the man stood up and introduced himself. In a shaky voice, he explained that he and his friend had come as volunteers to teach a "new paradigm without techniques" that had saved his life. He then gave a confessional speech, in which he described his struggle with depression, drug addiction, violence, and experience in jail. In the end, he announced that he and his girlfriend would be in Nepal for two weeks and would be holding a training in their new paradigm at a nearby hotel for anyone who was interested in attending.

In addition to foreign organizations there were also local Nepali youth groups run by Kathmandu-based volunteers. One such group circulated their activities to the Mental Health Sub-Cluster's shared email listserv, announcing that they had "conducted 7 trauma relief camps for 1500+ children in grades one to five in some of the highest and most remote hill and mountain villages of the region." By December 2015, the cumulative reporting from the

Psychosocial Working Group announced that a total of 334,191 "beneficiaries" had received psychosocial support services from over 66 organizations.[86] According to these lists, working activities included "capacity building to stakeholders," community awareness raising programs, community theatre, psychoeducation, "Psychosocial [sic] First Aid (PFA)," phone hotlines, and group and individual psychosocial counseling.

Many humanitarians had not worked in Nepal prior to the earthquakes but had responded to other major disasters in countries such as Sri Lanka and Haiti. Humanitarian staff circulated through zones of disaster, touching down in new locations where they had little to no knowledge of the local context, history, culture, or language. Among the new humanitarians, there seemed to be little awareness that Nepal had already gone through a civil war and a refugee resettlement program which had garnered an expansive psychosocial response. There was no reference to the extensive anthropological studies of illness, healing, and emotion that had been used to design a psychosocial approach in which universal diagnostic categories were correlated to Nepali ethnopsychology. There was no knowledge that prior researchers had created new languages for communicating distress with the explicit aim of destigmatizing mental illness. An extensive desk report on mental health and culture in Nepal was quickly drafted by anthropologists and global mental health scholars and circulated to the cluster groups, yet few people seemed to have read it. The humanitarian narrative of Nepal's mental health crisis seemed to operate in an imagined present devoid of history. At the end of one meeting, a Nepali colleague politely showed a representative from an American humanitarian organization a series of manuals on mental health and psychosocial counseling his organization had published in Nepali. She turned to the foreigners in the room and exclaimed, "See, I *knew* they had something already!" Couched in this statement was the reality that many humanitarians knew very little about Nepal or the local history of the problem they had arrived to solve.

"The Better"

In the months following the 2015 earthquakes people began to talk about "building back better" and what it could mean for the future of Nepal's mental health system. In the context of the humanitarian mental health response, there was much discussion of this in the weekly Mental Health Sub-Cluster meetings. As the group began to form over the following months, it became a place where Nepali and expatriate mental health specialists—psychiatrists, NGO staff, development workers, humanitarians, activists, and even anthropologists—would not only report their activities but could also talk about the future of Nepal's mental health system. Such meetings had never before happened during the years I had spent in Nepal.[87] So much money was flowing into postdisaster mental health and psychosocial support programs that it seemed almost anything was possible. I too felt infected by a kind of contagious hope and the feeling that suddenly change was imminent. As one Nepali psychiatrist exclaimed in the Mental Health Sub-Cluster meeting, "the earthquake has been a boon for mental health in Nepal!"

At one of the meetings, the expat project manager from an American humanitarian organization rose to share her thoughts. She spoke in a voice full of frustration, complaining about the general lack of coordination and unwillingness of groups to work together. She concluded by saying emphatically, "We must avoid colonial dependencies and try to create sustainable infrastructures for mental health!" The American humanitarian's opposition of "colonial dependencies" with the creation of "sustainable infrastructures" suggested an anxiety and awareness, at some level, of the continuity and potential similarities between the two endeavors, colonialism on the one hand, and humanitarianism on the other. The historical lineage from colonial medicine to contemporary forms of humanitarianism and development has been well documented by both historians and anthropologists.[88] Humanitarianism was routinely incorporated into the colonial project as part of the "civilizing mission," and colonial histories continue to "shape the geography of humanitarian intervention in the present," as humanitarian missions frequently occur in ex-colonies.[89] As Peter Redfield has pointed out in his work on the French humanitarian organization Médecins Sans Frontières, expat humanitarian workers often feel anxious about the resonance between their work and the history of colonialism in places where "any hint of paternalism or cultural arrogance threatened to open old wounds."[90] Building back better, then, was seen as a way of avoiding "colonial dependencies" and addressing the problem of providing a population with brief access to care and psychopharmaceuticals in regions where normally such resources were not widely available. While the work of disaster created the possibility for people to receive novel mental health and psychiatric services, it also raised complex questions about the afterlives of humanitarianism and the ethics of transient care.[91]

Soon a troubling issue began to surface in the cluster meetings: the problem of the abandoned mentally ill. Without family members to care for them, historically this population had often ended up on the street or incarcerated in the Dhulikhel jail. In 2015 the only existing help for this group of people was a small Nepali NGO run by a man named Vivek Ji, who brought the issue to the table. Vivek Ji was a well-known mental health activist in Nepal with personal lived experience of severe mental illness. I saw him regularly at both the Mental Health Sub-Cluster and the Psychosocial Working Group, where he would continually bring up the matter of the social abandonment of people with severe mental illness. Everyone enthusiastically agreed it was a problem, but what could be done? In the Mental Health Sub-Cluster meeting, one of the humanitarians mentioned that there might be a possibility of securing money to work on the issue. The group unanimously decided to form a working group to tackle the subject, and I, too, offered to help draft any reports or documents they might need. A palpable sense of excitement took hold. "You must strike while the iron is hot!" said a middle-aged Nepali woman in attendance. The facilitator of the group also approved of the idea, and it seemed that maybe the right people with enough power could also be brought into the conversation. But in the end, the representative of the humanitarian donor organization announced that funding could only be allocated for earthquake-related mental health issues.

Even after this failure, Vivek Ji continued to advocate and ask difficult questions. "What will happen to the abandoned children with mental disabilities? What will happen to the abandoned adults with severe mental illness?" he asked the room full of humanitarians. He was met with silence; there were no answers, no programs, no planned interventions. The facilitator of the meeting looked at him solemnly and said, "We don't have the capacity . . ." While the disaster presented the opportunity to build back better, ultimately the "the better" was defined by foreign humanitarian and development organizations, not local activists. The *Building Back Better* report's emphasis on training prescribers and community mental health workers over the construction of institutions to care for the abandoned mentally ill reflected the long-standing rejection of the asylum model and shift toward deinstitutionalization in the WHO and the field of global mental health.[92] Such limitations of "the better" point to the politics of the a priori—that is, how preconceived understandings, genres, and frames create but also foreclose possibilities for things to become otherwise.[93]

The seismic event set the work of disaster into motion. Its designation as a crisis worthy of care inspired people to donate money from all over the world. Humanitarians streamed into Nepal in order to "stop Nepal's mental health crisis before it happens."[94] Short-term psychosocial interventions were funded to heal trauma among earthquake victims with counseling and psychotropic drugs, and humanitarian agencies used the sudden increase in national and international attention and resources to fast-track development goals of improving the mental health system in Nepal. The WHO prepared the *Building Back Better* policy so that when a situation of crisis is designated as such, previously determined development priorities can be pushed through. The crisis is anticipated as an opening, a possibility to strengthen mental health systems. In this way, the earthquakes were a boon for mental health governance in Nepal. Many aspects of the mental health system were ultimately developed because of this policy. Additional psychotropic drugs were added to the free drug list, and the government created a budget for decentralized mental health care for the first time.[95] Yet it is also important to point out the limitations of having a predetermined understanding of "the better."

Throughout history, interventions into the psychic life of populations have been justified as a way to ease the existential distress of rapid modernization and cultural change, heal trauma and create new responsible citizens in times of conflict and disaster, and reduce the global burden of disease while increasing economic productivity. Over the past forty years in Nepal, foreigners have framed the need for mental health services in relation to a series of imagined figures. Just as the first biopolitical projects of population management in eighteenth-century Europe were justified through the figures of the Malthusian couple, the hysterical woman, the sexualized child, and the deviant adult, the biopolitics of mental health in Nepal emerged through the figures of the rural masses and the urban deviants, the victim of torture and violence, the unproductive worker and mentally ill person in chains, and, most recently, the disaster victim.[96] The use of crisis narratives to expand access to psychiatry and counseling in the aftermath of the earthquakes is only the most recent iteration of a longer story of donor-driven development that has taken psychic life as its object of intervention. Looking across this history of mental health governance, one wonders: What other visions of "the better" might have been possible beyond expanding access to pharmaceutical drugs? Yet despite the importance of critical thinking in dark times, in the moment of crisis it seemed there was no time for difficult questions.[97] As the NGO offices once again busied themselves with the project of training community mental health workers, a fleet of newly minted psychosocial counselors prepared to enter the disaster zone, tasked with the responsibility of healing the heart-minds of those who had lost everything.

Loss

In the morning the counselors and I set out on foot. Following the main road, a rough dirt track that had been punched out of the mountain, we arrived at a green hillside dotted with tin shelters so Indira could conduct a group counseling session with the members of an earthquake-affected community. Unlike others, this community had lost not only their homes but also the use of their land after being resettled to another area due to the ongoing risk of landslides. In response to this double loss, community members referred to themselves as having become "like landless squatters" (*sukumbasi*). The meaning of landlessness is powerful in Nepal, where identity is closely tied to belonging to land and territory.[1] Wealth is primarily invested in land, and being a *sukumbasi* is highly stigmatized.[2] Upon arrival, Indira explained the intervention to a confused and weary crowd. Why had she come? What relief materials would she provide? People wondered aloud.

"We won't be bringing you relief or any GI sheets," said Maya, the community psychosocial worker.[3] "We won't be bringing tarpaulin. We don't have all these things. We are here to bring relief to the hearts of all those who have problems . . . Know it well that we don't have any relief materials. Look, we have come empty-handed."

"It's only for psycho-counseling," a local man explained to the group. "They are not here to corrupt your minds. They are here to help you to spread public awareness. Their objective is to increase your confidence. That's why we should cooperate with them," he added.

With each new visit, the meaning of "psychosocial counseling" had to be explained. A group assembled in a circle beneath a tin shelter. The counselor, Indira, who had grown up in this district and had made a career working for donor-funded health development projects, began by asking, "How is your *man*, your heart-mind, doing?" and invited people to share with each other how they were feeling and enduring their loss. As Indira went around the circle, people spoke of worries about being able to pay their debt; about their children's education having been disrupted (literally "broken" or "ruined" [*bigreko*]); about their crops that were harvested but beginning to rot in the damp makeshift shelters they were occupying. Many had sons and even daughters working abroad in India, Malaysia, or the Persian Gulf, more had thoughts of sending their children abroad in hope of making some money to somehow start again. They were worried about how they would feed themselves. Consolation came in the form of the hope that maybe the government, some organization, or a donor-funded project would help them and a sense of comfort in the fact that at least everyone had suffered from the disaster collectively. People spoke of what they had undergone, of what they had lost, as their *karma*, as one's fate that was already "written" (*lekheko*). After each person spoke, Indira would comment on their words, alternately praising them for their ability to make plans for the future and asking them to reflect on what they could do to help themselves. Sometimes the loss was too much, and there was no response that could be given.

Many scholars have critiqued humanitarian psychosocial interventions as little more than a form of "therapeutic governance" and social risk management. As Vanessa Pupavac and others have noted, the concept of the humanitarian psychosocial intervention was originally inspired by the assumption that psychological well-being is connected to responsible citizenship.[4] By hedging risk through the management of psychic distress, Pupavac argues, counseling has become a new form of therapeutic governance that operates at the level of the individual psyche, with the aim of maintaining the social order by healing victims and avoiding the spread of violence and unrest. This new regime of care has been made possible by the diagnosis of PTSD and assumption of its universality despite the historical and cultural specificity of its emergence as a disorder.[5] Scholars have argued that psychosocial counseling not only employs irrelevant diagnostic categories but also pathologizes populations as automatically traumatized, discounting other, more politicized possibilities.[6] We find this in a particularly unsettling example of humanitarian mental health programs run by MSF in Gaza and the West Bank that are focused on treating PTSD among Palestinians living in the occupied territories.[7] By analyzing the humanitarian testimony published by these programs, Didier Fassin has shown how the language of trauma has been used to depoliticize experiences of violence and forms of resistance among Palestinian

youth. By foregrounding PTSD as opposed to political resistance to Israeli occupation, the stone thrower is turned into a passive victim of trauma through
a process of "humanitarian subjectification."[8]

Once humanitarian psychosocial interventions are established, they can
take on a life of their own. In locations of extreme scarcity, PTSD diagnoses
can be quickly commodified, entering into "a political economy of trauma"
in which suffering becomes the currency through which scarce goods and
services are accessed and negotiated.[9] As psychosocial counseling programs
open the doors to vital resources, new configurations of "therapeutic citizenship" have emerged in which claims to injury and victimhood through
sharing confessional narratives become the most viable way to secure (what
should be) the rights of the citizen, such as access to medicine.[10]

Given the widespread production of therapeutic citizenship in humanitarian settings, its absence in Nepal was surprising. However, participation in
postdisaster psychosocial counseling programs was not connected to access
to any coveted material resources. As one counselor said when reflecting on
her work, "we got questioned quite a lot about what kind of relief we were
carrying, as many people had gone there with relief materials. We said that
we had come to give relief to their heart-mind, so if they want then we could
give it to them." Clients would sometimes join a group session with the hope
that they might receive medical treatment, but they soon learned that general
medical care was not provided through the program. The absence of material
resources was a source of anxiety for counselors, who worried about how to
respond to people who might beg for basic medicines and medical treatments.
"Be clear about what can be expected from you," advised a Kathmandu-based
staff member during a counselor training workshop. "Our clients have a lot of
expectations" (*hamro clients dherai apeksa sanga chha*).

Tea and biscuits during a group psychoeducation session, reimbursement
for client travel to meet a counselor or psychiatrist, and free psychopharmaceutical medication when prescribed by the NGO psychiatrist were the only
tangible goods provided by the program. Yet because of the absence of awareness of psychiatry and its diagnostic categories as well as the stigma of madness (*pagal*) in rural areas, psychiatric treatments were not widely sought.
There was no diagnosis or proof of "deservingness" required for participation
in the program. Ultimately access to psychosocial support was linked only
to geographical territory—anyone physically present within the counselor's
working areas in the disaster zone qualified. Participation offered the possibility of referral to a psychiatrist if needed, but above all, the invitation to
talk with a counselor about one's loss and to share the worries they held in
the heart-mind.

While the psychosocial approach operated under the a priori assumption that facing loss and talking about suffering and grief leads to healing, this was in tension with a strong cultural taboo against the outward expression of negative emotions as well as traditional ways of working with loss in the Himalayas. In the villages, landslides, aftershocks, and the ongoing deconstruction of the earth generated existential dizziness and philosophical reflections on loss and the nature of the world, *sansar*. Faced with catastrophic loss, people did not dwell on suffering but, instead, emphasized that "the world is like this" (*sansar estai chha*) or "suffering-contentment is like this" (*dukha-sukha estai chha*). In Nepali, the word *sansar* is drawn from the Sanskrit *samsara*, the "course or circuit of worldly life, secular life, mundane existence, the world."[11] Unlike the concept of world as something one may either possess or lose, in *sansar* we find an understanding of world as impermanent, characterized by a constant oscillation between suffering and contentment, misery and joy, *dukha-sukha*. This way of conceptualizing the loss of a world and giving meaning to suffering—a process Gananath Obeyesekere has called "the work of culture"—can serve as protection against the development of psychic affliction.[12]

For local people, there was an awareness that speaking too much about a lost loved one, especially those who died a bad death, strengthens attachments between the dead and the living and can cause the dead to become trapped in a liminal realm between death and rebirth. Even in the aftermath of a major disaster, there was a general striving toward emotional composure and an emphasis on concealing the worries one held in the heart-mind.[13] Expressions of grief and remembering the dead were actively encouraged only in prescribed moments, such as when families and communities gathered to perform funerary rites or construct memorials for the dead. As Austin Lord and Jennifer Bradley have shown, for the Langtangpa community, who lost almost two hundred members when the April 25 earthquake triggered a seismic avalanche that buried their ancestral village, communal practices of remembrance and memorialization facilitated a powerful collective process of mourning and repair.[14] Such preexisting ways of working with grief and suffering immediately raise questions as to the usefulness of a Euro-American therapeutic approach that assumes ventilating emotion and talking about loss with a counselor will lead to healing.[15] Yet some people, especially those who had lost loved ones in the disaster, struggled to conceal strong emotions of grief and anguish. Ethnopsychiatrists and anthropologists have long questioned the universality of psychiatric diagnostic categories that imagine themselves to be "culture-free," arguing for the importance of incorporating the patient's cultural etiologies of affliction into psychotherapeutic and psychiatric treatment.[16] However, it is also possible that one's own culture and traditions may be a source of suffering as opposed to a therapeutic re-source.[17] From this perspective, counseling sessions offered an unusual shel-ter where people could express non-normative experiences of grief and the anguish of continued attachments to the dead without censorship.

If we pay close attention to the intersubjective interactions between coun-selors and clients, we can see that humanitarian psychosocial interventions in postdisaster Nepal functioned not as sites of therapeutic governance but as temporary shelters and spaces of critique. Assembled in the midst of ru-ins and rubble and interrupted by ongoing aftershocks, counseling sessions became sites of geophilosophy where people critically reflected on the mean-ing of loss, world, and existence as they stood on groundless ground.[18] As a method, critical phenomenology can be used to deconstruct concepts, such as the concept of loss, so that we might loosen our grip from the banister of our a priori definitions.[19] Hannah Arendt compared this practice of concept "defrosting" to a wind that shakes us out of our automatic understandings and assumptions, making us more "fully awake and alive."[20] Following Ar-endt's approach, Mattingly has argued that in its most radical form, critical phenomenology is "an experience-near process of concept destabilization."[21] By attending to the forms of thought that emerged in response to the di-saster and its destabilization, this chapter uses a critical phenomenological approach to explore how different conceptualizations of loss delineate pos-sibilities for repair after the rupture of a world.

Facing Loss

In August 2015, three months after the 7.3-magnitude "aftershock," landslides were frequent as the steep hills, destabilized by the earthquakes and drenched by the monsoon rains, were no longer holding together. The counselors and I traveled eight hours from Kathmandu to the district headquarters of Dol-akha, epicenter of the aftershock, and then into the mountain villages by jeep. At first the view from the road was beautiful—verdant green hills, water-falls, and the surging flow of a river filled by the monsoon rains. As we drove through the landscape, one of the counselors pointed out the window to show us a place "where three people died in a landslide, but an infant baby lived." We were silent.

We arrived in a small bazaar on the banks of the powerful Tamakoshi River. The multistory concrete homes that used to stand here were now twisted in piles on the ground. We went for a walk. That day a man had died in a landslide. His body was burning at the edge of the roaring monsoon river.

We watched the orange flames of the cremation from the suspension bridge in the rain. Bikas, one of the counselors, wanted to take photos of us posing on the bridge with our umbrellas. But it was difficult to smile. The counselors I accompanied, Deepak, Indira, and Bikas, were all district locals who wanted to show me around. We visited a pristine Red Cross tent hospital, with gray gravel flooring and an X-ray tent. I talked to the doctors there, one from Germany, another from France. The German doctor told me that MSF was also running a psychosocial program here and asked if we knew of their international psychosocial tool. He said that this tool had helped because it used to be that "any crazy person could come and do psychosocial counseling," that in Pakistan he saw "ten counselors make the children draw pictures of their parents' deaths and then the Hare Krishnas came and danced."

The German doctor's comment spoke to the long and troubled history of unregulated mental health interventions in times of emergency.[22] In the aftermath of disaster, it is not uncommon for a deluge of humanitarian organizations and volunteers to show up offering a range of treatments and approaches with little regard for cultural context, safety, or sustainability. This lack of regulation is what the 2007 IASC guidelines aim to address by providing standards of care and warnings against harmful practices.[23] Over the past twenty years, there has been a growing awareness that "debriefing"—that is, asking someone to narrate their traumatic experience in the immediate aftermath of disaster, as the German doctor described happening in Pakistan—is not a recommended form of support because it can strengthen painful memories in ways that ultimately lead to more suffering.[24] Instead, the IASC argues, psychosocial interventions in times of emergency should focus on connecting people to resources, securing basic needs, reducing stress, promoting adaptive coping, and, in sum, providing "a humane, supportive response to a fellow human being who is suffering and may need support."[25]

Two days later we slowly made our way farther up into the mountains by jeep, every few meters encountering a block in the path. At each impasse the driver jumped down with shovel in hand to remove stones and debris. Along the dirt road, there was not one structure that remained standing. Beside the ruins of their old homes, people had erected rough, temporary shelters of wood with roofs of corrugated metal, known by the vaguely exotic English euphemism "cottage." After a few hours, we finally arrived at the cottage where the counselors had arranged to stay. Unlike foreign humanitarian staff, local staff lived alongside residents, sharing their shelter, food, and exposure to risk in the disaster zone. Inside the darkened, smoke-filled structure, a woman welcomed us with plates of fresh cucumber and ears of roasted corn, plucked from the stalks that had grown over the ruins of her old home. Over time we would return to this place, which faced Gaurishankar, a stunningly beautiful seven-thousand-meter double-peaked mountain in the Himalayan range. It is said that the two peaks of Gaurishankar, one larger and one smaller, are a pair of lovers—Shankar, avatar of the Hindu god Shiva, and Gauri, avatar of his wife, Parvati. Beneath Gaurishankar, the towering green hills were streaked with landslides. Months later I found myself here again standing in the bright winter light with Maya, the local community psychosocial worker. Together gazing out across the valley, our eyes rested on a massive white gash. Turning to me she told me quietly, "The landslide began during the earthquake and didn't stop for three days." What does it mean to lose a world, and what role could psychosocial counseling play in repairing a world destroyed?

A world can be a place but it can also be a person. One day, Indira and I set out to meet with a well-off high-caste Hindu woman who had lost her daughter in a landslide. We sat outside in the courtyard in front of a pile of fallen stones and broken wood. Beginning the session, Indira said, "I feel happy seeing your face, I feel happy seeing *Ama* [mother], getting better than before. How is *Ama* feeling?" The wind was blowing, and as Indira spoke, she reached out to brush away a strand of hair that had fallen into the eyes of her client. Smiling bitterly, the woman replied, "This is how it is, child. Her image keeps wandering in front of my eyes at least once a day. I keep remembering her, whether it is day or night. Everybody yells at me and tells me not to remember her, but I can't help it."

The policing of memory and ongoing grieving for the dead is common in Nepal and is shared across both Hindu and Tibetan Buddhist communities. Remembering the dead is a complex action, for ongoing attachment to the deceased can cause the ghosts of the dead to suffer and attack the living. As opposed to the potential benefits of an understanding of impermanence as aid in the face of loss, here we see the shadow side of the work of culture in which ongoing outward displays of grief for a lost daughter are treated as a disturbance and a danger that must be curtailed. As Jonathan Parry has argued in his work on Hindu death rituals, "when death is an 'untimely' one, the expression of personal grief is liable to overspill the limits which culture tries to impose on it."[26] Similarly, as Desjarlais has noted in the case of Hyolmo Buddhists in Central Nepal, "the manifest, culturally prescribed reaction to death is one of restrained mourning, but more private feelings of loss often haunt the bereaved. These felt immediacies, which range from bodily pains to dreams of the deceased, are compounded by cultural constraints on the expression and interpretation of distress."[27] In this landscape of loss, counseling sessions became a space where personal grief and reflections on continued attachments to the dead were not only allowed but actively invited.

The idea that one must "face the loss" was directly taught to the counselors by their Nepali supervisors and the foreign psychologist associated with the organization. During a training session for supervisors in Kathmandu, Michelle, the foreign psychologist, took time to work through an exemplary case study of a group of Nepali migrants grieving the death of a friend who died while working abroad in Dubai. The death of Nepali migrants working in the Gulf countries and Malaysia is common, and incidents listed as "sudden death, cause unknown" are a leading cause of mortality among migrant workers.[28] In order to talk about how to address loss and death in the counseling session, Michelle presented a pair of wooden mannequins and used them to enact the scene of a session. One mannequin represented the death of the friend, the other represented the feelings of loss. A set of small wooden pawns represented the migrants and the counselor. At first, Michelle set up the scene with one mannequin, death, on its back in the middle of the circle of pawns. Turning to the counselors she asked, "What would you do?" A Nepali staff member approached the figures. She gently picked up the figure of death and lay it down to rest on her scarf at the edge of the room. "Now that it is out of the way, we can talk about nice things," she told the group. Unsure if I should participate, I raised my hand to ask if I might arrange the scene as well. Without thinking, I picked up the two mannequins, death and loss, and placed them upright in the center of the circle of pawns.

The sight of "death and loss" towering over the small figures of the friends and the counselors generated a visceral affective atmosphere in the room.[29] I got goosebumps on my skin. Michelle physically moved herself away from the scene. The room fell silent. Michelle said that this was indeed the "right thing" to do, to face the loss head on, despite the monumental difficulty of the task. Privately, Michelle and other foreigners commented to me that facing the loss was among the most difficult tasks for Nepali counselors to learn. Yet such difficulty was due not to an inability to learn, but to a radically different way of relating to death, grief, and loss. Within the counseling sessions multiple conflicting orientations toward loss coexisted. While the psychosocial approach insisted on "facing the loss" and expressing negative emotions in order to release them from the living, a Hindu-Buddhist philosophy of death and rebirth required suppressing outward expressions of grief to sever attachments and release the dead from the ghostly liminal realm and into the next life.

Back in the courtyard counseling session, Indira was repeating her observations of signs of improvement. "Your face looked different last time, but

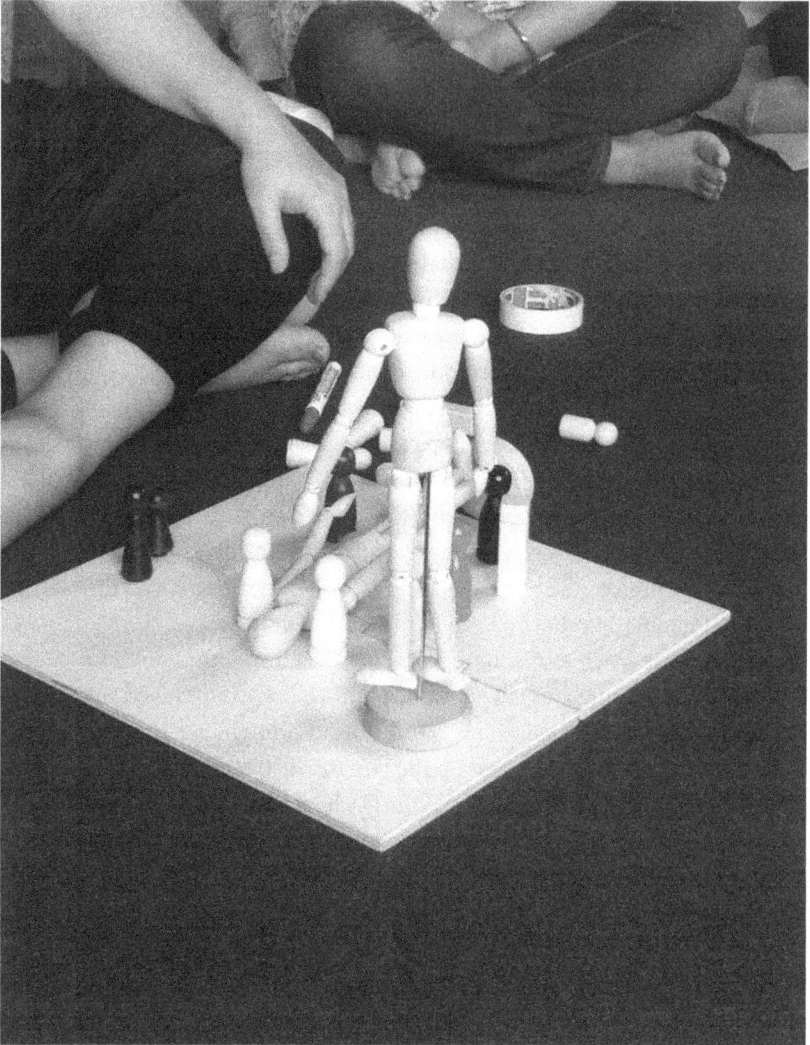

FIGURE 2.1. Learning to face loss. Photo by the author.

now it looks bright [*ujyalo*]. Seeing this, I feel like our *Ama*, mother, is feeling good now. How are you feeling?" Smiling and laughing, the woman replied, "Me? I feel scared to look in the mirror . . . when I look in the mirror, I see my own ghost [*aina herepachhi mero bhut ayechha*]." Gesturing to one side, still smiling, she explained that she avoided reflective objects like glass windows, for fear she might catch a glimpse of herself and in that reflection be forced to confront the image of her own grief.

Indira insisted, perhaps hoping that her words might bring it into being, "I find your face to be very bright; it looks so much brighter than last time. Your face looks very fresh and fair. I can see a very good face in front of me that looks much better than last time." Despite being trained to encourage people to express their sadness and worry, Indira's evaluation of the brightness of her client's expression spoke to a deeply held social value of concealing pain with positive affect. Faced with loss, people smiled and tried to laugh. They smiled as they narrated horrible experiences, they smiled as they spoke about life as an endless struggle of endurance and suffering, they smiled as they mentioned seeing their own ghost reflected in the mirror, and they smiled as they posed on a bridge in the rain by a body burning on a funeral pyre. In a place where outward expressions of happiness and bright, fresh countenances were highly valued, in the aftermath of disaster extreme emotional labor was everywhere.[30]

As the wind picked up around us, the woman tried to hold back her tears. "My face looked so different before the earthquake," she said. "But after the earthquake it has become ugly. Compared to before, it has become broken. But that's how it is, what to do."

"It is difficult for you," Indira said, as she searched her purse for tissues.

"No, no, I'm fine," the woman responded. "It is good. You all came here for me. May success always be with you; may god be always with you. Even though I have faced such tragedy, may you never face any hardship."

Indira leaned in, and wiping the tears from the woman's eyes with a tissue, she said, "I understand that this is hard."

"Life is full of sadness, what to do," said the woman. "We were living happily before. We had everything, and we were self-sufficient. . . . Now this has happened to us. An untimely death. . . . If she had died because of some disease then we could have at least searched for medicine. But there was a landslide. Even now the land is still sliding." Pointing into the distance to a far hill, she said, "It just went past that house there." As the land threatened to disintegrate around us, we were left to consider the meaning of the timeliness of death.

In Nepal, both Hindus and Buddhists practice intricate sequences of death rituals that help ensure the passage of the soul of the deceased from one life to the next.[31] These rituals are important containers for the expression of grief, loss, and mourning. For example, in Hinduism, the son is responsible for performing the thirteen-day death rituals that will enable his father to become an ancestor and to be reborn into a new body.[32] In this highly gendered ritual·space, women do not generally perform funerary rites.[33] A good death involves dying at the end of a long, good life and the proper completion of funerary rituals in which the corpse is cremated—a sacrifice to the gods that ultimately enables the "regeneration of life and the world."[34] A bad death is an untimely death, caused by accident, illness, or violence; it is a death in which the proper rituals cannot be performed due to family dissolution or the absence of the body.[35] Without being transformed through the rituals of death, those who die a bad death can get stuck in the liminal realm between death and rebirth where they become wandering ghosts, *bhut-pret* and *pisat*, who disturb the living with desperate pleas for their suffering to be appeased.[36] When trapped in an intermediate realm, the dead circulate their suffering through bodies and worlds, transferring affliction from the dead to the living.[37] Often the ghosts of those who die a bad death are said to inhabit the places where they die. In this way, the memory of an untimely death permanently marks the landscape, generating affective atmospheres that threaten to permeate the bodies of the living.

Indira was unsettled. Tears were welling up in her eyes. "I feel your pain," she said, moving her hand over her heart-mind. "It is hard to hear about your situation. I feel sadness, seeing tears in your eyes for your daughter."

The woman responded, "Because of me, even you had to face difficulties. What to do? Life is like this. Pain and pleasure are a part of your destiny; you have to face what is in your destiny. You can't always have pleasure in life, and you should not get worried even when you have pain. I hope that my daughter will never be reborn as a human" she continued. "I hope she will find liberation. There is so much misery and pain in human life."

Indira closed her eyes and listened carefully, head bowed, her hands drawn together beneath her chin.

"This is not a good life," the woman said. "No matter what happens do not take birth again in human form and make sure that you reach liberation. That is what I think."

Instead of understanding death as the opposite of life, here death is opposed to birth. As Diana Eck has pointed out in her work on Hindu concepts of death and liberation, "the great transition which death occasions is not from life to death, but from life to life."[38] In this way death is always accompanied by the possibility of rebirth into *samsara*, the world of suffering and illusion, or release into *moksa*, liberation. *Moksa* locates liberation from suffering in nonexistence, nothingness, boundlessness, and nonconceptuality and is known colloquially as "the far shore." The idea of "the far shore" is also articulated in the Heart Sutra, a religious teaching that appeared five hundred years after the death of the Buddha and that became foundational for both Mahayana (Tibetan) and Zen Buddhism.[39] Here liberation is synonymous with *sunyata*, the nothingness, emptiness, and groundlessness that is the relational, codependent arising of all things.[40] In both Hindu and Buddhist traditions, to reach "the far shore" is to transcend the endless cycle of death and rebirth, misery and joy, and to be liberated from the inevitable suffering that defines human life.

"The World Is Like This"

In the aftermath of the earthquakes, people who had lost everything repeatedly said in counseling sessions that "the world is like this" (*sansar estai chha*) or "the cycle of suffering and contentment is like this" (*dukha-sukha estai chha*). Speaking in a counseling circle in a temporary settlement in Dolakha, a man in muddy rubber boots shared the suffering his community had faced, his hand on the knee of the man next to him. "Right now, we are staying under sheds," he explained in the circle, continuing:

> We are dependent on our farming only. We have some corn and potatoes, but we don't have a place to store them. The floor is wet. We remember our homes. We had rooms that were neat and clean. It was dry. Actually, we are the victims but we can't always cling to this. However, we doubt if we can ever reach the state at which we were before. We are hopeful that some organization or project might help us to reach our previous state. . . . We are full of sadness, we are worried. At night we can't sleep. We are indeed facing adversity, but we can't always think like that. Whatever comes, we have to face it. Life is like this. So, we have to forget it and satisfy ourselves thinking that it's not like this for us only. Things like this happen all over the world.

The circle moved on from the man with the muddy rubber boots and soon came to a woman in a leopard-print sweater. Welcoming her turn, she shared her perspective with the group. "As long as one is alive, one endures [*bamchunjel, sahaunjel*]," she said with a sly smile. "What to do. . . . If you look at the world, it is like this [*sansar estai chha*]." *Bamchunjel* is a compound word, drawn from the verb *bamchnu*, meaning "to be saved, escape; be set free; be alive."[41] *Sahaunjel*, from the verb *sahanu*, means "to suffer, endure, bear; tolerate."[42] In this way, to say that "the world is like this" is to say the world is such that in order to survive, in order to live, one must struggle, suffer, and endure.

Soon another woman spoke. She said, "Home collapsed; misery-joy is like that [*dukha-sukha estai chha*]." A man added, "The government gave us some things, but how will the government help us? Misery-joy [*dukha-sukha*]." He said he had three sons—two were working in India. He hoped he could build a small house with help from the government but doubted it would really happen. *Dukha* means "trouble; misfortune; pain; grief; worry."[43] While *sukha* means "happiness; pleasure; leisure; health."[44] If *dukha* is the task of carrying one thousand heavy loads from morning till night, then *sukha* is the ability to pay others to carry your loads for you. Together *dukha-sukha* is best understood as the ceaseless alternation between suffering and contentment, misery and joy; it is the impermanence of all things.

To understand what it means to say "the world is like this," it is worth considering what "world" is. This is a question that was taken up by Martin Heidegger in a series of lectures in which he set out to define *world* through a comparative examination of the particular relationship that different beings (stone, animal, man) have toward it.[45] It is in this work that Heidegger famously argues that "[1] the stone (material object) is *worldless*; [2] the animal is *poor in world*; [3] man is *world-forming*."[46] In Heidegger's universal metaphysics, world is something that is possessed in greater and lesser degrees and accessed at varying levels of richness, depending on one's capacity to bring the question of being into consideration.[47]

As opposed to a notion of world as something beings possess or access to greater or lesser degrees, in the Himalayas we find a concept of world as illusion and impermanence. In the Nepali language, *sansar* can be translated both as "the universe" and "the round of birth and death."[48] In both Hindu and Buddhist traditions, the aim of living is to achieve liberation from worldly life and thus exit the endless cycle of misery-joy, *dukha-sukha*, that characterizes the condition of mundane human existence, *samsara*.

Liberation, *moksa*, is the "freedom from attachment to the round of birth and death."[49] In Hinduism, *moksa* is one of the four aims of human life (known as *purusarthas*), the other three being *kama* (pleasure), *artha* (wealth and prosperity), and *dharma* (right action). While *kama*, *artha*, and *dharma* are pursuits for those who remain in the world, *moksa*, the fourth and final *purusartha*, can be achieved only through the wisdom gained by renouncing the world.[50] Thus, to choose to be "homeless in the world" is to actively work toward achieving liberation. In Nepal it is common to see such world-renouncers. Dressed in simple orange cloth, with matted hair and ash smeared across their foreheads, the *sadhus* (acestics) walk barefoot through the streets of Kathmandu carrying small tins in which they collect donations. During the Hindu festival of Shivaratri, a celebration of the night of Shiva, *sadhus* travel from far and wide to make a pilgrimage to Pashupatinath, the temple complex and holy site of Lord Shiva, whose image and ethics they seek to embody.

In the lived practice of Tibetan Buddhism in Nepal, liberation is also achieved through a process of severing attachments to worldly life, yet this is done during a series of rituals that take place during and after the process of dying. Central here is the use of the *Bardo Thödol*, "Liberation upon Hearing in the Between," a text that is read aloud to the dying person and helps guide them through the *bardo*, a terrifying liminal space between death and rebirth. As Desjarlais writes in his ethnography of death and dying among Hyolmo Buddhists in Nepal, "if a reader or listener understands the texts' teachings well, it is held, he or she can achieve liberation from the samsaric world."[51] The *Bardo Thödol* is thus a detailed guide to the process of dying and the navigation of the intermediate bardo state between death and rebirth or death and liberation.[52] What does it mean to lose a world if world is understood to be illusory and impermanent and liberation is freedom from attachment to the world?

Since the incorporation of the diagnosis of PTSD into the third edition of the *Diagnostic and Statistical Manual* (*DSM-III*) in the 1980s, there has been increasing focus among researchers on the link between disaster and the development of nightmares, flashbacks, and increased vigilance that interrupt one's daily life after exposure to a traumatic event. However, as anthropologists have shown, psychological responses to existential threats also depend on the concepts people have on hand—such as "PTSD," "depression," or even a notion of "karma"—that shape the way they understand and experience suffering, their identity, how they interact with the social world, and the treatments they identify as necessary for healing.[53]

To say that "the world is like this" at first glance suggests a passive and apolitical response to disaster. The tendency for those who adhere to a karmic understanding of life to uncritically accept suffering, domination, and inequality has been critiqued by Nepali scholars as an obstacle to development and modernity. Dor Bahadur Bista, the "father of anthropology in Nepal," famously argued that "the absolute belief in fatalism, that one has no personal control over one's life circumstances, which are determined through a divine or powerful external agency," has had a devastating effect on social and economic development.[54] Fatalism, Bista argued, should be replaced by a notion of free will, agency, and self-determination so that Nepal might liberate itself from Brahmanism, the dominance of high-caste Hindus, and achieve its full potential as a nation.[55] Yet as Sara Lewis has argued through her work with Tibetan refugees in Dharamsala, the concept of karma, expectations of suffering, and an understanding of world as illusion can serve to support recovery and resilience as opposed to psychotherapeutic approaches that insist on debriefing by returning to the source of suffering again and again.[56] At the same time, to say that "the world is like this" also speaks to the differential expectations and thresholds of livability between those for whom disaster is a surprise and those who have long been living in precarious conditions.[57]

Aftershocks

On our way back from a group counseling session, a 5.1 aftershock hit. It sounded like a bomb going off. The noise came from directly beneath us. Despite the risks of traveling, the next day the counselors set out to conduct another group session in a settlement referred to simply as "beneath the steep cliff." Once we arrived, Indira formed a counseling circle, and people immediately began to speak about fear of landslides. They were worried about their children, who had to cross a landslide on the only route to the school. And yet if they didn't cross it, they wouldn't be able to study, they explained. The parents wanted their children to study; it was incredibly important even if the only option was a minimally staffed and severely underfunded government school. Then suddenly the land across the valley on the opposite hill started sliding. It sounded like an airplane, and a white rip in the earth ran down the hill.

Soon we headed to a nearby government school to conduct a school program. Despite the red X that had been painted on the outside of the building, marking it as structurally unsound, the teachers continued to teach students inside. One of those teachers was Dawa, an energetic young man who taught English classes in the school. Dawa also rented a room in the cottage where the counselors and I stayed, and over time, we became friends as we bonded over his love of the English language. As we were sitting around inside the cracked school building waiting for the program to start, Indira casually asked Dawa about his own experience of the disaster. Although we were in a room full of people, Dawa told his story in English so that only I could understand. He said that on the day of the earthquake, he was attending a teaching workshop and all of the teachers had assembled in the training hall.

> I watched the wall shaking and tried to go under the table, but all the other teachers were under the table and there was no space for me. I thought there was no one left on earth and I cried. My eyes were full of tears. I went back to my village and all the houses had been destroyed. I am still feeling very afraid of earthquakes. Two days ago, there was an earthquake of 5.1 and I was teaching. All the students were crying and I couldn't control myself. They were really afraid of the earthquake. One of our staff got injured. Except our life, nothing is left. The students don't have bags, they don't have books. It is very difficult to live. This area is very dangerous as well. Everything is cracked. The students come from very far away and it is dangerous. All Nepalese are in tragedy. It is very difficult to live.

In a counseling circle a young woman spoke of her experience in similar terms. She said she was walking with her brother when the shaking began;

then she fainted. Falling stones. When she awoke, she thought, "Maybe I have gone mad [*pagal*], maybe everyone has died and I am alone." Although Dawa and the young woman ultimately found that they were not the only survivors, their fears ask us to consider the madness of being alone and what it would mean to be the last one left on earth. If ethics is conceptualized as responsivity to a breakdown or a demand, it is the seismic rupture of disaster that brings out the materiality of ethics, generating tremors that radiate through earth and bodies and giving form to thought.[58]

In the 1950s, researchers created the term *disaster syndrome* as a way to describe immediate postdisaster somatic and psychological states of disorientation, often involving a sense of being in a daze, frozen, or stunned.[59] As time passes, disorientation can develop in multiple directions depending on one's well-being and level of social support prior to the disaster as well as one's personal and cultural resources in the management of loss. Counselors and clients repeatedly emphasized that a way to cope with the fear of loss of one's own life was to never be alone, to always surround oneself with the presence of others. In a counseling circle the Forest Chairman (*ban adhyaksa*) sat listening to the heart-mind worries of his community, turning his necklace of *mala* beads in his fingers. When it came to his turn, he said that he was often alone, that he had fear in his heart-mind, and that he felt like he was dying. "My heart-mind shakes, my body trembles, my heart feels like it's moving [*manma hallinchha, jiu kamne, mutu hallieko jasto lagchha*]," he said. "In the afternoon I meet with my friends and chat, but the minute I am alone . . ." his voice wandered off.

In the aftermath of disaster, the presence of others can be a powerful form of protection against the development of disabling psychic afflictions.[60] This was intuitively known in rural Nepal, where being alone was already seen as a form of pathological behavior and where people recognized that to stay alongside each other could offer momentary stability in a trembling world.[61] In the face of ongoing landslides, aftershocks, and threats of loss, to be alone was equated with madness and the end of the world, while to be in community with others made it possible to endure a future of unknown risk. During group sessions, Indira ended with a round of collective deep breathing exercises. This had been taught to her, and these were tangible practices she could recommend and give to all clients as work they could do to relieve tension on their own. I noticed that the older women, long exposed to indoor smoke from burning wood at the hearth, struggled to breathe during these exercises.[62] There is a common Nepali saying that "as long as there's breath, there's hope." As we stood on the hilltop side by side, breathing together, the unpredictable landscape seemed to resonate in momentary harmony and stillness.

Defrosting Loss

An earthquake is a form of ontological destruction. Ground gives way, sliding. Land cracks. The materiality of earthquakes and recurring aftershocks
makes ethical demands on life and generates forms of responsivity. Within a
Himalayan landscape infused with Hindu and Buddhist philosophy, we encounter a distinct set of reveries, images, and forms of knowledge that "stem
directly from matter"—that is, from the material properties of the seismic
rupture and its disorienting sensations of groundlessness.[63] In the round of
the counseling circle, the disaster generated reflections on life, world, loss,
and liberation. Yet in the rural farming settlements of the Hindu-Buddhist
Himalayas, reflections on a world in destruction did not dwell on how such
misery could be possible but instead met devastation with the acknowledg-
ment that "the world is like this" (*sansar estai chha*) and that death offers
the possibility for rebirth or liberation from the world.[64] The sentiment of
acceptance communicated in these simple statements echoes the ideas of the
ancient Indian philosopher Nagarjuna, who wrote in the *Mulamadhyamakakarika*, "How could there be destruction without becoming? How could there
be death without birth? There is no destruction without becoming."[65]

As repeated aftershocks made bodies and heart-minds tremble, people
struggled to navigate their way out of dangerous states of grief and disorientation. They did this by seeking the company of others, by tempering attachments, and by acknowledging the impermanence of all things as the nature
of *sansar*, world. In the deceivingly humble statements of members of a rural
farming community, we discover a Himalayan philosophy of impermanence
that can serve as a source of psychic protection when facing the loss of a
world—whether that world is a place or a person. This philosophy emphasizes the importance of detachment in facilitating repair, for it is attachment
that ultimately leads to suffering, among both the living and the dead. This
way of conceptualizing loss suggests that repair is facilitated by accepting impermanence. It is by severing attachments that a world that is lost may be free
to transform into its next incarnation.

In his work on Buddhism and depression in Sri Lanka, Obeyesekere similarly observed that people suffering from grief and loss were often able to
"generalize their despair from self to the world at large and give it Buddhist
meaning and significance."[66] Here he argued that when dysphoric affects were
conceptualized in such terms, people did not experience their suffering as depression but instead saw it as a defining feature of the world and opportunity
for transformation. Using the metaphor of constellations in the night sky,
Obeyesekere called the transformation of painful, free-floating affects into

publicly accepted meanings and symbols "the work of culture."[67] We can see the work of culture at play in Indira's group counseling sessions as people drew on culturally shared meanings to work through their loss and expressed their suffering in Hindu and Buddhist terms.

While this way of working with loss can protect against the development of psychic affliction, sometimes, when lived experiences of grief overflow normative frames, the work of culture can fail. In Nepal, many people who died untimely deaths could not be given complete death rituals, leaving open the possibility that they might become wandering ghosts, *bhut-pret*. As a result, those who grieved the death of their loved ones feared that by talking about grief they might strengthen attachments and cause further suffering to the dead. For people struggling to conceal their grief in a social world where one hides negative emotions, counseling sessions served as temporary shelters where taboo sentiments could be expressed without judgment. In the space of the counseling session, loss was something to be "faced," expressed, verbalized, and given to the counselor to hold so that one might release built up emotion, accept attachment, and begin the long process of repair.

Just as the work of culture provides a way to describe the process by which free-floating affects are transformed into a constellation of publicly accepted meanings, the work of disaster seeks to give language to the process by which emergent situations—such as the unexpected trembling of the earth and its dangerous and disorienting effects—are transformed in various ways through the concepts and frames we use to understand them. A critical phenomenological approach focused on concept destabilization seeks to unsettle the guiding concepts that may on the surface seem to be so obvious and automatic that we cannot think to question their meanings.[68] Yet it is only by exploring the differences between humanitarian and local conceptualizations, both their limitations and unexpected possibilities, that we are able to see how different understandings of loss reverberated across a Himalayan fault line, shaping embodied experiences of grief and disorientation and guiding the distinct practices that are identified as necessary to repair the world.

3

Solidarity

"Tell them how much we have suffered to do this work, how far we have to walk to reach the clients, what kind of places we have to stay in—tell them!" Bina said, referring to both her Kathmandu supervisors and to you, the reader of this book. In the work of counseling, most of the time was spent simply trying to reach the clients. Psychosocial counseling was not only emotionally but also physically exhausting. First, traveling from Kathmandu to earthquake-affected districts like Dolakha, Ramechhap, or Okhaldhunga by bus, shared jeep, or "micro" van took between five and eight hours, on roads both paved and dirt. In the district of Dolakha, home to a major hydropower project and longtime recipient of numerous development aid projects, roads had been carved out of the towering hills.[1] Here the counselors were able to travel mostly by local bus to their working areas. But local bus travel was also difficult. Fuel was scarce during the blockade, vehicles were limited, and counselors would regularly travel for up to six hours on dangerously over-packed public buses as they moved from one Village Development Committee (VDC) to another.[2] Sometimes in desperation counselors hitchhiked rides on the back of trucks and tractors. Once they had reached their base site, they would walk, guided by the local community psychosocial worker (CPSW), between thirty minutes and two hours to reach the nearby home of a client. It was not unusual to travel all day only to meet with one client for thirty minutes, if that. At first, I lamented the fact that most of our time was spent reaching the clients as opposed to the "real" work of counseling, yet slowly I began to realize that this, too, was an integral part of the therapeutic encounter.

There was something in the embodied experience of walking, of crisscrossing the towering hills, of traveling for hours just to reach a single client that added meaning to the therapeutic work for both clients and counselors.

The challenging geography, unstable landscape, and lack of infrastructure were not only limitations to be overcome but also affordances that shaped the work of counseling. As James Gibson has defined it, "the affordances of the environment are what it offers . . . what it provides or furnishes, either for good or for ill."[3] The physical act of walking, exposure to risk, and the struggle to reach clients created affordances for care and solidarity that people recognized as such. "You suffered and came here for me [*mero lagi dukha garera aunubho*]," clients said. Clients acknowledged that the counselors had struggled to reach them, that they too were staying in temporary shelters, traveling by foot and on packed buses. This movement, exertion, and exposure to risk was a form of solidarity with an efficacy all its own.

Walking is central to life in Nepal in very specific ways, for it is a place of towering mountains, extensive footpaths, and a history of limited road infrastructure. While some areas are connected by motorable roads, vast swaths of the country remain largely accessible only by foot. In this mountainous landscape, walking overflows with symbolic meaning. Often walking carries negative associations, for it is generally those who cannot afford to ride or who live far from roads who must walk. To live in a "remote region" (*durgam ksetra*) is an official government classification but has also become a socially stigmatizing label. As Sara Shneiderman has noted, *durgam* means not only remote but also "impassable" and is understood in contrast to *sugam*, or "easily accessible."[4] The meaning of remoteness is so deeply lodged in the social imaginary that, as one Nepali friend explained, when playing volleyball as a child the position where the ball would never land was called "Rukum," a *durgam* district in the hills of midwestern Nepal. Here "Rukum" was shorthand for places where things never arrive.

"Carrying loads and walking" (*bhari bokera hidne*) is a commonly spoken phrase that serves as a commentary on the everyday struggle of *pahadi* life and conjures ubiquitous images of porters carrying *dokos* (large wicker baskets) strapped to their foreheads as they traverse the steep terrain. At the same time, there are many forms walking might take in rural Nepal, from homecoming journeys, wedding *janti* (the procession from the groom's home to gather the bride and bring her back), and *yatra*, religious pilgrimage, to the newer forms of trekking introduced by the tourism industry, to the aimless roaming, wandering, and exploring known as *ghumne*. In eastern Nepal, older generations still recalled a time when they would walk to Kathmandu, a journey that took three weeks.

Walking through a landscape destabilized by aftershocks shaped the work of counseling and the way I came to know the counselors. As my fieldwork with counselors took place within a trembling landscape, my collaboration with them unfolded vis-à-vis shared exposure to the unstable ground beneath us. Lee and Ingold have argued that "the potential for shared understanding through movement, through walking together, is part of the richness of field-work on foot."[5] When walking together, people share the same visual field and rhythm of movement, opening up the possibility for a shared point of view based on copresence.[6] At the same time, the ability to share a perspective is always already limited not only by the impossibility of ever fully accessing the subjective experience of another but also by the very different stakes involved in those who walk alongside each other.[7] As Jason DeLeon has pointed out in his work on the necropolitics of the US-Mexico border, "walking-with" is a limited method in the context of border crossing, where there are dynamics of extreme inequality between the undocumented migrant who crosses the US-Mexico border by foot under threat of deportation, and the American citizen-anthropologist who might walk alongside him.[8] Yet in spite of our asymmetries, together as the counselors and I walked side by side along mountain paths, crossing valleys and climbing over hills, we shared a horizon of walking *toward* suffering.

The earth's unpredictable movements and shifting atmospheres tempered the quality of therapeutic encounters.[9] Counseling did not only take place within a particular sociocultural and political-economic environment but was also formed by the geography of the Himalayas. For as Ingold has shown through his phenomenological work on perception of the environment, the environment is not merely "out there" but is a force that mediates knowledge, thought, and relations.[10] To consider the role of the earth in counseling is to follow the psychogeographies of care in the aftermath of disaster—both the embodied experience of crossing a disaster zone to reach clients and the counselor's own internal psychic landscape. Sigmund Freud famously described the psyche in geological terms, comparing the mind to the archaeological ruins of an ancient city in which past and present structures coexisted simultaneously.[11] In Freud's image, the psyche is depicted as a landscape in which past memories and experiences are overlaid onto current structures that together shape one's present emotional world. Years later, in 1955, the French Situationist Guy Debord introduced the term *psychogeography* as a playful exploration of the relationship between emotion and the environment.[12] Central to psychogeography was the *dérive*, "the drift," a method of wandering that involved walking through the city and allowing oneself to be affected by the flow of experience and encounter. In a similar way, walking-with counselors served as an ethnographic method through which to approach the relation between psyche and geography and the merging of internal and external landscapes in the postearthquake psychosocial intervention, as counselors faced existential risk to provide care to others.

The fact that Nepali counselors were required to walk long distances and face risk to provide care while foreign humanitarians remained protected laid bare the inequalities of the humanitarian endeavor. Within humanitarianism, as in many forms of charity, hierarchies of power are deeply embedded at multiple levels—between foreign humanitarians and local staff, between donors and NGOs, between supervisors and field staff, and between field staff and local communities.[13] The existence of such asymmetries in humanitarianism makes solidarity a rare and fragile achievement. In the *Oxford English Dictionary*, *solidarity* is defined as "the fact or quality, on the part of communities . . . of being perfectly united or at one in some respects, esp. in interests, sympathies, or aspirations."[14] The French sociologist Émile Durkheim famously studied solidarity as a broader form of social cohesion, which is variously mediated by either shared values (in the case of small-scale societies) or the necessity of social interdependence (in industrial societies). He called these two types mechanical and organic solidarity, respectively.[15] The type of solidarity I am concerned with in this chapter is closer to what the anarchist theorist Peter Kropotkin has described as "the sense of justice, or equity, which brings the individual to consider the rights of every other individual as equal to his own."[16] Yet as Dean Spade argues in his work on crisis and mutual aid, there are few possibilities for solidarity in models of aid based on charity.[17]

This chapter explores the question of solidarity in humanitarianism by following three counselors as they crossed a Himalayan disaster zone to reach clients. Through a critical phenomenology of walking that describes how the embodied work of counseling took form in relation to the social, cultural, and material environment, we come to know each counselor's story and explore the lived experience of facing risk to provide care.[18] The movement of counselors across a still-trembling landscape to listen to worries people held in their heart-minds had been set into motion by the work of disaster— the rupture of the earth and its conceptualization as a crisis requiring novel forms of treatment. Transnational humanitarian hierarchies became embodied in the physical and emotional labor of counselors who traveled by foot over steep hills and stayed in tin shelters alongside local people. Alternating between descriptions of the experience of walking through a Himalayan disaster zone and the internal psychic landscapes of counselors, this chapter shows how infrastructural limitations, geography, personal histories, and the cultural meanings of walking came together to create unexpected affordances for solidarity between counselors and clients in an otherwise hierarchical, charity model of care.

Barefoot Counselors

For the women I walked with, psychosocial counseling was a particular form of gendered labor that demanded empathy, sacrifice, and physical strength. Their work required them to navigate the act of walking in a social world where women's movement was clearly circumscribed. As I had learned in eastern Nepal, women in villages did not circulate so freely. I recalled my friend in Khotang, daydreaming about a handsome driver she had secretly been talking to on the phone. She wished she could go to the city with him where people didn't watch one's every move. "In the village if you walk around too much, people will say, 'She walks too much,'" she explained. Here "walking too much" was a moral judgment and euphemism for immodesty and loss of *laj*, an idealized virtue and gendered emotion that involves a mix of shame and embarrassment.

At the same time, since 1988 there has been a tradition of FCHVs who circulate through their local wards providing vaccines, information about family planning, and treating common childhood illnesses in rural areas.[19] These women walk dressed in a government uniform and are highly respected. Throughout Nepal, FCHVs provide the essential services that keep the cash-strapped public health system going, yet they receive little payment. Both FCHVs and psychosocial counselors in Nepal are connected to the lineage of the primary health care movement that first emerged in the field of international health 1970s. Following critiques that health development programs had largely ignored primary health care in favor of disease eradication, the early primary health care movement was inspired by innovative solutions to health care delivery that emphasized community participation and the training of laypeople to provide basic health services in resource-poor settings.[20]

China's "barefoot doctors," laypeople trained to provide basic health services in medically underserved rural regions, became an important case study in the WHO's search for innovative alternatives in public health care delivery.[21] Launched in China by Mao Zedong in the mid-1960s, the "barefoot" model trained agricultural workers to provide medical care, including delivering babies, immunizations, and prescribing basic medicines.[22] The shift from expert physician to community-based health worker aimed to democratize medical knowledge, decentralize medical care, and expand access to services at low cost in regions without preexisting medical infrastructure or adequate numbers of doctors. China's barefoot doctors and other examples of community participation in health care from countries such as Cuba, Tanzania, Costa Rica, and Bangladesh helped inspire the primary health care movement, which was officially promoted by the WHO in the Alma-Ata Declaration of 1978.

Among the most well-known contemporary examples of the power of community health care workers has been the success of the "accompaniment model," an approach developed in Haiti by anthropologist-physician Dr. Paul Farmer and his nonprofit organization Partners in Health.[23] Community health workers play a central role in "accompaniment," as the figures who accompany patients in their personal journey from illness to health. At the practical level, this work involves regular home visits, medication monitoring, and material and social support. Inscribed in this model of care is a sense of doing work with one's feet on the ground—that is, work that is grounded and directly engaged in addressing suffering and injustice. In this way, to be a barefoot doctor has always had moral implications.[24] In Nepal, the work of psychosocial counseling in the aftermath of the disaster was conceptualized in similar terms, as counselors walked long distances to meet clients in their homes and listen to the worries they held in their heart-minds.

While the rise of the community health movement inspired the Declaration of Alma-Ata in 1978, its influence in global health would soon wane.[25] It was only in the 2000s, in response to the HIV epidemic, that the WHO officially endorsed task-shifting, or the redistribution of tasks from expert medical professionals to community-based health workers and laypeople with basic training.[26] Task-shifting was celebrated by WHO Director-General Margaret Chan as "the vanguard for the renaissance of primary healthcare" and a highly effective way to increase access to services in resource-poor settings that face a shortage of health workers and an increasing demand for care.[27]

Like the barefoot doctors of the 1960s and 70s, in Nepal psychosocial counselors are laypeople with a secondary school education who receive around six months of training in mental health and counseling before they are sent out into the field. In a country where there are few psychiatrists, NGO-trained counselors provided basic counseling services and referrals to psychiatrists by traveling throughout rural communities and meeting clients in their homes. In a very real sense, minimally trained counselors are the infrastructure of global mental health, a field that has identified task-shifting as the most viable solution to the "treatment gap" in low- and middle-income countries.[28] In Nepal, the ability to walk and traverse remote regions was a key element that made the decentralized work of community mental health care possible in the aftermath of disaster. Although they were near the bottom of the organizational hierarchy, nonexpert psychosocial counselors carried the greatest share of responsibilities for care while simultaneously facing the extreme mental and physical challenges of working in a disaster zone.

Psychogeographies of Care

Anthropologists have shown how infrastructure is linked to practices of sociality, for it fundamentally mediates interactions between people, space, and objects and "shapes the rhythms of everyday life."[29] Road infrastructure not only enables transportation but in many places also stimulates desire and collective dreams of progress, modernity, and freedom.[30] Roads and their enchanting promise of speed and connectivity have "affective force."[31] Such is the case in the Himalayas, where road conditions have long been a potent symbol of national development (*bikas*) and its lack.[32] In this way, the materiality of the mountainous terrain—roads and their absence—not only determined how counselors reached clients but also lent meaning to the practice of care in the aftermath of disaster.

Compared to that of Dolakha, road infrastructure in the districts of Ramechhap and Okhaldhunga was considerably less present. Counselors instead had to travel between their working VDCs by foot. In Ramechhap we would sometimes walk for six, eight, or ten hours as we traveled over high suspension bridges and well-worn paths, crossing steep hills, winding through vast forests of coniferous trees, and sometimes carefully skirting the narrow trails that hugged the sides of steep cliffs, in order to reach the clients. As Bina explained, one of the hardest things about the work of psychosocial counseling was learning how to walk.

> Before, I didn't used to have the *bani* [habit]. I wasn't used to going to the field. . . . I wasn't used to walking. I didn't have the habit of walking and carrying my bags [*jhola bokera hidne bani thiena*]. The first time I went to the field I came back after only a few days. On the way, there was so much mud everywhere—it was extremely difficult. My whole body hurt, I was carrying this huge bag; it was massive. It was so difficult for me to carry this bag and walk. I also didn't know the roads. I was completely alone. And afterwards I felt like, I cannot do this work. I wasn't confident, I was suffering, the sun was burning down, and I said, "I am not doing this!"

When Bina talks about walking as a *bani*, she simultaneously conjures the multiple meanings of the word, which can be translated as "habit" as well as "practice," "temperament," "disposition," "inclination," "character," "lifestyle,"

FIGURE 3.1. Looking ahead at the day's walk, across the suspension bridge and up and over the hills. Photo by the author.

FIGURE 3.2. A woman carries a jug of water in a *doko*. Photo by the author.

and "addiction."[33] In this sense *bani* is intertwined with a particular form of life. In Nepal it is commonly said of porters, who spend their days carrying heavy loads, that they are able to do so because they have the *bani* (thus replacing a structure of exploitation with a quality of character or disposition). When Bina said she had acquired the *bani* of walking, she also meant that she had developed a new disposition, that she had become the type of person who is accustomed to walking far distances and carrying their own belongings. In the Himalayas, the figure of the one who walks and carries heavy loads holds powerful symbolic connotations.

Once we had reached the working VDC, finding a safe place to stay was often challenging. Despite having been told by their supervisors only to stay in secure structures, the counselors regularly occupied cracked buildings because there were few alternatives. This was not the case for foreign humanitarians. One option available to aid workers was the "humanitarian hub," a sterile tent complex amid chaos. It cost USD 25 per person per day to stay there. Equivalent to a day's wages, $25 was an amount Nepali field staff could not afford. My white skin and light hair granted Indira and me entry into the hub without questioning. We wandered in through the gates and past the security guard, bewildered. Inside, we waited to speak with the receptionist. Indira raised her hands together in a formal greeting of *namaskar* and began to introduce herself. The young Nepali receptionist responded with a pained and embarrassed expression. In his grimace I sensed that he did not think people like Indira belonged there. An Australian man appeared. He complained about the Wi-Fi connection and demanded a solution immediately. The receptionist darted away. I asked Indira if she would like to stay, but she told me she would prefer to sleep at a friend's house. We parted ways for the night.

Inside the humanitarian hub, there were hot showers. The sleeping quarters were partitioned into capsule rooms made of gray cloth with doors that zip shut. No bigger than a single bed, each room came equipped with a mattress, blanket, and razor-sharp Swedish knife, for reasons unknown. The hub felt like a strange ship, adrift and at sea. Outside the high fence of the compound and beyond the security floodlights, the landscape lay in ruins. Inside, I slipped into another world like a dream. In the dining hall an iPad displayed the words "Spanish Night" and was playing Flamenco music. We were served couscous, chicken, beef stew, bread, and imported fruit juice. In this surreal scene, we come face to face with humanitarianism's asymmetrical value of human life.[34]

I had heard of the existence of the "humanitarian hub" from the foreign project manager, who mentioned it was a place with hot showers where humanitarians stayed while working in the field. Humanitarian hubs are field

FIGURE 3.3. A painting of the humanitarian hub. Umesh Shrestha, *Under the Himalaya: Experience of Students*. Photo by the author.

accommodations organized by the International Humanitarian Partnership (IHP), to support the work of humanitarians in disaster and crisis settings.[35] Hubs may be temporary camps or more permanent structures but generally include housing, laundry facilities, a kitchen and canteen, a water purification system, showers, toilets, access to electricity, and security.[36] This option was not available or even known among the Nepali field staff, who were expected to arrange their own lodgings and did not have the luxury of temporary escape from the landscape of disaster. Above the dining tables hung a painting of the humanitarian hub itself. The image depicted a tranquil scene of an empty camp. Young girls pass by on their way to school, dressed in uniforms. One girl turns to her friend and says, in a red speech bubble, "Hey Parvati! Listen The IHP (International Humanitarian Partnership) is Really Working well in this Critical Condition." The schoolgirls peer over the fence in curiosity. In the distance the mountain Gaurishankar can be seen through a frame of lush green trees against a backdrop of clear blue sky. In the image there are no ruins, no signs of disaster. Only the safe, calm beauty of nature, femininity, and the vacant camp.

The next day, I met Indira. While the other people in the hub were picked up by drivers in white jeeps, we hitched a ride on the back of an open milk truck. "It's better than the public bus!" she yelled over the revving engine. We clung to the metal rails between boxes of clanking bottles and set off for the day's counseling sessions.

In his work on solidarity and crisis, Dean Spade has argued that there are two main forms of crisis response in times of disaster: mutual aid and charity. Charity relies on a hierarchical model in which those with resources decide who is deserving of aid and in what form. In this way charity is diametrically opposed to mutual aid, "the collective coordination to meet each other's needs, usually from an awareness that the systems we have in place are not going to meet them."[37] Mutual aid flattens hierarchies and relies on "survival work" organized by volunteers who are dedicated to the community as opposed to externally funded interventions and professionalized humanitarian services that are tied to specific predefined issues and eligibility criteria and operate through top-down decision-making.[38] If charity is focused on saving victims, then mutual aid is about building solidarity with those in need through collective action and self-determination, without expectations of payment or reward.

One can quickly sense the absence of solidarity in the humanitarian hub, where Nepali field staff and community members were excluded from areas of respite from existential risk, a luxury that was guarded by high fences and sharp knives. Yet within the work of the postdisaster psychosocial counseling program, the boundaries between charity and mutual aid were less rigid. Even within a humanitarian intervention based on a charity model, solidarity with those affected by the earthquakes was still possible. Among Nepali counselors, solidarity took multiple forms, such as walking long distances, staying in the temporary shelters of local people, and suffering to reach the clients. At the same time, solidarity was fragile; always threatening to break down.

The geography of the landscape and lack of infrastructure worked in unexpected ways that sometimes opened up possibilities for solidarity, in spite of the hierarchies that constantly threatened to annihilate it. Here the difficulty of movement across a steep and unstable landscape lent meaning to the work of counselors, who exposed themselves to risk and faced emotional challenges in order to reach the clients. In this way, the environment was not only an obstacle to counseling, but an affordance that gave unexpected meaning to its work. Counselors exposed themselves to risk and learned the *bani* of walking through rugged terrain, and in this embodied gesture, clients recognized that someone had traveled a long way to listen to their worries, that someone had walked and suffered for them.

Walking as Moral Experience

The winter following the earthquakes was freezing, especially for those who now occupied temporary shelters of tin and wood. Local newspapers began

FIGURE 3.4. Walking to reach the clients. Photo by the author.

reporting cases of death by hypothermia in the affected districts. Working in Dolakha from December to February meant that the counselors also had to endure the biting cold alongside the earthquake-affected communities. It was now winter, and Indira and I had arrived at a claustrophobic settlement at the edge of a new road, built in a narrow pass between two steep cliffs. Land-slides were everywhere but had mercifully missed this place. Although eight months had passed since the earthquakes, the settlement was still littered with debris and the remains of broken houses.

We entered the house where we would stay the night. Passing through a shadowy corridor, we reached the darkened inner room of tin and wood where the meals were cooked. A single solar-powered lightbulb provided a dim light. There hadn't been electricity since the earthquakes. The space was very rough and very cold. Indira and I sat on a wooden cot and warmed ourselves around a heavy iron stove, its embers glowing red and orange. The room receded into darkness.

That night Indira and I would sleep in a bare dark room on wooden beds covered with rugs and old blankets. While I prayed that there wouldn't be a landslide, Indira's youngest son called from Kathmandu to say the electricity was out and he couldn't do his homework. When she got off the phone, she told me how hard it was for her to be so far from her children all the time. Indira had been "walking in the field" (*fieldma hidera*) for the past twenty years.

We had traveled a long way to reach this place, but once we arrived, there were few clients. Most of the work was not "the work" I had imagined, but everything leading up to it that made the therapeutic interaction possible. Indira was not well and struggled to walk. She was afraid of earthquakes and felt she should not climb too high into the mountains as an earthquake might come again. She had seen only a handful of people for more than one session of counseling. Often days would pass without seeing anyone. Sometimes, we would spend hours attempting to meet a client for a brief session. Ninety percent of our time was spent traveling across the rough and broken terrain. I began to wonder if I would be able to endure the work—the crowded buses, the temporary shelters, constant sickness, walking all day to meet only a few clients, absorbing the suffering of others.

We made our way back to the village facing Gaurishankar, this time its peaks were covered in snow. In the village, it was ice cold at night, and in the morning, everything was covered in a layer of frost. You could see your breath inside, as the tin-and-wood-slat structures provided little protection from the elements. I returned to Kathmandu feeling heavy and tired. I felt exhausted by the struggle that was living, for the people I met in Dolakha, and for Indira as well. How sad it all was, how frightening. The places people were inhabiting—the village at the bottom of the canyon, the landslide just feet away. There was a constant striving, an extreme physical exertion to get even the smallest things. To walk with Indira was to be inside of this.

Indira had made a career as an NGO field worker. At age sixteen, she started working for a rural health development program. She spent almost twenty years as a rural health worker in Dolakha district, a period that spanned the violence of the People's War. In this job she learned to collect data for household surveys and organized "mothers' groups" where she led discussions with rural women on maternal and child health, covering topics such as hygiene, handwashing, vaccination, nutrition, vitamins, and postdelivery visits to the doctor. During the People's War, Indira received training in trauma counseling and began conducting programs for mothers and children who suffered during the conflict. The networks she built and the respect she earned with local leaders in Dolakha during her long-term position there was a central asset in her work as a postdisaster psychosocial counselor.

"I am the kind of person who likes taking risks and gaining work experience. I have the guts to work," Indira told me as we perched on the sunny balcony of her Kathmandu home. Indira was a high-caste woman in her thirties, yet the struggles of work seemed to have aged her. Although she grew up in Dolakha, by the time I met her she was living in a five-story, concrete, joint-family home on the outskirts of the city. During her employment as a rural health worker, Indira became a mother. As she put it, "I conducted programs while carrying my children on my back and holding my bags in my hands. . . . It was difficult. But now I have the experience of working, even in difficult situations. If we want to try to move forward, then we can even conduct programs while carrying our children on our back. I have experienced this." Indira often spoke about the difficulties of being both mother and field worker. Again and again, she would tell the story, not only to me but to anyone who would listen, of how she used to carry her children on her back and her bags in her hands as she worked, traveling from village to village by foot. Indira's emphasis on what she carried and how she traveled suggested an ambivalent relationship of "cruel optimism" toward her work, a job she took pride in yet caused her to suffer.[39] Reflecting on the relationship between gender and work, Indira spoke into my recorder, using the formal genre of Nepali speechmaking, *bhasan*:

You also experienced how hard Nepali women work. How much difficulty they face. How hard they work for their communities, carrying their own bags in their hands. In Nepal, there are many women who can't work as field staff. Many have the conception that women should only stay in the home. I hope that I can also set an example that women don't need to restrict themselves to the home only. They can also work like men and go out to the fields and the villages. . . . We will be an example of women who can go out in the field and work even in difficult situations.

Indira's situation had indeed been difficult. During the earthquakes she was in Kathmandu. Her family evacuated their home and stayed, as many in Kathmandu did, in a tent outside. During the evacuation her father passed away. On the thirteenth day of the thirteen-day death rituals, Indira was called for an interview at the NGO, where she had recently applied for a job as a counselor in the postdisaster psychosocial program. To do the interview at that time seemed impossible, but she went anyway. She was selected and deployed to Dolakha district.

When we walked through Charikot, the formidable, highly built-up district headquarters of Dolakha, Indira knew and greeted almost every person we passed. Walking with her through the bazaar was slow going, as she would stop to acknowledge important people and give her formal introduction to those she had not yet met. Indira had a politically minded prowess and paid careful attention to maintaining public relations with local leaders. Her strong and outgoing public persona contrasted with the side I saw when I visited her in her home in Kathmandu. There Indira was reserved, carefully embodying *laj*, the quiet, restrained shyness of the proper daughter-in-law. This was a stark difference from the tough persona I saw in the field and the Kathmandu training hall, where she was always the first to answer questions. Indira struggled to balance her desire to be a salaried and respected frontline worker with her role and responsibilities as daughter-in-law, wife, and mother as she faced the extreme physical, mental, and material challenges of fieldwork. As a result, for Indira, walking in the field was an embodied experience infused with personal moral and ethical significance.[40]

One winter afternoon we sat on the double twin beds in Indira's freezing rented room in the district headquarters of Dolakha. Wrapped in the thick synthetic velvet of her new set of Chinese blankets, we could see our breath in the air as we spoke. Indira proudly showed me her résumé. The dossier included a stack of laminated and signed certificates for trainings she had completed over the course of her career. However, the years of work had come at a price, especially her most recent position. During our time together in the field, Indira was frequently unwell. She suffered from chronic gastric problems, respiratory infections, fevers. Toward the end of the project, after we were no longer working together, Indira fell while walking in the field and broke her arm. "I feel that I can keep working as long as my health supports me; landslides, cliffs, and rivers are the tough parts," she had mentioned ominously months earlier. In spite of, or perhaps because of, these challenges, Indira spoke with pride about her postdisaster work as one of her biggest achievements. "We worked hard, even during the blockade," she explained. "We were able to provide our services even when we couldn't find any vehicles. We went by foot to those places and helped people there. The biggest achievement is to fulfill the goals and objectives that you have set. This is also a source of self-satisfaction. . . . I have experienced that we can work and give our services to the community, no matter what."

What comes before the counseling session begins may be just as important as what happens within its duration. As psychoanalytic theory has long argued, such beginnings—the scheduling of the meeting, the patient's journey to the office, the waiting room, the greeting, the small talk, the décor, the patient's mood, the therapists' own psychic knots—can all play a role in setting the therapeutic stage even before the session has begun.[41] Such is also the case in counseling sessions in the aftermath of the earthquakes. The therapeutic encounter cannot be confined to the delimited space of the session but must also include the steep and shaky paths that lead up to it.

Internal Landscapes

It was very beautiful in the hills of Ramechhap. Bina and I were surrounded by the deep forest, and the early spring weather was beginning to warm. To get there, we had walked with a local psychosocial worker for eight hours, first down a hill face, then across a suspension bridge, and then up and up through the villages. On the way, we stopped once to rest and to meet a client. Soon we left the villages behind and entered a large and beautiful forest of coniferous pine. Tapped for sap, the tree trunks were marked with scars like feathers. Since Bina had developed the *bani* of walking, she no longer experienced walking as difficult but had come to enjoy it.

Walking with Bina felt like an adventure because of her ability to transform the struggle of reaching clients into *ramailo*, fun. For although the work required walking in unfamiliar places, for Bina it also offered an opportunity for personal growth, to see new things, and to enjoy the beauty of her country. While walking along the paths Bina would sing, tell stories, and pose for photos on her phone. "When the clients say they are getting better, I feel so happy and I don't even care how long I had to walk to reach them. Once I reach their place, I forget everything," Bina said. Instead of being depleted by the work, Bina drew energy from it.

Bina had an innate ability to understand others and empathize with them. She made you feel as though she had known you for years even if you had just met. Bina recognized these qualities in herself. "I can go to an unknown environment and talk as if I am familiar to the people there," she explained, when I asked her what she considered to be her personal strengths. "People compliment me regarding this, and I also believe that I have this talent. Whenever I go to new places, people tell me that I talk to them as if I have known them from before. I get along well with people very fast. I regard this as a talent." Bina felt she personified a feminist ethics of care, or in her words, "the necessary virtues [*gun*] that a woman should have." As she put it, "I like to take care of others. This is also one of my virtues, *gun*. I ask people about their well-being even if I don't know them. I have this skill, the ability to care for and help others. I help people, even if I don't have much."

Sometimes while I walked with Bina through Ramechhap, we would stay in the temporary shelter of Parmila, a local psychosocial worker based in the area. Not yet married, Parmila lived with her parents in a small bazaar town situated within one of Bina's working areas. Her family's temporary shelter was made of bamboo with a floor of cold beaten earth. Mice had invaded and were eating holes in the blankets. Others were renting the land as well, and a row of four or five dwellings shared the hollow bamboo walls. Parmila was thin and had not been eating much recently. In the midst of this, sometimes Parmila's mother would suddenly embrace her daughter tightly. I said it made me miss my mother. Bina said she didn't have a mother or a father so there was nothing she ever knew that she could miss.

Bina had a hungry childhood. She was born to an extremely poor indigenous Tamang family of ten in a remote village in Solukhumbu, the district where Mount Everest lies. For money, her parents cut trees to make Nepali paper.[42] "We used to feed ourselves with the money that we got from it and if the money wasn't sufficient enough, we didn't eat anything . . . We used to work there for the whole day and at night we would stay inside huge stone caves. We didn't have a proper house. Our father used to bring sugar by selling that paper. We found it very tasty when we dissolved the sugar in a small bottle of water and drank it." When the situation became unlivable, Bina's father relocated the family to Sikkim in the eastern Indian Himalayas where his mother lived, and Bina began to attend school. When Bina was seven years old, her father died suddenly from an asthma attack while walking to the fields without his inhaler. Two years later, her mother also passed away. Supported by her elder siblings, she completed her bachelor's degree in the

late 1990s and returned to Nepal with her brother. By that time the People's
War had begun. She settled in Solukhumbu and got a job as a "house mother,"
taking care of orphans in a home funded by a foreign NGO. Soon she began
to volunteer, teaching preschool in the local government school in the after-
noons. Eventually she moved to Ramechhap district, where she bought her
own land and opened a home for disabled orphans. Bina had become an orphan herself after losing both her parents at a young age, and this experience
seemed to inspire in her a desire to help others. Uninterested in marriage and
living far from relatives, Bina created her own family in unconventional ways
by gathering her friends and adopted children around her.

Bina often recalled to me that the first lesson she learned as a psychosocial counselor was that it was OK to cry with clients. She was soon surprised
to find that her training as a counselor also helped her understand her own
emotions. After the earthquakes destroyed her house, she suffered from out-
bursts of anger. Sometimes she would become enraged at her friends for no
reason and would yell at them to shut up. At night she suffered from headaches, fear, and *jham-jham*, tingling sensations in her body.[43] She felt restless
and lonely. "I was not even able to think properly," she explained. She found
that the role-playing exercises she participated in during the counselor training program helped her control her anger.[44] "I used to get very angry. Too
much. And when speaking, when I was angry, I used to yell at people a lot.
Since I was a child, I have always been angry. But after I started doing this
work my anger has lessened." I had seen Bina erupt into anger on only one
occasion, yelling at a staff member on the phone after a mistaken action with
a client who had been a victim of sexual assault. Her rage expanded and filled
the room as her voice mounted into a high-pitched shriek. It was through her
work as a counselor that gradually she was able to feel less anger. "I realized
that if you don't have mental balance, then you suffer from many problems,"
she explained. By experiencing healing through her participation in counseling training, Bina began to believe in the value of psychosocial counseling.

Bina was not the only one who expressed that becoming a counselor had
been a source of personal growth. After years of taking prescription sleeping
pills for insomnia, another counselor mentioned that he was finally able to
sleep without medicine after receiving support from his supervisors as part
of his training. Both within the postdisaster psychosocial project and in other
psychosocial programs, counselors said that their training had helped them
to manage their own worries and struggles, increased their confidence in
themselves, and enabled them to "become developed" (*bikasit*). In this way,
becoming a psychosocial counselor not only helped counselors manage their
own emotions but also had the potential to generate new forms of subjectivity.

Just as the challenges counselors faced on the mountain paths shaped therapeutic encounters, so too did the counselor's own internal landscapes of struggles, accomplishments, losses, pain, and past relationships impact how they interacted with clients and helped them with the problems they faced. Even as Bina applied the insights of counseling to her own psychic suffering, she also continued to carry her personal history with her. Yet Bina's childhood experience of the loss of both her parents was not only a source of ongoing emotional pain but also shaped her identity as a counselor and her ability to empathize with others.

Fragile Solidarities

While solidarity with clients became possible through shared exposure to risk, walking through the disaster zone to reach clients, or through similar personal histories and experiences, it was a fragile accomplishment in the context of humanitarian intervention—both within the NGO and between humanitarians and local communities. Solidarity's fragility surfaced in the tents of the "humanitarian hub" where foreign humanitarians slept in warm beds, guarded by sharp knives, high fences, and floodlights. It became tangible when a client was offered money for a bus ride at the wrong moment, and perceived the gift to be an insult. It became palpable as it seeped into dreams.

One night Bina dreamed of a black caterpillar. A few days later, she mentioned it to me. In the dream she saw herself sleeping. Next to her, she noticed a black caterpillar, picked it up, and flung it away. When she told me about the dream Bina was unsure about its meaning but sensed that the color black was linked to something bad. She had never had a dream like that before, and it worried her especially as traditional dream interpretation in Nepal emphasizes dream symbols as predictions of the future. When I asked what she thought the dream could mean, Bina suggested it might be related to her insecurities during fieldwork. "I have been involved in fieldwork. While doing so, I have said good or bad things to others. While doing the counseling, I may have made some mistakes as well. Maybe the dream has something to do with it."

Although counselors attended numerous trainings, they often felt unprepared for the level of suffering among the clients they met in the field. Part of the model of psychosocial counseling is that it can be done by minimally trained staff and thus scaled-up in places with few expert mental health professionals. Counselors in the program received short trainings in basic counseling skills prior to the start of their work and at various points throughout its duration. The trainings consisted of role-playing exercises and reflexive prompts through which various lessons about counseling were taught. And yet, "however much training we had, we didn't have much practice with real clients," Bina later explained to me. It was only after working in the field for six months that she began to gain confidence. As Bina began working in remote areas, she slowly gained a new understanding of the meaning of counseling. There she found the opportunity to learn as she suddenly found herself helping all kinds of clients: "I met every type of client—those who can't sleep, those who cry a lot, those who run away, those who hit others, those who have insomnia, those who faint—I met every type of sick person. But for me, I enjoyed meeting these people because I learned so much. Although it was very challenging, I also had the opportunity to practice."

I associated Bina's dream of the black caterpillar with the fragile solidarities we had built with each other. I was there alongside her, walking with her and accompanying her, but I was also observing her work to communicate the challenges on the ground to the supervisors and foreign project manager in Kathmandu. Although I was there to advocate for the counselors, they remained concerned that I might say something critical. If Bina was afraid to make a mistake, it was also because I would see it. I began to wonder if perhaps I was the black caterpillar—if only she could fling me away so easily. Yet in choosing to tell me about her dream, Bina also opened a space for us to reflect on her insecurities about the work as well as the implications of my presence for her. For the counselors I was an ambiguous figure, insider and outsider, friend and stranger. While sometimes my presence created anxieties about their own work and lack of experience in the field, at other times the counselors seemed hungry for guidance, grateful for accompaniment, and welcoming of any form of feedback they could receive.

On the night of the dream of the black caterpillar, Bina had repeatedly asked me for guidance as we lay on our two wooden cots in the dark. She wanted supervision and feedback about her work. She said no one had come to observe her work in the field before, and she was concerned about whether or not she was doing things correctly. Later, in a counselor training held in a small bazaar town, the supervisor asked the counselors what they thought my role in the project was—they replied that I was someone they could communicate their problems to and that I would relay their messages to the people at the top. To travel as the counselors did, to sleep where they slept, and to walk alongside them drew the counselors and I together in an NGO culture of hierarchy where supervisors and foreigners rarely accompanied counselors in the field in this way. The counselors recognized this, and our shared experience brought us closer. "You also have given us energy, by walking together with us," Indira said.

The fragility of solidarity became especially visible while I worked with a third counselor, Anjana. We were sitting in a small room with a green carpet in the top floor of a rural health post. The windows were open, but the air was hot and still. Facing us was a client who had come for a counseling session. She was an older woman, dressed in a hot pink *cholo*, red *lungi*, and checked handkerchief, with a beaded necklace of flowers around her neck.[45]

"My *cottage* isn't even nice," she said. "There isn't even a door. Rain comes in." The woman told us that her back and chest hurt and it was hard for her to breathe. She was given medicine but had no idea what it was, saying only that she took pills, "one red one, one white one." We learned that one of her sons went abroad but wouldn't send her any money. She was in debt. The only one to help her was her older sister. With tears in her eyes, she spoke about how the earthquakes took her house. Throughout the meeting she continuously repeated "*mare pani marhos*" (if you're going to die, die). Anjana struggled to find the right response. As the session ended, she offered the woman 200 ru-pees from the NGO so she could pay for transportation and buy a snack. She asked her to sign a form before accepting the money, but the woman refused the gift. "Why don't *you* take it," said the client, hurt and angry.

As I walked with Anjana in the remote villages of Okhaldunga, there was a general mood of distrust and hopelessness that seemed to color many of her interactions with clients. Often Anjana, with her minimal training, was unable to provide solutions to the complex problems people presented, and the meetings ended in frustration. Anjana felt that she needed more empathy, support, and guidance from her supervisors. "I used to think that supervisors are the people who are supposed to help me and support me in difficult cir-cumstances, but I have now realized that they don't support you in that way." Faced with extremely challenging client cases that often surpassed even her supervisors' experience, Anjana felt increasingly alone in the work.

Anjana and I traveled by bus throughout the western part of the district of Okhaldhunga. The region was notorious for its bad roads, and to travel from the district headquarters of Okhaldhunga Bazaar to Anjana's working areas took eight hours, the same amount of time it had taken to drive from Kath-mandu to Okhaldhunga itself. As we made our way, we inhaled clouds of dust from the road that had engulfed our bus. Passengers, nauseous from the road, threw up into small plastic bags and tossed them out the windows. After the long journey, Anjana immediately began to meet with clients, as the next day she would already be on her way to another VDC, so she could complete her work before the upcoming holiday. Anjana felt that she was constantly rushing. Previously she had been criticized by a supervisor for not seeing enough clients in her working areas. According to Anjana, she had helped another counselor in the district with her caseload but received no credit for it. "I would not have felt so bad, but I have also left my small children at home. My young children are also earthquake victims! I even thought about quitting the job, but then I realized that they are the ones who didn't understand me; I know that I worked. So, I consoled myself by saying that I should value my work even if others don't." The need to fill the quota propelled Anjana into anxiety. She worked nonstop, seeing as many clients as possible to meet expectations for reporting. Accusations that Anjana had not worked hard enough were painful, for they implied that all of the sacrifices she had made—being away from her young children, exposing herself to risk—had been for nothing.

Humanitarian interventions are marked by stark asymmetries. In the post-disaster psychosocial intervention, hierarchies of power shaped all aspects of the work—from the relationships between foreign humanitarians and local staff to the interactions between counselors and local communities. Within such humanitarian hierarchies, solidarity was not easy to achieve. By moving between the material and psychological conditions of the work of disaster, this chapter has shown how facing risk and walking long distances over unstable land to reach clients lent meaning to therapeutic encounters. The embodied work of counseling in a Himalayan disaster zone reconfigures humanitarian conceptualizations of aid that assume repair of a ruptured world is best accomplished through the sheltering of expert humanitarian workers. Here we discover a sharp contrast between repair as enabled by access to special protection in the humanitarian hub and repair as facilitated through shared exposure to risk.

A critical phenomenology of walking in the aftermath of disaster requires attending to how the social and material environment affects ways of feeling, caring, and relating to others in a context of uneven exposure to risk. As counselors circulated through the disaster-affected districts, they listened to worries held in the heart-minds of others while facing their own challenges in the disaster zone. The embodied experience of walking to reach the clients was not a peripheral aspect of counseling but a central element that shaped the therapeutic work. By expanding the spatial frame of the therapeutic encounter from the bounded session into the crisscrossing mountain paths that lead up to it, we attend to the desires, struggles, risks, and ambivalences that counselors carried into the counseling sessions after crossing a landscape in ruins. Michel de Certeau writes that "walking is a space of enunciation," a form of speech in which the walker enunciates their desire through movement and traces left of paths traversed.[46] This chapter can then also be read as a "long poem of walking" along uncertain and trembling paths to provide care to others.[47]

4

Efficacy

In December 2015, I sat in a hotel in Naxal, a busy commercial neighborhood in the center of Kathmandu. I had come to attend a training for the psychosocial counselors from the postearthquake counseling project. It had been six months since the project began, and the donors were calling for the final reports before ending the work. There was talk of the possibility that some of the donors might renew their projects for an additional year, but this was not yet known. That day one of the NGO staff, Vishnu Sir, came to talk to the counselors about "quality reporting." We sat in a circle of chairs around the edge of the room, the sounds of traffic permeating the windows. A faded painting of Mount Everest decorated the gloomy walls. "Report *kasari lekhne* [How do you write a report]?" Vishnu Sir asked the group. The counselors volunteered topics that should be included, and Vishnu Sir noted their answers in a list on a white board at the front of the room. Vishnu Sir then asked the counselors to define the meaning of a "quality report." Indira, one of the psychosocial counselors, eagerly raised her hand. A quality report, she replied, requires describing "how much achievement there was, and after that, what kinds of challenges came, right? And after that, analysis." Vishnu Sir explained that up to that point, there was "only data measuring output," but that now they needed to understand the outcome. How do you make it qualitative?"

"Qualitative *kasari banaune*?" he asked the group rhetorically, code-switching from Nepali to English to emphasize donor accountability–related terms like *evidenced-based*, *data*, *numbers*, and *observations*.[1] He said what was needed to justify what the counselors wrote in their reports was evidence because without evidence one could also write lies. With this problem in mind, he asked the group, "How do you make it evidence-based? It must be evidence-based." "Evidence-based *kasari garne*? Evidence-based *hunuparchha*." He continued, "For *evidence* we must have *data* with us. When one says *data*, it means *numbers*, right, and how many *sessions* were done also could be *data*, in which place was the work done also could be *data*, how many times it was done could also come as *data*, was the *counseling* with an *individual* or with a *family* or with a *group*, and what *observations* came? *Observation* is *important*, what changes did you see?"[2] Evidence was required for the purpose of reporting to donors and communicating the quality and effectiveness of the intervention through written proof. This need was connected to what Marilyn Strathern has termed "audit cultures," in which accountability to donors is increasingly required to justify funding and investment.[3] Maintaining funding was of course a real and pressing concern for the NGO, because without donor-funded projects, the staff had no source of income and the organization would collapse. Yet the emphasis on reporting also led staff to make ambivalent jokes that maybe they were really "data counselors" and not real counselors at all. The reporting done by the counselors took on a role of critical importance and was defined by a tension between, on the one hand, the personal value of counseling sessions to clients and, on the other, the financial value of the work done by the organization. This dual set of concerns was reflected in the ambiguous term *quality report* itself, which could simultaneously be read to mean both "a report on the quality of work done" and "a good quality report" that conforms to the requirements of donor accounting.

For the Kathmandu-based NGO supervisors and the foreign project manager, the most important question was always about the effectiveness of the humanitarian psychosocial intervention. The project manager wanted to know what the counselors were doing on the ground and if it was helping people. Were the counselors using the techniques they had been trained in correctly? If not, what kinds of "indigenous" techniques might they be using? The relatively inexperienced counselors themselves also wanted to know if their work was efficacious and if they were applying their recently learned techniques correctly. However, evidence for humanitarian efficacy was in no way straightforward. Uncertainty over the cause of a client's improvement and the problem of measurement were issues that Bina, a psychosocial counselor, directly reflected on in conversation. "While doing follow-ups, people say that they have gotten better and recognize the work done by our organization," Bina explained. "I feel good when they say that it has helped them quite a lot. But I sometimes wonder if it is really me who has helped them because I don't have much experience. When they thank us, I sometimes find it hard to believe that they got better because of us. When they thank our organization,

at times I doubt if it was really because of us or not. . . . We don't have anything that can accurately measure the work that we do. They are treating
themselves with shamans as well." Frequently during therapeutic encounters,
both clients and counselors would talk about improvement. Indira would ex-
claim enthusiastically to a client, "you are 50 percent improved" or insist that
someone's face "looked bright," or a client would repeat again and again how
much taking a particular medication had helped him and that with more
medicine he believed he could be cured. Clients would often comment in
conversation that they felt counseling was helping them improve and sometimes described how certain symptoms began to recede after meeting with
a counselor. Yet for freshly minted counselors with little confidence in their
skills, uncertainty remained. In this way, the field of global health's turn toward task-shifting was sometimes met by task-shifters with disbelief in their
own abilities.

    This chapter explores the question of humanitarian efficacy through the
stories of four clients who participated in the psychosocial intervention. The
interactions I describe took place both during the humanitarian intervention and three years after it ended. In each case, experiences of "efficacy" became an object of attention and reflection for clients and counselors and were
marked by confusion, uncertainty, ambivalence, and ambiguity. Here I take
inspiration from Jason Throop's phenomenological study of the articulation
of experience, in which he argues that in "looking for certainties, coherences,
and structures we [anthropologists] have often overlooked the ambiguities,
the confusions, the gaps, and the ambivalences that arise in the midst of our
own, and our informants' experiences as lived."[4] In postdisaster Nepal, the
primary cause of uncertainty had to do with the fact that clients' experiences
of suffering and healing overflowed humanitarian frames, rendering evidence
for efficacy difficult if not impossible to assess.[5]

    In his essay on "framing and overflowing," Michel Callon discusses the
problem of "externalities"—the positive and negative effects on a set of agents
that were not involved or envisioned in the original design of a project.[6]
Externalities include things like the impact of toxic chemical pollution on
communities located near a petrochemical plant, if the effect on nearby communities was not initially taken into consideration, or, in our case, the positive and negative effects of postdisaster counseling interventions on clients
with chronic suffering. Callon argues that externalities are fundamentally a
problem of framing and the identification of overflows, yet identifying and
measuring overflow is difficult because it requires intermediaries (such as
anthropologists) who can travel across and break through the borders of the
frame. Here ethnography serves as an important boundary-crossing device

for describing the externalities and overflows of the humanitarian frame of efficacy that assumed suffering would be directly linked to the event of the earthquakes.

While the humanitarian intervention was designed to heal the trauma of earthquake victims, few people could neatly trace the origin of their afflictions to the day the earth ruptured. Many clients suffered from chronic problems which predated the earthquakes—such as interpersonal abuse, social suffering, poverty, or severe mental illness—and received transient care because they happened to live in the disaster zone. For these clients, the emergence of a postearthquake mental health crisis did not map onto the temporality of their afflictions, which began long before the disaster. Through the work of disaster, their suffering became momentarily transformed into a problem of humanitarian concern, leading them to discover the possibilities of psychotropic medication and counseling, which they pursued alongside other modalities of treatment and care. Yet after the humanitarian intervention ended and earthquake victims were no longer subjects of public attention, people with chronic suffering were once again left on their own in a region where medication and counseling were no longer readily available. Even when their pain was clearly linked to the loss of a loved one in the earthquakes, grief did not adhere to donor timelines. By attending to experiences of clients that overflowed humanitarian frames, this chapter demonstrates the limitations of conceptualizations of efficacy that are bound to predefined temporalities of crisis and imaginaries of victimhood.

Efficacy and Effectiveness

Since Claude Lévi-Strauss's study of symbolic healing, medical anthropologists have been interested in the black box of therapeutic efficacy.[7] Allen Young has defined therapeutic efficacy as "the ability to purposively affect the real world in some observable way, to bring about the kinds of results that the actors anticipate will be brought about."[8] James Waldram has further complicated this definition by pointing out that determinations of efficacy are not straightforward, but shift in relation to varying hopes, expectations, perspectives, definitions, and standards of evaluation.[9] The diversity of perspectives on efficacy are especially pronounced in the context of humanitarianism where, as senior policy advisors have pointed out, "there is no clear or shared definition of what success looks like in the humanitarian endeavor" and donors, project designers, counselors, and affected communities and persons may hold divergent expectations.[10] In humanitarian interventions the measurement of effectiveness is also caught up in unequal relations of power, for it is those with the ability to provide funding who ultimately define what counts as evidence for effectiveness and when it should be assessed.

After selecting some data on counseling sessions to share with the Nepali supervisors and foreign training psychologist, one of the issues they chose to focus on was the discernment of efficacy during the sessions. The foreign psychologist decided to discuss ways that the counselors could better understand their clients' experience of the effectiveness of counseling sessions, instead of merely offering their subjective evaluation. Lorraine Daston and Peter Galison have argued that objectivity is an "epistemic virtue."[11] "To be objective," they write, "is to aspire to knowledge that bears no trace of its knower— knowledge unmarked by prejudice or skill, fantasy or judgement, wishing or striving."[12] Daston and Galison focus on the cultivation of objectivity as a virtuous way of seeing, describing, depicting, and knowing. Here objectivity is a set of practices and techniques of the self that work to suppress the influence of subjectivity through careful training and repetition over time. As the counselors learned about the requirements of "quality reporting" and practiced creative modes of measurement, they also began to cultivate the epistemic virtue of objectivity in themselves.

In the trainings that followed, counselors were taught to take measurements of clients' perceptions of improvement and began to incorporate the use of scales into their counseling sessions. They would ask the client to rate their perceptions on a scale of 0–10, including how much the client felt they had improved, what percentage of illness remained, and even how much the client liked the counseling session itself. "But what if the client is illiterate and doesn't know how to recognize numbers?" a counselor asked during a training, anticipating the difficulty of rendering experience in abstract terms among people she imagined might be unaccustomed to doing so. In response, the Nepali supervisor instructed the counselors to go out and collect other objects that could be used as a scale during the sessions. The next day the counselors came back to the training hall, presenting rocks and sticks of various sizes. Indira brought three balloons, which she inflated in decreasing sizes. But in general, counselors were instructed to draw a line on a sheet of paper, marked by the numbers 0–10 to present to the client before and after a counseling session as a way to illicit the client's perception of his or her own improvement over time as well as the perceived efficacy of the session that day.

Unlike humanitarian interventions for malnutrition that prove efficacy by documenting changes in weight and arm circumference, the efficacy of psychosocial interventions is less tangible and cannot be easily measured.[13] Evidence for the effectiveness of humanitarian psychosocial interventions is inconclusive, and determining how to measure efficacy in these intangible, time-limited interventions is under debate. Since the 1990s, randomized control trials (RCTs) have become the gold standard of measurement of efficacy in global health interventions, and this turn to "evidence-based medicine" has been adopted by the field of global mental health as well.[14] Yet in the context of humanitarian psychosocial interventions after disaster, a control group cannot be justified, and many projects employ their own methods and measure their outcomes based on disparate criteria, such as the creative elicitation of client feedback previously described.[15] As a result, the lack of evidence for the efficacy of humanitarian mental health and psychosocial interventions has even been put into question by leading practitioners themselves.[16] In response to this problem, researchers have developed a method of using biomarkers to determine effectiveness by measuring changes in hair cortisol concentration levels before and after the intervention.[17] Such modes of measurement avoid the problem of the subjective experience of efficacy by turning to hormonal proof in the body. Yet while postintervention reduction of cortisol can be proven statistically, little can be said about what specific aspects of an intervention were meaningful or effective for a particular person and why.

The desire for statistical proof of humanitarian effectiveness reflects a concern with accountability. Once global health interventions began to be funded largely by private investors, accountability to donors became a central requirement of health development programs. RCTs are valued by the field of global health over all other forms of data for their statistical power and assumed scientific objectivity, which, in the audit culture of neoliberal governance, directly translates into a language of accountability to donors as well as justification for "scalability." As a result, anthropologists have argued that contemporary global health interventions and the organizations that implement them are often more concerned with the production of "good numbers"—data that is capable of proving efficacy statistically and securing further funding—than in the provision of care.[18] While the NGO's local methods of measuring therapeutic efficacy could not produce "good numbers" with statistical power, they focused on documenting clients' lived experiences of efficacy through other means.

Thus far this chapter has used the terms *efficacy* and *effectiveness* interchangeably; however, they carry different meanings. In clinical trials an important distinction is made between studies of "efficacy," defined as "the performance of an intervention under ideal and controlled circumstances," and studies of "effectiveness," which refer to the performance of an intervention under "real-world" conditions and settings.[19] In the field of humanitarian psychosocial interventions, the common term of reference is "effectiveness," reflecting both the complex conditions in which interventions take place as well as the influence of the RCT model as the gold standard of evidence. Despite their accelerated speed, humanitarian interventions must still prove that money invested by donors is cost-effective by demonstrating, measuring, and accounting for effectiveness.[20] In this way we can define the humanitarian concept of efficacy as a concern with effectiveness and all that the term indexes.

In the hierarchy of evidence in global health interventions, ethnographic research falls at the bottom of the pyramid and is often dismissed as subjective, unreliable, anecdotal, and otherwise ungeneralizable beyond the situation. The presumed insignificance of ethnographic ways of knowing in global health is an artifact of the powerful cultural shift toward standardization and evidence-based medicine that reconfigured Western medicine from the 1980s onward.[21] Yet as Vincanne Adams has argued, the "singularity and idiosyncratic complexity" of the ethnographic case study provides a different kind of evidence "that is sometimes more truthful, proposing alternatives to the evidence-making from metrics work."[22] In the section that follows, we begin in the intersubjective space of the counseling session. The case described is one of many examples of the indeterminacy of evidence for humanitarian efficacy that I encountered while working with counselors in the earthquake-affected communities. This indeterminacy was often present in clients' experiences of improvement, and yet it escaped representation in the smoothed-over forms of accounting required by donors. Sally Engle Merry has pointed out that "it is the capacity of numbers to provide knowledge of a complex and murky world that renders quantification so seductive."[23] Instead of yielding to the seduction of quantification, this chapter draws from work on the phenomenology of experience to show how ambiguous experiences of humanitarian efficacy were articulated and given meaning in the midst of intersubjective interactions between counselor and client.[24] Despite counselors' efforts to measure the impact of psychosocial counseling, the complexity of clients' lived experiences of both affliction and healing continuously overflowed humanitarian frames and the forms of measurement that aimed to grasp it.

Ram's Graph

We first met Ram at Saraswoti's temporary shelter, where we were preparing to eat lunch before Anjana started her afternoon counseling sessions. In an inversion of the usual direction of counseling, Ram had walked at least one hour to reach the counselor that day. Saraswoti, a CPSW on the project, offered Ram food, which he accepted. However, as Saraswoti was Brahmin (high-caste Hindu) and Ram was Dalit (the lowest caste group in the Hindu caste system), she did not invite him inside her temporary shelter to eat, a gesture that would otherwise have been extended to any other guest. Although caste discrimination is illegal in Nepal, it persists in everyday life, ranging from the regulation of space and touch to extreme acts of anti-Dalit violence.[25] During my time in Nepal, anti-Dalit sentiment was widespread and was often treated as common sense by members of high-caste Hindu communities. For example, while I was conducting fieldwork in eastern Nepal, a government schoolteacher exposed his prejudice when he explained to me the supposedly innate inferiority of Dalit people by using a metaphor of bamboo. "There are two kinds of bamboo, one thick and one thin," he said. "No matter how much you fertilize the thin type [i.e., Dalit], it will never grow."

Ram ate his food outside, sitting on a stool that Saraswoti had given him. I sat with him, grateful to escape the hot, smoke-filled space of Saraswoti's temporary shelter. After Ram ate, Anjana, herself a member of the Rai ethnic group and thus officially outside the Hindu caste system yet historically granted more rights than Dalit people, appeared and gave him water so he could wash his own plate, bowl, and cup—a task that was expected of him as a way to avoid polluting the family of the higher-caste CPSW while washing the objects he had touched. Such tacit forms of discrimination were common in the postdisaster intervention, as they were in everyday life. Despite the fact that counselors themselves did not explicitly support discrimination against Dalit clients, they also did not intervene when such incidents occurred throughout the course of their daily work. After a decade spent in mental health NGOs in Nepal, I had met only one Dalit psychosocial counselor. Across all organizations, the vast majority of counselors, psychiatrists, upper-level staff, and supervisors were high-caste Hindu. If walking long distances and facing risk to reach clients were forms of solidarity that lent meaning to the therapeutic encounter, the paths leading up to Ram's session were marked by gestures not of solidarity but of exclusion.

After lunch we walked to the still-standing, badly cracked community building where Anjana would conduct her counseling session with Ram. At the time of the meeting, Ram was in his mid-twenties and married with a two-year-old child. He lived with his parents, a common arrangement, but his wife had left him, taken their child, and moved to Kathmandu. He had passed his school-leaving exam and interspersed his Nepali with English words. Ram wore clean, new clothing and appeared healthy and well put together. During the counseling session, as with the other clients, there was never any mention of Ram's diagnosis or specific discussion of the name of the medication he had been prescribed by the NGO.

Anjana and Ram sat facing each other in plastic chairs. He proceeded to narrate the story of his affliction, which he said began fifteen years earlier in the form of chronic sinus problems caused by cold weather and "invisible, evil reasons" (*adrsya, bigarko karan*). When Anjana asked him what he meant by "invisible reasons" he replied, "*adrsya* means there was magic and witchcraft involved, *jadu tuna*. People don't believe in these things as this is the twenty-first century. But still these things exist. That's why the medicine was not working on me." He had traveled to multiple private and public hospitals in Kathmandu to receive biomedical treatment for his sinus problems, but no physiological cause was found. "Then it was found out that it was revenge from a girl," he explained.

Ram spoke about a romantic relationship that had ended badly. According to him, his problems began when black magic and spells sent to him by his ex-girlfriend had caused a doctor in Kathmandu to give him a dangerous and poisonous medicine. From that point on, he became convinced that people were trying to kill him. The earthquakes were not the origin of Ram's affliction; instead, his suffering was intertwined with a story of love and madness, a common narrative in South Asia.[26] His romantic relationship had grown over a year of clandestine letter writing between the couple, a literary form of romance especially popular in Nepal during the era before access to phones, the internet, and the widespread use of social media.[27] When the girl's family found out about their correspondence, they put an end to the relationship and arranged a marriage for her with someone else. After this, Ram described feeling afraid that her male family members would come after him, a fear so intense that it led to a breakdown in the district headquarters in which he was convinced her family members were trying to kill him.[28] In self-defense, he armed himself with a Nepali *khukuri* knife and publicly announced that he would kill anyone who tried to attack him. He ended up in the district hospital, where he was given an injection and was sedated.

After this incident, Ram began to slowly improve. He went to Kathmandu to work in construction. Seeing he had become more stable, his father arranged for him to get married. Despite Ram's protest, the marriage took place, and soon after, his wife became pregnant. Ram's marriage was an unhappy one, and he quickly left the village again to return to work in construction in Kathmandu, where he came in contact with a charismatic church program in Jawalakhel, a rapidly gentrifying neighborhood that is popular with foreign aid workers.[29] Ram was told that if he became a Christian, he would be healed. "The main reason to go to the church was to get better," Ram explained.

> The program was about healing illness. One elder sister [*didi*] told me if that person [the foreign pastor] puts his hands on you, then your illness will be cured. . . . The pastor said that all the chronic diseases and nerve problems will be cured and there is no need to have the doctor's medicines. He put his hand on my head, and he made me fall down. . . . Other people were also falling down when he was laying his hands on them. He was showing magical power. . . . I thought I was healed and cured so I left my medicine. But after three months, my problem started again.

Ram's experimentation with charismatic Christian healing, which he described as "superstition," soon came to a close. He returned to the Hindu religion but continued to feel he was being tortured by an "invisible power."

After discussing the topic of invisible power at length, Anjana changed the subject to the efficacy of medication. For the previous eight months, Ram had been prescribed medication from the NGO as part of the postdisaster humanitarian intervention, and Anjana wanted to find out if the medicine was helping him. "My problems will not be cured by the medicine only," Ram said firmly. Ram articulated his ontology of illness by referencing the concept of *nasako rog* (nerve illness), a diagnostic category that had been introduced into Nepal during the first era of mental health development programs in the 1980s in an attempt to redefine the meaning of mental illness by conceptualizing it as a physiological disease requiring pharmaceutical treatment.[30] "My nerves are already dried up," Ram explained. "They are almost dead and my brain is barely functioning. But that medicine is helping to make my body swell and to reopen my shrunken nerves. It is helping me to fall asleep and it has helped me to get my appetite back. I talk a lot and it is also helping me to talk less." Anajana, drawing on a technique of systemic family therapy–inspired questioning that she had been taught in a training, asked Ram what he thought he would be like if he stopped taking his medication. Ram replied that he had been doing yoga for a few months and that "even if I am taking the medication, 50 percent of my health has improved because of yoga."

"I also feel you have improved a lot." Anjana responded. "You look very good now. Compared to the time when I first met you, you have gained some weight and your face looks much brighter now. Am I right?"

Ram agreed with her observation but then continued to discuss his fear that people were trying to harm him with "invisible power," magic, and witchcraft. He explained that he had recently spent NPR 15,000 (about USD 150) on a ritual *puja*, for which he had sacrificed multiple animals and had stopped taking his medication, but that again his affliction had returned, so he resumed his medication. In response, Anjana explained that he should feel free to seek any treatment that makes him feel better, whether yoga or *puja*, but that he should not discontinue his medication. Ram agreed that he would not stop taking his medication, regardless of the other treatments he sought.

As the session came to a close, Anjana decided to elicit Ram's perception of the day's session, with the aim of producing concrete evidence of efficacy for her quality report.

"How are you feeling now?" she asked.

"I feel light [*haluko*] as I could talk about many things," Ram replied.

"You said you feel light. What does 'light' [*haluko*] mean?" Anjana asked.

"I could share my feelings. You took it all in a very positive way. So, I feel comfortable."

Anjana then produced a piece of white paper, drew a horizontal line, and, numbering it from 0 to 10, asked Ram to rate how he felt about the day's session. She told him that it could be good or bad, and that he could even rate the session below zero.

"I really think it was good, I mean it from my heart," Ram told Anjana.

"When you say 'good,' where do you rank it on this scale of 0 to 10?" Anjana pressed further, showing him the paper.

"I feel it has reached from 1 to 10 now," Ram replied ambiguously.

Moving into the end of the session, Anjana handed Ram another white sheet of paper and a pen and explained that she wanted to do an exercise. She asked him to draw and measure the percentage of his problems he felt had been caused by *jadu tuna* (magic and witchcraft).

"How much do you feel is in your life, your body?" Anjana asked.

"Shall I start with the demon problem?" Ram replied, as he began to draw lines on the sheet of paper. Observing him with a satisfied expression, Anjana praised Ram's handwriting. Carefully drawing the X and Y axis of a Cartesian plane, Ram created a bar graph. Showing Anjana, he explained, "Ninety percent of my illness is due to *jadu tuna*, black magic. After doing yoga, I have improved by 50 percent."

"So 40 percent of the problem is left in your body?" Anjana asked.

"Yes. Forty percent is left," he replied.

Turning the activity of measurement into an opportunity for reflection, Anjana re-created Ram's rendering on her own paper, drawing two circles, one large and one small, and labeling them "60 percent" and "40 percent," respectively. She then asked Ram, "So, now do you want to increase or decrease this 40 percent?" "I want to reduce it," Ram replied. "How do you want to reduce it?" Anjana asked. Ram replied that he would like to continue taking his medication, and that he planned to visit a *mata*, a female shaman, in Kathmandu because of the influence of black magic.

Two-dimensional instruments of visualization—such as graphs, diagrams, figures, and prints—are abstractions developed precisely in order to extract "all that counts" through a process of simplification. As Latour has noted, "in the debates around perception, what is always forgotten is this simple drift from watching confusing three-dimensional objects, to inspecting two-dimensional images which have been *made less confusing*."[31] In this way, the creation of the graph and the scale enabled Ram to translate a complicated and ambiguous experience of affliction and healing into a numerical language that could be used in Anjana's report. However, these simple techniques of rendering also facilitated a shared reflection on the quality of the interaction. By graphing the impact of black magic on his body, Ram made his desire for improvement visible. In this way, although we can critique numerical measurements as reductions of the complexity of lived experience, we also find that sometimes quantification might serve unexpected therapeutic purposes in which experiences of suffering and visions of recovery are transformed into concrete representations and plans for the future.

Ram's graph, in which he illustrates the percentage of illness in his body caused by black magic and the positive impact of his yoga practice, illuminates not only the difficult task of measuring therapeutic efficacy but also the limits of humanitarian conceptualizations of efficacy that are bound to predetermined expectations of victimhood and temporalities of crisis. Like that of many other clients seen in the postearthquake period, Ram's suffering had become visible through the work of disaster. His psychic struggle, which he referred to as the "demon problem," began not with the earthquakes but with a broken heart. His experience of affliction involved a dizzying range of possible causes—heartbreak, nerve illness, black magic, witchcraft, and demons—each operating according to their own ontology of illness. As counselors pointed out, in a context of medical pluralism it was difficult to know if clients were improving because of counseling and medication or through some other coexisting therapeutic modality. Reflecting the unique "social ecology" of medical pluralism in the Himalayas, Ram received a few counseling sessions but also took psychotropic medication, experimented with charismatic Christian healing, practiced yoga, visited shamans, and made ritual sacrifices.[32] By focusing on intersubjective interactions between counselor and client, we are able to zoom in on the ways in which the tools of measurement are brought to the field, how they are used, and how complex and ambiguous experiences of improvement are simplified as evidence for humanitarian efficacy in the midst of the therapeutic encounter.

What effect does Anjana's counseling session have on Ram's life? From a phenomenological perspective focused on counselor-client interaction, we get a feel for the mood of the therapeutic encounter; we note perceptions of improvement and track the negotiation of evidence. Anjana's open and nonjudgemental attitude and her unquestioning acceptance of Ram's narrative of black magic, witchcraft, demons, and ritual healing stand out, if only because they confound prevailing ethnographic accounts of health workers in contexts of development and humanitarianism in Nepal and South Asia.[33] Ram himself said that he felt light (*haluko*) after the session and that he found it good because he was able to share his feelings and Anajana "took it all in a very positive way." However, the true measure of efficacy will occur outside the session, in the ongoing flow of Ram's life. As Thomas Csordas and Arthur Kleinman have argued, "the therapeutic process cannot be understood as bounded by the therapeutic event precisely because it is ultimately directed at life beyond the event."[34] Yet "life beyond the event" is not easily measured within the accelerated temporality of humanitarian interventions.

While Ram's experience of affliction and healing complicated Anjana's attempts at measurement with medical pluralism, this was not the only way in which clients' lived experiences overflowed humanitarian frames of efficacy. Three years later, I returned to Nepal to follow up with clients who had been seen as part of the intervention. While I did not meet with Ram, I met with others. By this point, the humanitarian psychosocial intervention had long since ended. The final report had been written for donors celebrating the successes of the program and identifying lessons learned and areas for improvement. Because the program had come to a close, there was no longer any desire or administrative need for the measurement of efficacy. Yet if we truly wish to understand humanitarian efficacy, we must insist on the value of exploring life beyond the event. In what follows we will travel beyond the bounded spatial and temporal frames of the therapeutic encounter to consider the impact of postdisaster psychosocial counseling on the lives of those who received it. When examining the question of humanitarian efficacy from a different endpoint, clarity breaks down further.

Vishal's Medicine

Three years had passed and Bina and I were driving down a long rough road. It was monsoon season. As we passed through the forest and the villages, the smell of sweet smoke, wet leaves, and decomposing matter drifted in through the open window. We had made plans to meet Vishal, one of Bina's former clients. After the earthquakes, Vishal had received counseling sessions and antidepressant and antipsychotic medications following an episode of bizarre behaviors that involved wandering wild and alone in the forest. After two hours, we reached a desolate stretch of road along the edge of a cliff overlooking a field of rice paddy. Vishal appeared at the edge of the road, covered in mud. When he saw the jeep, he broke into a broad smile. Vishal was almost unrecognizable since Bina and I had last seen him years earlier. Strong and working in the fields again, he had just come from planting rice.

Vishal jumped into the jeep, and we drove to a *chautara*, a stone resting place overlooking the green terraced valley below. Since the program ended, Vishal had continued to take his medication regularly and had returned to full health, at least as he defined it. When Bina first met Vishal for counseling three years earlier, he defined his vision of health as the ability to care for others. When he imagined a life free of his affliction, he described himself as being able to take care of his animals again, to be able to cut leaves to feed his goats, and to work the land. Now, three years later, he was able to cut fodder for the animals, plant crops, plow his fields, and help his young children by taking them where they needed to go.

However, Vishal's return to health had come at a great cost. While the NGO provided free medicine during the postdisaster program, three years later, Vishal was spending NPR 1000–2000 (USD 10–20) per month on medication, which was a lot for a farmer who, as he put it, "has only expenses and no earnings." In order to continue his psychiatric treatment, he had taken out loans from people in the village and sold the very goats he had hoped to care for. In Nepal, to sell one's animals is no small matter. As Radhika Govindrajan has shown in her work on human-animal relations in the central Himalayas, in the small farming settlements of this region goats and buffalos are often considered to be members of the family.[35]

Although additional medicines had been added to the government's Free Drugs List after the earthquakes as part of the *Building Back Better* framework, all of the ex-clients we met in the area were buying their medication at a private hospital in the district headquarters at great personal cost—by taking out loans, selling animals, scrimping, and saving.[36] Three years later ex-clients made sacrifices so they could to continue to take the psychotropic medication they had discovered by chance after the seismic rupture. When I asked the Kathmandu-based psychiatrist who ran a monthly Saturday private outpatient clinic in the district headquarters why so many people were buying their own medication, he said that the drugs on the Free Drugs List were often not available, and besides, clients sometimes needed drugs that weren't on the list. The preference for treatment in a private hospital was also related to its reputation and specialized services. As the director of the hospital put it, "People who come to the private hospital know they will have to pay for medicine. The reason they come is because the quality of treatment is higher, and because they know they will be able to see a psychiatrist and won't have to go to Kathmandu." Because mental health care had still not been fully incorporated into public hospitals at the district level, in 2019 in many rural areas it was only possible to consult with a psychiatrist through one-day-a-month private practices set up by individual doctors who visited from Kathmandu.

Vishal, like so many of the clients who were treated in the program, had never conformed to humanitarianism's imagined figure of the earthquake victim. When Bina first met with Vishal he was suffering from strange sensations in his body. He had left his responsibilities to his family to wander incoherently through the forest. However, after becoming a subject of care and attention through the work of disaster, Vishal received counseling and psychiatric treatment for the first time in his life. Three years later, Vishal was back at work in his rice fields, and even his brother-in-law mentioned that he was shocked by his transformation. Although Bina enthusiastically believed that her counseling sessions with Vishal helped him, Vishal seemed to barely reference them. Vishal attributed his improvement not to counseling but to medicine.

Yet as Vishal spoke with us about the positive effects of medication, he also expressed concern about becoming dependent on psychiatric drugs precisely because of their efficacy. While he strongly believed that the medication helped him, he was unsure how long his treatment should last and wondered if he would have to take medicine for the rest of his life. Although he hoped his psychiatrist in the district headquarters might eventually reduce his dose, he was afraid of what might happen if he went off his medication. He worried that things might become difficult again, that he might abandon his family once more and return to wandering in the forest, becoming wild (*jangali*). Much of the focus of global mental health is on expansion of access to psychiatric drugs by training health workers to identify disorders with diagnostic tools developed by the WHO's Mental Health Gap Programme.[37] As in the field of psychiatry more generally, in global mental health and humanitarian psychosocial interventions, there is little discussion of how and when to taper patients *off* psychiatric medication.[38] The work of disaster provided Vishal with psychiatric drugs, which he might take for the rest of his life. Because psychotropic medication alleviates symptoms but is not a cure, for Vishal, therapeutic efficacy was also accompanied by ambivalence.

FIGURE 4.1. Vishal's medicine. Photo by the author.

Vishal's psychiatric treatment was an externality of the humanitarian intervention.[39] It was an unintended consequence of a short-term program that was not designed with him in mind. Yet the brief access to medicine that the humanitarian intervention provided had a profound effect on Vishal's life. Even when the temporary program ended and medicine was no longer available free of cost, Vishal took it upon himself to find ways to continue his treatment in a therapeutic landscape defined by scarce psychiatric resources. Can we say that the humanitarian psychosocial intervention was effective for Vishal? If, as Young argues, efficacy is defined as the ability to produce the results that actors expect will be generated by a given treatment or intervention, then Vishal's case might not qualify at all.[40] Vishal falls outside the humanitarian frame of the imagined victim the program was designed to serve. While we can conclude that for Vishal aspects of the intervention were efficacious, these positive effects were an unintended consequence—that is, an externality that overflowed the frame.[41]

Ganga Maya's Pain

When Bina and I reached Ganga Maya's house, everyone was working in the fields except for her daughter-in-law. The young woman explained that she couldn't call her mother-in-law to tell her we had arrived because they weren't on speaking terms, and besides, Ganga Maya didn't have a cell phone. Eventually the daughter-in-law called her husband to see if he might call his father and send his mother to meet us.

"Who is at the house? Who are these people? What do they want? Why are they here?" Ganga Maya's son asked loudly on the phone. "Is it about *amako mental* [mother's mental]?"

Soon Bina received a call from Ganga Maya's husband, who was talking fast and yelling. He was angry because after the earthquakes an NGO came and gave Ganga Maya medication, and she fainted, fell, and couldn't work. "No, no, that was another organization," Bina tried to explain. "We aren't going to give her any medicine; we just want to see how she is doing." Eventually, he agreed that his wife, Ganga Maya, could meet with us.

An hour passed before Ganga Maya appeared. She was sweating and wearing a green *cholo* and red *lungi*, splattered with mud from the rice paddy. Around her neck were strings of green glass beads with a golden ornament at the center. A scarf was wrapped tightly around her head. It was an extremely hot day, and she had been working hard under the blazing midday sun.

Outside the house, we bantered hello. "*Tapai motaunubho!* [You've gotten fat!]" exclaimed Bina warmly, an expression used when someone appears to be in good health. Ganga Maya told us that everything was much better now; she had been in a bad place before, but things had improved. Yet when we followed her inside the new house her family had rebuilt after the earthquakes, the room was filthy. The bed was a tangle of dirty blankets, and there was trash strewn across the floor. Spilled lentils lay scattered on the ground in a corner. In the back of the room, there was a small padlocked cabinet of biscuits that Ganga Maya had started selling so she could afford to buy meat. The three of us sat down on a straw mat on the floor, and Ganga Maya began to talk about the state of her health. She said she had pain in her uterus and asked if she could talk about it with us.

In words identical to those she had shared when we first met three years earlier, she again told us that the pain began after the traumatic birth of her youngest son. Then in a low whisper she added that it was very painful when her husband tried to have sex with her but that he does it anyway, especially when he's been drinking *raksi* (liquor), which he does every night. Although she told us when we first met that she was suffering from uterine prolapse, three years later she had still not received treatment for it. "I say I will go but it's expensive, and I don't have any money, and my husband won't give me any money either," she explained. "But what to do, it is like this. It's time to die anyway. I'm sixty-two years old [*Ke garne? Estai chha. Marne bela bho*]."

Bina's thoughts returned to the time of the earthquakes when Ganga Maya tried to commit suicide. She asked her if such thoughts still come. Ganga Maya said that they still come sometimes but that since she started taking medicine regularly, she felt better. It's when she stops that the thoughts return. When I asked her what kind of medicine she was taking, she could only recall that it was a small white pill. Ganga Maya explained that she first learned about this medicine when an NGO staff member came to her home after the earthquakes, took her to a hospital, and paid for the medication. "Wasn't it you?" she asked Bina, bewildered. Since the end of the humanitarian intervention, Ganga Maya continued to take medication, which she purchased from the private hospital in the district headquarters. Despite Bina's empathic counseling, three years later Ganga Maya still struggled with suicidal ideation and an abusive sexual relationship with her husband. Like Vishal, she attributed whatever minimal reductions in suffering she experienced not to counseling but to medication. When we left, Bina was visibly upset. This was not the situation she had hoped to find.

Like Ram and Vishal, Ganga Maya's afflictions also overflowed the humanitarian frame of the imagined "earthquake victim" and its predefined temporality of crisis. Instead, her suffering was enmeshed in relationships marked by ongoing abuse and dysfunction and compounded by economic precarity. Through the work of disaster, Ganga Maya's pain temporarily became worthy of humanitarian concern, and during that time, she received medication and counseling sessions from multiple NGOs that appeared at her home. But the humanitarian psychosocial intervention was not designed to help people in situations of *ongoing* poverty and abuse, and so this case resulted in the medicalization of social suffering. While we must acknowledge that Ganga Maya found respite in the medicine she discovered after the earthquakes and continued to seek it out, it is also clear that temporary access to pharmaceuticals alone would not solve the deeper social, economic, and personal sources of her desire for death. In the final section, we turn to a client whose suffering was a direct outcome of the earthquakes. Could the efficacy of the intervention on this client's life be measured within humanitarian frames?

Rekha's Dreams

Rekha was thirty years old when the earth ruptured. She had three children, but now there were only two. She survived the unthinkable nightmare of being buried under debris when her house collapsed. When the earth began to shake, Rekha grabbed her infant son and ran but couldn't return to reach her daughter in time. Rekha suffered from head and body injuries and was taken to the district hospital and then on to Kathmandu for further treatment. When Bina met her, she had returned to the village but was still physically weak and shaky. Deep in grief, she cried while awake and while asleep. At night she saw her daughter in dreams. "In my dreams she runs toward me saying, 'Mother,'" she said, "but when I try to pick her up, she disappears."

When I met Rekha in the months after the disaster, she told me that talking to Bina had helped her accept that "the world is like this, that no one is immortal; that everyone has to die one day." By that time, Bina had been working with Rekha for six months and had already provided four counseling sessions. "I don't know what I would have become if you were not there," Rekha told Bina three years later. "Nobody was there to help at that time. Everybody was busy with their own work. No one used to talk to me about what happened or try to console me. Until you came, I used to think only in one direction."

In the months after her daughter died, Rekha participated in counseling sessions with Bina, but she also spoke of other ways of working with grief that fell outside the frame of "mental health care." Rekha told Bina that in one year's time she planned to conduct a *puja* in the name of the lord Shiva to purify herself and then build a small temple in the memory of her daughter where she could pray. "Her soul has not died even though the person has died [*usko atma mareko chhaina manchhe marepachhi*]," she explained. "I feel like she might be walking behind me, following my steps." Worried that her daughter's soul was wandering, Rekha hoped that building a temple might bring her daughter peace. Like Anjana's response to Ram's discussion of demons and sent sickness, Bina was not troubled by Rekha's ontological claims that the soul of the dead might still be present among the living. Instead, Bina empathized with Rekha, encouraged her plans, and said that she too would like to offer flowers in Rekha's daughter's name.

In 2019 Bina and I visited Rekha at home to see how she had been doing since the intervention's end. Although Rekha had planned to construct a temple for her daughter, four years after her daughter's death, she had not done so. Rekha invited us inside a darkened room, where we sat with her and her mother-in-law on a large wooden bed. As she spoke, the young son she was able to save on the day of the earthquake darted in and out smiling and then became shy—sliding his back against the wall into a corner, looking at us looking at him.

"Since the program ended, how has your *man*, your body, your everyday life been?" Bina asked.

"It's going well, but things will never be like they were before," Rekha replied. "I work, but I'm dizzy [*ringata lagchha*]."

"What do you think is causing the dizziness?" asked Bina.

"I still remember, I remember . . . how much I remember [*kati sam-jinchha*]," said Rekha.

Rekha saw her daughter in a recurring dream. In the dream, her daughter came to her as the age she would have been now. She came not crying, Rekha said, but laughing, her hands together in namaste, asking for food but never speaking. "She is *sukha* [content], I think," said Rekha. "I make her things to eat. The last time she came she asked for water, her open hands were cupped together. She comes to the threshold of the door but never enters. The other day I saw her, and yesterday morning. [*Kati yad aunchha*], how much I think of her, when taking the children to school, how much I think of her. . . . Others think everything is fine, but only you know what is in your *man*, your heart-mind. Only you know what is there."

Another young girl came into the room and stood by the door as we talked, watching, listening. Rekha gestured to her and said, "She is eleven, the same age my daughter would be now. They went to school together." The girl had a blank look on her face.

"What else can you say? Everyone will go someday. Crying, how much I've cried! Five years, how many tears went? I don't even know. Now they say there aren't any tears left in my eyes. These days when I cry only a few tiny tears come out. Tears don't come. Tears . . . I think they've run out," said Rekha.

"*Dukha, dukha* [suffering, suffering]," her mother-in-law murmured, from somewhere in the darkened room.

"It happened so quickly. The older child and the small one was here, in front. I was carrying this one, this child, carrying him and then escaped. . . . I took one out and left her, but she was already gone." As Rekha recounted her story, I got the sense from her gestures that we were sitting in the very place where it happened.

"Who do you share your hardships with?" Bina asked.

"No one. They don't want to hear. I keep it to myself. I don't tell anyone, I just keep it to myself. I don't speak about it with anyone. I used to talk to friends about it. But now I've stopped," said Rekha. "If you hadn't come at that time, I don't know how I would be today."

"It's OK to remember and to cry," Bina said. "When you think of her and you feel like crying, you can cry. While crying, if many tears come, you might feel lighter afterwards. If you ever want to offer her flowers, to offer her water, you can also do that. If instead of forgetting you would like to remember, that is also OK."

"I can't forget, but now at least it is a little further from my heart-mind [*man dekhi ali kati tara*]," Rekha replied.

According to Rekha, Bina's counseling sessions were meaningful because they provided a rare space where she could speak about her grief when no one else would listen. For Rekha this form of listening had a significant impact on her life, so much so that she wondered what she would be like if she hadn't received Bina's care. At the same time, the temporality of Rekha's grief could not be contained by the humanitarian frame of efficacy, for while it may have started with the earthquakes, it did not seem to have an end. In his essay "Mourning and Melancholia," Freud argued that mourning entails working through grief, such that eventually a person might "sever" their attachment to the lost object, ultimately making new attachments possible. When the severing of attachment is unsuccessful, the mourner instead internalizes their lost loved one and enters into a state of extended melancholia.[42] From this perspective, the inability to loosen one's attachments to the lost object (i.e., loved person) leads to a state of pathological grief. Today, we can see the influence of Freud's distinction between "normal" and "pathological" grief in the diagnostic category of "prolonged grief disorder," which has recently been added to the eleventh edition of the *International Classification of Diseases* (*ICD-11*).[43] However, years later, when Freud lost his own daughter to influenza, he revised his argument. In a short letter to Ludwig Binswanger written on the anniversary of his daughter's death, Freud wrote, "Although we know that after such a loss the acute state of mourning will subside, we also know we shall remain inconsolable and will never find a substitute."[44] Five years after the day her daughter died in the earthquake, Rekha's grief had begun to drift away from her heart-mind, but it had not subsided. She described this feeling, the endlessness of grief, as an ongoing sense of dizziness, *ringata lagyo*.

Humanitarian Efficacy

In her work on the efficacy of Tibetan medicine, Sienna Craig has emphasized the need to "pay close attention to the ways history and politics, language and culture imbue an herb, a clinical encounter, a training curriculum, or research methodology with the capacity to produce a desired outcome."[45] While Craig is writing of the unequal relationship between biomedicine and traditional medicine in the Himalayas, such considerations inspire us to question the history, politics, and theory of change that imbues the humanitarian psychosocial intervention with its presumed effectiveness. As Joshua Breslau notes in his work on disaster psychiatry in Japan after the Kobe earthquake, from the beginning such interventions have been motivated by the concept of trauma and the assumption that when provided early on, counseling can prevent "the long-term psychological effects of stressful events."[46]

When humanitarians intervene on behalf of precarious lives that inspire sympathy, they do so under the assumption that "PTSD is a theoretical certainty in cases of natural disaster in any cultural setting."[47] However, as we have seen throughout this chapter, in postearthquake Nepal suffering often did not begin with the event of the disaster.

For the project manager and the counselors, the most important question was efficacy. After walking long distances over the hills and valleys of the disaster zone to reach clients, counselors wanted to know if the work they were doing was actually helping people. Ethnographic research revealed that evidence for therapeutic efficacy was marked by confusion, ambivalence, and ambiguity. Clients sought multiple forms of treatment in a social ecology where psychiatry and counseling coexisted alongside shamanic healing rituals. But beyond the confounding presence of medical pluralism, for many clients their suffering could not be located within the concepts of trauma and PTSD that motivated the humanitarianism intervention's raison d'être.

While humanitarianism is a moral field driven by compassion for the suffering subject, it is also a business model concerned with performance and tangible results.[48] Humanitarian psychosocial interventions must prove effectiveness in order to justify their investment value and demonstrate cost-efficiency to donors. To document effectiveness for donors requires the measurement of efficacy. However, evidence for effectiveness is not clear-cut when temporalities of suffering and grief do not align with donor timelines and a range of treatments occur alongside the psychosocial intervention that may also influence its course. In the humanitarian intervention, there were different and overlapping categories of clients, such as those with chronic or preexisting mental health problems, those suffering from abuse, and those whose suffering was directly connected to the disaster. While the psychosocial intervention was designed solely for the third group, it constantly served people in other categories, for unlike many other humanitarian contexts, in Nepal anyone could receive care as long as they were in the disaster zone. While this openness avoided violent forms of triage and the production of therapeutic citizenship, the heterogeneity of clients who overflowed the frames of humanitarianism complicated measurements of effectiveness.[49] Callon argues that once overflows are identified as the rule, then it may become possible to anticipate, incorporate, and contain them through the purposeful practice of reframing. What would it mean for humanitarian psychosocial interventions to *plan for externalities*, to anticipate that in all disaster settings the discovery of people with chronic afflictions and comorbidities will be the norm?

Long ago phenomenologists warned that objectivity and quantification reduce the complexity of experience into manageable, simplified, and sometimes dehumanized forms.[50] Anthropologists have made similar claims when they have argued that lived experience is marked by indeterminacy and excess that can never be grasped in its totality and that ethnography focused on the singular idiosyncrasy of a case may be more truthful than forms of objective measurement and metrics.[51] While the broader field of global mental health champions RCTs as the gold standard for measuring the efficacy of a psychosocial intervention, it may be the case, as Elizabeth Roberts has argued, that integrating ethnographic research (with all its unruly ethnographic "excess") might ultimately help "ask questions that produce better numbers and better knowledge."[52]

In Ram's graph, Vishal's pills, Ganga Maya's pain, and Rekha's dreams, we find that lived experiences of both suffering and healing continuously overflowed the humanitarian frames that aimed to grasp them. Three years after the intervention had ended, some ex-clients had found a way to continue the medication they had been prescribed through the postdisaster project. Others had sunk back into the same abusive relationships that had been the source of their suffering to begin with. Many attributed efficacy not to counseling but to medication. Yet some said that talking to a counselor had been meaningful. As Ram put it, "I feel light [*haluko*] as I could talk about many things. . . . I could share my feelings. You took it all in a very positive way. So, I feel comfortable." Or as Rekha said, "If you hadn't come at that time, I don't know how I would be today." Despite prevailing anthropological critiques of the totalizing violence of humanitarianism, such comments demand that we also acknowledge an unmeasurable dimension of care: that momentary lightness of being, *haluko*, felt by a singular life that has been touched by the concern of a stranger.

In the final chapter, we go back in time once more to the scene of the postdisaster therapeutic encounter to examine the ethics of care. Here we consider both the violence of humanitarianism and the gentle words and gestures between counselors and clients that sometimes lead to feelings of "lightness." In doing so, we will return to Vishal and Ganga Maya's stories, among others.

5

Care

It was winter, and Indira was bundled in a puffy jacket and knit hat to fight the biting cold. Searching for clients in the hills of Dolakha, she found Kiran, a young man she had met before. They sat, legs crossed, on a woven mat in front of the corrugated tin wall of his makeshift shelter. It was their third meeting, and Indira began by saying, "The other day we spoke. After the conversation, I see that your face has become a little brighter, *ujyalo*. You look happy. Is my guess correct?" In response to her observation, Kiran began to talk about how everything was worthless.

Kiran explained that his problem was fear. This fear had started not with the earthquakes but while he was working abroad as a migrant in the Persian Gulf, one of the few possibilities for employment available to Nepalis from lower socioeconomic backgrounds. Life as a Nepali migrant in the Gulf can be brutal and sometimes deadly, as workers are often confined to labor camps where they earn low wages, exercise little freedom, and are frequently exposed to dangerous working conditions of extreme desert heat.[1] Kiran linked his fear to an emotional shift that began in the workers' camp one day when he was struck by a paralyzing feeling of terror and paranoia. "One day I was sleeping while the others had gone out on their duty." He explained. "I hadn't done anything wrong, so why would they arrest me? Yet for no reason I felt that the police would come and take me away. I tried to convince myself that nothing would happen, but when I turned on the TV and watched the news, I only became more terrified." Kiran began having trouble getting out of bed. He would break out in a cold sweat at the thought of having to bathe, even though he found the cool water calming.

Kiran returned home to his village, but the ever-present feeling of fear, which he referred to simply as "it," continued. *It* would worsen when he was alone. Sometimes while he was resting, his heart would begin to race. Lying in bed, heart pounding inside his chest, he would grasp his wrist and check the pulse. "I am afraid I will die—just like that," he said. "When *it* happens to me, I am afraid because there aren't any doctors here. At least there are some people in the village who could carry me to the hospital if something happened." The deep breathing exercises and mind diversion techniques that Indira taught him had helped, but his fear persisted, slowly becoming intertwined with other worries. Would he die suddenly from a heart attack? If he had a heart attack, would he die because there was no doctor nearby? Would he be able to get out of bed? Would he ever feel energetic again? Could he forget his fears? Could he live up to his family's expectations? What should he do? How should he do it? He told Indira with sincerity, "My biggest medicine is alcohol. I have started drinking it not for taste, but for treatment." Raising one eyebrow, Indira did not hide her disapproval.

A discussion of Kiran's fear opened onto a panorama of interconnected political and economic issues and sources of affliction, all of which predated the earthquakes. In Nepal, labor migration to Malaysia and the Gulf countries is widespread and is the leading source of employment for Nepalis. As of 2020, personal remittances accounted for almost 25 percent of the country's annual GDP, and this number has only continued to increase in recent years.[2] On any given day, Tribhuvan International Airport in Kathmandu will likely be crowded with lines of young men, name tags around their necks and blessings of red *tika* on their foreheads, leaving to work abroad in Dubai, Qatar, or Malaysia so that they might earn enough to build a future. Temporary labor migration is the lifeblood of the Nepali economy. Yet labor in a foreign country, while lucrative, is not without risks. Beyond the difficulty of years of separation from one's family and community and the immense social pressure to return home successful, working conditions in these countries are often unsafe and abusive.[3] From this perspective Kiran's fear of arrest was not just a paranoid fantasy; it also reflected the lived reality that labor migration for Nepali people involves exploitative work in places with few legal protections for migrant laborers.

The 2022 Nepal Labour Migration Report, a study of the impact of migration on health, identified anxiety, depression, tuberculosis, headaches, suicidality, accidents, and injuries as the major health-related issues faced by migrant workers in the Gulf countries.[4] The report also noted the high incidence of sudden, unexplained death among Nepali migrant workers abroad, which is often registered by foreign governments as death by "natural causes."[5] Since 2011, over 600 Nepali migrant workers have died abroad each year, with 1,395 deaths in the 2021–22 fiscal year alone. The report states that the risk of death is due to unsafe living and working environments, which range from cramped and dirty lodging and long working hours to exposure to extreme heat in agricultural and construction work and physical and psychological abuse.[6] These risks and stressors, combined with "high expectations of family members back home, poor living conditions, loneliness, lack of social support and poor social life abroad," can have serious implications for mental health.[7] In 2023, an article in *The Guardian* reported that "almost 12% of Nepali migrant workers who die abroad, mainly in the Gulf and Malaysia, take their own lives."[8]

Kiran's fear of dying of a heart attack in a village without close proximity to a hospital was similarly grounded in reality, for many places in rural Nepal still have severely limited access to medical infrastructure. While it may be unlikely that Kiran would in fact have a heart attack, due to the remote location of his village, it is certain that he would not reach a doctor in time if he did. Kiran's fear multiplied into a cascade of worries about the ability to do something with his life in a society where migration is both an economic necessity and a social expectation, especially among men of his age. Desperate to manage his anxiety and paranoia, he soothed himself with alcohol.

What would his life be like if one day his problems magically disappeared? Indira asked Kiran to imagine. This was called the "miracle question" and had been taught to the counselors during their training in Kathmandu. "If I was cured," he said, "I would feel fresh and energetic. I would have a good appetite, because when you feel good you like to eat." But the problem was that Kiran never felt fresh. He felt as if he was constantly stoned on *ganja* (cannabis). Kiran said he enjoyed making plans to plough the fields and do other work nearby, but every time he listened to the news, he would hear about a new accident and his heart would start racing again. As the session came to a close, Kiran told Indira directly that he wanted more treatment and asked if he could come with her, somewhere, to access further care. "OK," she responded. "We have already talked two to three times with you. If you want to talk more with us, then we have a one-year program here, so we will talk to you again." Faced with Kiran's request for care, Indira responded that the program had been extended for one year. But what would happen after a year had passed and she could no longer make promises of return?

Care

While humanitarian interventions seem increasingly necessary in an era marked by disasters, conflicts, and the neoliberal withdrawal of the state, the tendency to allocate such care based on victim status rather than rights produces a "regime of care" that only responds to those who are able to evoke

compassion.[9] In Nepal, humanitarian compassion was reserved for earthquake victims and could not be extended beyond the territory of the disaster
zone. As Miriam Ticktin has shown in her study of the politics of humanitarianism in France, determinations of who is worthy of humanitarian care
are based on limited definitions of humanity that exclude anyone who is unable to become legible as a proper (i.e., passive, apolitical, innocent) suffering subject worthy of sympathy.[10] It is well known that this "regime of care"
has unintended consequences, such as the production of subjects who may
wish for victimhood and seek illness and injury in exchange for scarce resources like food, cash payments, medicine, or asylum in order to survive.[11]
This paradoxical inversion in which rights are secured through suffering is
grounded in the sanctity of "bare life," that figure of the human that has been
stripped of *bios*, political existence.[12] In this way, humanitarianism functions
as a domain distinct from politics, as its purpose is to respond to life only in
its bare, apolitical form.[13]

The disconnect between the imagined subject of care and the reality on
the ground was also the case in Nepal, where many clients who received psychosocial counseling after the earthquakes confounded humanitarian expectations of the "disaster victim." Over the course of eighteen months, the counselors made their way through the earthquake-affected districts where they
encountered not only earthquake-related suffering but many forms of affliction. Frequently, counselors met clients who spoke about sources of distress
that predated the disaster and would also outlive it, such as interpersonal
violence or social abandonment. Yet within the demarcated territory of the
disaster zone, the problem was not the exclusion from care but the fact that
care would end. In Nepal, if there was an element of violence to humanitarian
care, it was the violence of time.

After the earthquakes, humanitarian care was unevenly distributed and
always constrained by the timeline set by the donor agencies in which "victimhood" required a practical endpoint. In the psychosocial support cluster
meetings in Kathmandu, humanitarian partners were reminded to make a
"dignified exit." Even the most sensitive and engaged foreign project managers could not escape the constraints of the logics of their field—whether
development or humanitarian—in which "phasing out" was always required.
On the ground, counselors avoided discussing the possibility of the project
ending to their clients, a bitter truth that no one enjoyed speaking about.
When I asked, in the NGO headquarters in Kathmandu, what would happen
to clients who had been prescribed free psychotropic medication once the
project finally came to an end, the Nepali project supervisors were unable to
answer with clarity. Ultimately, the duration of the program was out of their

hands. As one NGO officer said in a mix of English and Nepali to a group of counselors during a counselor training, "Donors *bhanne* [say], 'Beggars can't be choosers'"—that is, NGOs can't control how long a project exists. What are the ethics of giving care, only to take it away?

The anthropology of care has often focused on the violence that is perpetuated in its name. This work has revealed the disconnect between biopolitical care that seeks to control and "normalize" populations, and the Indigenous, marginalized, and minoritarian practices of care that endure in spite of the state's efforts to discipline and eradicate these forms of life.[14] One of the most significant differences between these forms of care hinges on the anonymous project of biopolitical care as opposed to ways of caring that are attuned to the singularity of the Other.[15] As Lisa Stevenson describes in her work on the psychic life of biopolitics in the Canadian arctic, for Inuit people who were forcefully taken from their families for the treatment of tuberculosis and referred to with disk numbers in place of their names, the "care" provided by Canadian public health interventions came to feel more like murder.[16] One consequence of the anthropology of care has been its ability to open up the concept by upending normative assumptions of what care is and should be.[17] Practices of care are thus never predefined but are instead shown to take a vast array of forms.

According to the *Dictionary of Untranslatables*, the concept of "care" is not easily translated across languages.[18] While the English term *care* derives from the Old High German *kara*, which means "care, grief, lament, and sorrow," today *care* refers both to the act of protecting oneself and others from harm and the state of being concerned about someone or something.[19] The inability to disentangle care and concern in the English language is reflected in the work of disaster as it played out in Nepal, when the earthquakes and their conceptualization as a crisis generated a sudden shock of care for the mental health of Nepali people. As the feminist philosophers Berenice Fisher and Joan Tronto have defined it, care is "a species activity that includes everything that we do to maintain, continue, and repair our 'world' so that we can live in it as well as possible."[20] Yet what such care consists of will depend on the varying, often conflicting, visions of the world we wish to build and the actions seen as necessary for repair. To care is an ethical act in which each element—becoming aware of the needs of others, taking responsibility for care, the practice of giving care, the ways of responding to the care that is given, and decisions regarding the termination of care—is morally and ethically charged.[21]

In Nepali, the English concept of care is distributed across at least six different terms. For example, *hernu* means "to look" but also "to take care of" in the sense of "looking after," and the term *herbichar garnu* is often used in the context of medicine to refer to the act of taking care of a patient and providing expert treatment. Likewise, *kurnu* is used in similar ways but is also connected to the caretaking done by servants when an employer is away, as revealed in the linked term *kuruwa*, which means "caretaker," "attendant," or "watchman." Alternately, *palnu* means "to care for" but within a different temporality, as in the sense of "to raise" and "to grow," and is used in reference to the relational act of taking care of family members (both children and parents) as well as animals and plants. Finally, the word *wasta*, defined as "concern," "care," or "worry," is used to describe the way one "cares about" a particular person, thing, or issue. The humanitarian conceptualization of care as a form of aid driven by sentiments of compassion is more closely aligned with the Nepali concept of *daya*, which means both "kindness," and "mercy, pity, charity, compassion," than with any of the available terms for care.[22] As Bina said when reflecting on her own strengths as a counselor, "I really like to *care* for others," she explained, using the English term; "this is also one of my virtues." (*Arulai* care *garnu malai ekdam man parchha. Thyo pani mero gun ho.*) Bina's codeswitching from Nepali to English when speaking about care was not only an index of her linguistic knowledge but also suggested that psychosocial counseling itself involved a unique, and foreign, practice of care that did not quite fit into other familiar concepts.

In what follows I examine the limits and possibilities of the formations of care that were generated by the disaster and its transient humanitarian response. I argue that although humanitarianism enacted forms of violence by meeting chronic suffering with transient care, the encounters between counselors and clients that were inaugurated by the work of disaster also created unexpected possibilities—to discover novel treatments, hope for different futures, and experience the caring virtues (*gun*) of kindness and gentleness. Across four stories, I describe various forms of psychic suffering that were entangled with ongoing social and political issues in Nepal, such as the risks of labor migration, abuse in the family, social abandonment, the border blockade, and lack of medical infrastructure. In each story, the counselor comes face-to-face with what the phenomenologist Emmanuel Levinas has described as the ethical demand of the Other, as clients asked directly for more care and more treatment when there was none that counselors could promise. For Levinas, responsibility is defined as the impossibility of turning away from the Other who suffers and cries out in pain.[23] If one is able to hear this cry *as* a call for help, then the encounter with the Other creates an ethical demand to respond.[24] In the aftermath of the disaster, counselors were faced with a responsibility to the Other regardless of what the humanitarian intervention could or could not promise. As a result, in spite of the temporal limitations of humanitarianism, within the frame of the counseling session we can also find moments of gentleness that should not be overlooked. Unlike the concept of care that can be co-opted by institutions and put to use for normalizing, disciplinary, and depoliticizing ends, gentleness, as the philosopher Anne Dufourmantelle argues, ultimately "resists perversion."[25] To notice kindness, gentleness, and hope in broken institutions is to engage a reparative approach to care in times of disaster.

Ethical Demands

Bina and I met Vishal in the upstairs room of his mud home, which had survived the earthquakes. Prior to the disaster, Vishal had largely abandoned his daily farmwork and family responsibilities and begun to wander incoherently in the nearby forest, an experience of madness he described as *jangali* [wildness]. A month had passed since he had been prescribed olanzapine, an antipsychotic, and fluoxetine, an antidepressant, by the NGO, two medications he took along with his own memtone memory tonic, an Ayurvedic medicine for "memory loss, stress, depression, headache, sleeplessness, anxiety and forgetfulness." Vishal spoke as if heavy with sleep, a side effect of the powerful drugs he had been prescribed. He said that before he started taking medication, he felt restless, dizzy, and physically unstable. He had sensations of burning pain throughout his body. Often, he felt he had suddenly gone deaf. Then the pain would begin to spread throughout his body as he saw strange yellow forms, "something rotating in front of my eyes," before becoming overwhelmed with dizziness. At other times, Vishal would get lost in his thoughts and experience what he described as "strange feelings." However, since he began taking the medicine, he felt his illness had started to slowly improve. "We have some goats," Vishal said, his eyes lighting up. "I can look after them, I can give them grass. Even if the fodder is far away, I can still carry it back home for them. After getting a little better I have been able to do this." Vishal defined his health as the ability to take care of others (*palnu*), to raise his animals and make them grow. Vishal strongly believed that with continued medication, he could return to full health.

"So, when you become completely healthy again, what do you hope to do?" Bina asked.

"There is nothing in particular," Vishal replied. "But if I am cured and become healthy, then I can help my elderly mother in the fields."

With Bina's prompting, Vishal began to imagine what life could be like in the future, and to see the existing support and love he already had gathered around him. Vishal's family strongly supported his treatment, and when Bina asked about their reaction to his improvement, he said "They feel good and they are happy. They want to see me even better after the treatment, they want me to take the medicine on time." Again and again, as if repeating a mantra, on at least nine separate occasions throughout the session, Vishal voiced his feeling of hope and his belief in a cure.

Bina listened patiently, often repeating back the phrases he said to her as if checking that she understood correctly.

"After meeting you and talking with you, and after taking the medicine, I am feeling a little better," he said slowly. "And after having more medicine, I believe that I will be cured."

"That's very good thinking," Bina replied. "So, you are feeling better and comfortable after talking to us and taking medicine?"

"Yes," he answered. "With continued use of the medicine and by taking the medicine on time I will be cured. You have given me this hope and I believe it."

Bina neither confirmed nor denied his belief in a cure, although it was likely that without the program, Vishal's access to medication would be greatly limited. On the day of the session, he informed Bina that he had only one more dose of medicine left.

In Vishal's case we find an example of the hope provided by talking with a counselor and the discovery of a medicine capable of reducing negative symptoms as well as the violence of transient humanitarian interventions that provide brief access to care only to take it away. Vishal expressed trust in Bina and deep faith in the power of biomedicine to cure him, and based on the small improvements he had experienced since beginning his treatment, he actively wished to continue his psychiatric medication. Often the strongest arguments in favor of global mental health are made on the basis of severe forms of mental illness, such as schizophrenia and bipolar disorder, which respond well to pharmaceutical treatment. The diagnostic labeling and successful management of symptoms through medication can also serve to alleviate long-standing stigma around madness, which in Nepal is referred to as *pagal* (insanity) or *baulaha* (crazy), although here is described by Vishal as *jangali* ("wild, savage, uncivilized," or "wild man").[26] An image of the stigma of *pagal* in Nepal is encapsulated in an old faded photo I once stumbled across in an archive. In the photo, a thin woman dressed in rags has her back to camera. A red rhododendron blossom is stuck in her messy hair. She wears a sash of blue glass beads across her body but seems to have no shirt on. A group of men, women, and girls have surrounded her in a tight circle to stare at her abnormal behavior with looks of fascination, concern, disgust, and amusement.

Vishal's attitude toward pharmaceuticals resonates with many of the observations made by Brandon Kohrt and Reverend Bill Jallah in their discussion of the utility of diagnostic labeling and pharmaceutical treatment for severe mental illness in Liberia, a country with similarly limited psychiatric services. For Reverend Jallah, receiving a psychiatric diagnosis of bipolar disorder allowed him to actively challenge highly stigmatizing cultural labels for his abnormal behavior and enabled him to seek psychiatric treatment. Kohrt and Jallah argue that anthropologists who critique the cross-cultural relevance of psychiatric categories, the medicalization of social problems, and the nefarious role of profit-driven pharmaceutical companies in global mental health must also acknowledge the multiple relationships users may have to their psychiatric diagnoses and medications in diverse cultural and economic contexts.[27] While Vishal was not given a new concept through which to understand and experience his affliction (or himself), he repeatedly emphasized his feeling of improvement and his belief that that medication would supply him with a cure. The central issue at stake in Vishal's case was whether or not he would be able to continue to access the medication he had found so helpful once he was no longer deemed to be living in a disaster zone.

In this particular program, clients who counselors felt might need medication were taken to Kathmandu free of charge, where they would meet with the NGO psychiatrist for a consultation. Once the psychiatrist had given a diagnosis, clients were eligible to receive their medication for free through the NGO. Back in the village, they either had to purchase their own medication for reimbursement or the local community psychosocial workers were expected to be notified ahead of time to deliver the medicine. But when the program phased out, this access and monitoring would also disappear. Even during the program, unless a client started looking for more medication at least ten days before it ran out, it was not guaranteed that it would actually be available in a nearby pharmacy, nor was it guaranteed that the available pharmaceuticals would be of trustworthy quality due to the lax regulations of the off-patent formulations that dominate the market in Nepal.[28] The availability of drugs (along with fuel, cooking gas, and construction materials) became further limited when violent political protests over the new constitution erupted in the Madhesh region of the southern Tarai, causing a four-month unofficial blockade at the Indian border from September 2015 to February 2016, and sending Nepal into a spiral of scarcity. "What will happen when the project phases out?" I asked Bina as we left Vishal's house. Would his family have the funds to ensure he continues his medication, which he may have to take for life? Bina hoped that maybe there would be a further extension of the project.

The chance that clients might be left without access to medicines after humanitarian care ends is one of the key drivers of the WHO's *Building Back Better* model. This model seeks to harness the temporary concern for mental health in times of crisis to build sustainable mental health systems in places that receive humanitarian mental health and psychosocial support. The idea is that if lasting mental health infrastructure can be constructed in the midst of emergency, then people will continue to have access to psychiatric and counseling services even after humanitarian intervention ends. In Nepal, the better to be built was largely focused on training prescribers and increasing access to psychopharmaceuticals. However, as we have learned from the previous chapter, three years after the humanitarian intervention ended, Vishal was unable to continue to access his medication free of cost even though a number of antipsychotic drugs had been added to the Free Drugs List after the earthquakes. In spite of this barrier, he and many others found ways to continue the novel treatments they discovered through the work of disaster, often at great personal cost.

∗ ∗ ∗

Bina and I hiked down the dusty trail of a steep hill to reach the still-standing mud house of an elderly woman, Ganga Maya. It was the second time Bina had met with her. Local resident and CPSW Tara, herself living in a transitional shelter made of corrugated metal, led us to Ganga Maya's home. Bina and Ganga Maya sat cross-legged on a woven mat on the floor inside her modest house. The mud walls were painted in a classical style, red mud on the bottom, white mud on the top. "Namaste, *Ama*," Bina said, her hands held together in prayer, the typical Nepali greeting. Compared to Bina's robust health, Ganga Maya's body was small and thin. Her face held a sorrowful expression, and her eyes were downcast. "How are you feeling today?" Bina asked gently. Ganga Maya replied, "You came, so now my heart-mind is a little refreshed [*sital*]."

"I don't know what to do," she said to Bina. "I am sick. I just sit and cry. What to do [*ke garne*]. I belong to a poor family. We have to work for our livelihood. So, I work here and there. This is reality. What to do. Whatever is written we have to face it, right? I have children but no one is here with me. I don't know where they are. I stay here alone."

Ganga Maya had recently tried to commit suicide in the nearby river. She was saved by people nearby who pulled her out of the rushing water. Ongoing arguments over money had preceded the event, including the distribution of NPR 10,000 (USD 100) of earthquake relief money, which members of her family accused her of hoarding. She said her husband refused to spend his earnings on her and asked her to pay him back for every expense that she incurred. "Where can I get the money from?" Ganga Maya said. "I am already old so no one will give me work. All these things give me mental problems. All the reasons are domestic issues. What can I do? I think this is my fate." Ganga Maya said that her husband was often away at work and that he rarely came home except to sleep. She proceeded to tell the following story.

> My husband has a very bad habit of talking bitterly. That's the reason I don't want to stay here. I get pain in my lower abdomen. I pulled the placenta my-self . . . I get pain while with him as well. If I say I cannot do it, he gets angry. That's why I cannot tell him that. So I want to stay away from him, and some-times I feel it would be better if I die . . . it's been a very long time. That hap-pened when I gave birth to my third son. He is now sixteen years old. Labor started at noon and I gave birth at midnight. At that time nobody took me to the hospital and no one gave me any medicine. The newborn was in front of me. He was crying and his lips were getting dry and blue. So I didn't care about the consequences and pulled the placenta to separate the baby. When I pulled, everything came out. Then with the help of another woman, I put everything back in myself.

Ganga Maya told Bina that although she had seen a *dhami* about her uterine pain, her husband did not support her seeing a doctor. "A daughter's karma is a life already lost [*chhoriko karma hareko juni*]," she explained, quoting a well-known Nepali proverb and critique of life under patriarchy. Later she continued, "I wish to be cured. I want to live out my days without any health problems. I wish I didn't worry so much. I am taking medicine for that. But when I had that medicine, I used to fall asleep everywhere."

"Did you take the medicine after proper consultation with a doctor?" Bina asked.

"No, without any consultation. We were talking just like this. I told my problem, and they gave me the medicine." Ganga Maya had been prescribed amitriptyline, an antidepressant, by another NGO also providing mental health and psychosocial care in the earthquake-affected district.

Ganga Maya's story of suffering occupies a different kind of temporality. It does not describe a sudden disaster in which everything is lost; instead, she speaks of something slower. These are the mundane disasters of everyday life—an abusive relationship with her husband, the memory of a traumatic birth, severe pain due to uterine prolapse, nonconsensual sex, insoluble fam-ily conflict, patriarchy, poverty. According to Ganga Maya's narrative, her physical suffering began with the near death of her newborn son and had gone untreated for sixteen years. Suddenly, after the earthquakes, multiple psychosocial counselors came to her home to provide counseling, antidepressants, and support to travel to a hospital. Her ordinary, everyday suffering had become hypervisible through the frame of crisis.[29]

The disaster that commands attention and demands care revealed old wounds, afflictions, and chronic pain that had been normally disregarded as unexceptional forms of suffering in a country with the second-lowest per capita income in South Asia after Afghanistan.[30] While clients seen in the immediate aftermath of the earthquakes described problems that had a clear connection to the disaster, the majority of those seen over the following eighteen months were being treated for afflictions, sometimes severe mental illness, that predated the earthquakes. While the earthquakes undoubtedly placed these people and their families into situations of further precarity, their ongoing suffering had only become visible as a problem worthy of concern through the work of disaster and its transient ethical demands. The "right to intervention," justified on the basis of "superior ethical principles" and predefined universal values, has also produced a contemporary situation in which a spectacular crisis is required for care, and a disaster might become a boon.[31] Ganga Maya's story of suffering that momentarily became an object of care through the work of disaster shows us the violence of its interpretive frames.

Throughout the session Bina seemed to draw on every technique she could remember from her short forty-eight days of training. She guided Ganga Maya through deep breathing exercises, encouraged her to reflect on the advantages and disadvantages of worrying, asked her to imagine how she would feel if a doctor cured her uterine pain, and helped her articulate a concrete plan about how she could get to a doctor. As they reached the end of their time together, Bina proceeded to draw two faces on a blank page of her notebook, one happy and one sad. This was an intervention she had been trained to do by the NGO as a way for the counselor to learn more about the client's emotional state. Turning to Ganga Maya, she asked, "Which one do you like?" Ganga Maya chose the smiling face. Bina then invited Ganga Maya to consider what she could do to become more like that face. Ganga Maya said, "If my family talks nicely, then I would be happy. I get upset when my family talks badly. . . . I feel hurt."

I had seen the happy face / sad face exercise used on one other occasion, in a psychosocial intervention for a group of teenage girls in a government school where a case of "mass hysteria" had occurred. The counselor leading the intervention asked the students to publicly select which face they preferred on a chalkboard in front of their peers, and I too was asked to participate. I recall being struck by an overwhelming feeling of anger at being forced to take part in an activity that felt like a disciplinary exercise in so-

cial conformity and a public performance of happiness. As I approached the
chalkboard where the two faces were drawn, I sensed an intense pressure
to select the happy face, although I did not want to. The pressure to choose
the smiling face seemed to be yet another iteration of the strong social expectation of outward displays of happiness in Nepal, where I had repeatedly
observed people smiling even while speaking of extreme suffering. I experienced the happy face / sad face exercise as a violent act, a public disciplining
of depressive affects in which there was no choice but to comply. When a
student did eventually choose the sad face, the counselor asked her why. The
girl responded that "sad people must also be given love," before changing her
check mark to the happy face.

Back in the session with Ganga Maya, Bina drew another image, this time
of two houses. Inside each house she drew a table with a television on it. Bina
said that one house represented Ganga Maya's house, and the other represented the house of her neighbor. She then asked Ganga Maya if it would be
OK to move the furniture inside her neighbor's house.

"In other people's houses, it's their wish where and how they want to keep
their things. How can I tell them?" said Ganga Maya. "In my house I can do
things whichever way I like."

Bina praised Ganga Maya's insight, explaining, "Just as we can move things
in our house and not others', so we can change ourselves but we cannot force
others to change. Isn't it? *Hoina*?" Bina continued, "Happiness is within us.
Happiness given by others is just temporary; it remains only for a short time."

As we hiked back up the dusty trail, Bina spoke angrily about violence
against women. "In Nepal husbands treat their wives badly. They make them
wash their clothes, cook their food, and don't give them opportunities because
they don't want them to get too smart," she said. "In Nepal, wives can't do
anything without their husband's consent!" Ganga Maya's story of her abusive
husband seemed to have personally touched something in Bina, who herself
had chosen not to marry and started a master's degree in gender studies at
Tribhuvan University in Kathmandu. In 2014, the WHO reported that Nepal
had the third-highest rate of suicide mortality among women in the world.
While subsequent research has complicated this claim (statistics on suicide
in Nepal remain fuzzy because of lack of reporting), as Bina moved through
her working areas in the disaster zone, many women disclosed thoughts of
suicide to her.[32] All described complex situations of interpersonal violence
and family dysfunction, often involving incidents of sexual violence as well as
other forms of ongoing verbal and physical abuse.[33]

In their brief session Bina was confronted with the long duration of Ganga
Maya's pain, her abusive relationship, and ongoing suicidal ideation. Tasked

with the ethical demand to treat chronic suffering with time-limited resources and minimal training, Bina tried to help Ganga Maya imagine ways
she might begin to actively change her despairing situation. Yet it was not
clear if Bina's intervention, with its middle-class references to televisions on
tables, its emphasis on happiness as a personal choice, and its normative dis-
avowal of depressive affect, had resonated with Ganga Maya, who seemed
reticent to accept Bina's counsel. When Bina asked at the end of the session
if Ganga Maya had started to feel she should seek happiness, she replied ambiguously. "Yes, it's a two-day's life [*dui dinko jindagi*]," said Ganga Maya, referencing a popular saying on life's short and unpredictable nature. "Life is
short, so we must try to live happily," Bina replied, adding that she would help
Ganga Maya see a doctor and would meet with her family members, which
Ganga Maya had asked her to do. "We are with you to help you in this," said
Bina. Faced with the ethical demand to respond to the Other who cries out in
pain, Bina promised Ganga Maya an uncertain resource in the humanitarian temporality of crisis: that she would return to see her again the following week.

✶ ✶ ✶

Phul Kumari, age eighty-one, sat on the ground in the courtyard in front of
the ruins of her home. She said that she felt afraid that she would die in her
sleep by being crushed by the remains of her house. She was less worried
about dying per se than about dying a slow and painful death. Her problem,
she said, was that her sons, who lived on the same property, had not built her
a shelter to stay in, and she had not been invited to stay with them in theirs;
so, she remained alone inhabiting the ruins of her home. "I lie down in my
bed and from there I can see the sky," she said, as the roof to her shelter was
only partially intact. "I watch the sky and I think about my fate."

Phul Kumari's pain stretched back many years and revolved around an
ongoing feud with her son and daughter-in-law. Again and again, she said
that she felt alone and abandoned by her family. The last time she met with
Bina, she told her that she wanted to kill herself but that she was worried
about what people would say. She said these thoughts come to her heart-
mind, gesturing to her chest. Bina was attentive. She sat close to Phul Kumari
and leaned her body toward her. When the old woman told her that she had
recently fallen, Bina took her hand to examine the swelling. Phul Kumari
called her *babu*, child, and Bina called her *ama*, mother.

The presence of kinship terms in counseling sessions was widespread and
reflected their broader use in Nepali society. In Nepal, kinship terms are commonly used in public spaces as a mode of address that immediately establishes

oneself in relation to others. As Mark Turin points out, using terms such as *didi, bahini, dai, bhai, bua,* and *ama* (older sister, younger sister, older brother, younger brother, father, and mother) with complete strangers is a way to create social intimacy while respecting social hierarchy.[34] Alternately, the choice *not* to use kinship terms with strangers or colleagues establishes social distance and formality. Bina and Phul Kumari's use of kinship terms is important, as it created a level of social intimacy between them while respecting an age-based hierarchy. At the same time, given Bina's own identification as an orphan and Phul Kumari's abandonment by her children, it is possible that in this instance the use of the terms *ama* and *babu* may also express transference and countertransference elements.[35]

In her essay "Love, Guilt, and Reparation," the psychoanalyst Melanie Klein argues that "making reparation" is "a fundamental element in love and in all human relationships."[36] In Klein's conceptualization, repair means both "to repair something" and "to make reparation to someone."[37] Reparation is thus a way to overcome the depressive position and restore a sense of unity with the loved object, at least in one's imagination. While Klein formulated her theories based on work with children, she notes that fantasies of reparation are repeatedly played out in interactions with others across the lifespan. As she writes, "In acting towards another person as a good parent, in phantasy we re-create and enjoy the wished-for love and goodness of our parents. But to act as good parents towards other people may also be a way of dealing with the frustrations and sufferings of the past."[38] For Klein, to play the part of a loving child or parent is to engage in a reparative fantasy that allows the subject to undo what they fear has been destroyed and to restore the loved object to a state of goodness and wholeness.

Toward the end of the session, Phul Kumari told Bina, "You talk so nicely and politely. You talk in such a way that you show me reality as if in a mirror," she said as she spread her hands across the ground in front of her. "When you talk I feel that I have everyone, my children, my relatives, and my grandchildren. I feel like my heart has broadened with joy, it is like a *nanglo* [a large round rice-winnowing pan]. When you leave, it is again the same loneliness." Responding to this direct comment on separation and the end of care, Bina said, "There is an old saying that 'compared to a distant god, a ghost close by is more useful,' *tadhako deuta bhanda najikko bhut kam lagchha.*" "Yes, that's it, *babu,*" Phul Kumari agreed. "Distant gods . . . ghosts close by . . . the ghosts close by are more useful." "Yes," said Bina. "We are distant [*hami tadhako ho*]. We will visit you when we can." Within the frame of the session, reparative fantasies could be enacted, but Bina and Phul Kumari both understood that they could never serve as a replacement for one's relationships in the real world. Despite knowing this, it seemed hard for Phul Kumari to bear a repetition of yet another abandonment. "Oh my child, when will you come again?" She cried out as Bina prepared to leave. "I will wait for you to come! Oh, my daughter!"

Three years later Bina and I followed up with both Phul Kumari and Ganga Maya. We quickly realized that talking with Phul Kumari would be impossible, for the situation with her family remained so tenuous that meeting with her might put her at further risk. Despite the fact that all of Phul Kumari's neighbors knew that her son mistreated her, they still refused to intervene. Phul Kumari's son was a *neta*, a local political leader, they explained, and a *gunda*, a thug. Her neighbors told us that they regularly saw her crying, even while walking through the village. Yet they would not comfort her—or could not, out of fear. It is no wonder that when Phul Kumari met Bina in the months after the earthquakes she told her she felt her heart broaden with joy. As described in the previous chapter, meeting with Ganga Maya again was similarly tense, as her family seemed mistrustful of outsiders and did not approve of the medication she had been prescribed by an NGO after the earthquakes. When we left her home, we stopped in a small shop for lunch. Inside, a young girl tried to get the details about what we did and who we saw. When we declined to answer, she said, "Everyone knows who you are going to see if you went down to that village anyway." While transient humanitarian care enacted forms of violence, for both Ganga Maya and Phul Kumari, it also provided a temporary shelter in which it was possible to receive support without the burden of stigma or fear of retribution.

The Intersubjective Otherwise

After traveling for hours on packed buses and crossing over steep hills on foot, the counselors arrived at the shelters of unknown strangers to ask about the worries they held in their heart-minds. As counselors and clients sat together under trees, in empty fields, in quiet patches of sunlight, and in the cracked rooms of mud homes, stories of fear, panic, sadness, anger, pain, past betrayals, future uncertainties, strange physical sensations, and broken relations came rushing out. Therapeutic encounters are ethical encounters, if, following Levinas, ethics is defined as responsibility to the Other.[39] When counselors met clients with psychic afflictions that stretched back far before the seismic rupture, they came face-to-face with the ethical demands of people with chronic suffering, who asked for more medicine, more treatment, and more sessions though they, the aid workers, could promise none. Instead, within the brief encounter, the counselors did what they could to help clients find hope and begin to see their lives from a different perspective.[40]

With the "miracle question," counselors asked clients to imagine what their lives might be like if suddenly, magically, they woke up one day and their problems had disappeared. What would be different? What small changes would they notice? As Kiran explained to Indira, if a miracle happened and he was cured of his fear, "I would feel fresh and energetic. I would have a good appetite, because when you feel good you like to eat."[41] Or as Ganga Maya told Bina, "If my husband didn't speak bitterly to me, it would make me feel good. If something goes wrong, it would be nice if my husband said, 'Let it go, it's OK, these things happen.'" By offering the miracle question, counselors invited clients to momentarily suspend reality and liberate themselves from hopeless situations by imagining what an alternate future might look and feel like. The miracle question operates from the assumption that language plays a central role in the construction of reality—by describing life after a miracle, the client begins the process of "talking it into being" with the therapist.[42] If the miracle question is delivered skillfully, the dialogue between client and counselor can become a site for the co-construction of an alternate future. If delivered poorly, the miracle question can backfire and leave the patient upset, bewildered, angry, or worse. In spite of the risk of this approach, re-searchers have argued that the miracle question is especially useful in times of disaster, as it can help people focus on small, feasible goals, identification of strengths, and the construction of future possibilities as opposed to a poten-tially traumatizing, problem-centered conversation about loss.[43] In this way, the miracle question stands in stark contrast to the practice of "debriefing" that was popular in the previous era of disaster psychiatry.[44]

In this particular humanitarian intervention, the stated aim of questions like the miracle question was to awaken a new form of consciousness in the client, help them learn new things about themselves, and discover that they have more agency over their lives than they had originally thought. As Mi-chelle, the foreign psychologist, explained during a supervisor training in Kathmandu, "The job of a systemic counselor is to disturb the old thinking pattern and change the focus. The client is suffering and suffering and sud-denly you interrupt. You are not fulfilling the expectations. Instead, you dis-appoint the expectations of the client, shake him up, and then he comes out of his pattern. This is an intervention." The phenomenologist Alia Al-Saji has similarly argued that moments of hesitation in everyday lived experience can open up the possibility of interrupting previously held assumptions, percep-tions, and habitual ways of being-in-the-world, thus paving the way toward new ways of living.[45] Despite the limitations of transient care, what if even a brief encounter with gentleness, a feeling of hope, a moment of hesitation, or an invitation to imagine could open up the possibility for life to become otherwise?

The otherwise has emerged as a hope-filled concept in the wake of what Sherry Ortner has referred to as decades of "dark anthropology," for it allows us to move beyond the paralysis of critique and sketch a path toward alternative ethical and political futures that have not yet come into being.[46] As Laura McTighe and Megan Raschig write, the anthropology of the otherwise seeks "to glimpse that which has been prefigured but not formed; to speculate possibility beyond our dystopic present, or to hold open relations or actions that don't quite fit into liberal understandings of politics." Povinelli first described "the otherwise" as forms of "alternative social projects" that emerge and endure in the unlivable and lethal spaces of late liberalism.[47] Here such hopeful spaces of potentiality can involve organized movements of resistance or simply the act of maintaining a particular form of life when faced with its possible extinction. While Povinelli locates the otherwise in "scenes of abandonment," she also questions the implications of positing a form of world making that is created by lethality.[48] As opposed to processes of world building that begin with prefigurative politics, Zigon argues that "new worlds emerge over the long term through the everydayness of our political and ethical activities with one another."[49] In Zigon's work on drug user politics, the otherwise is neither a rupture with the past nor utopia nor even something that is necessarily "better" than what came before.[50] Instead, he argues, the otherwise is something—such as marginalized practices of care, freedom, and community among anti–drug war agonists—that sticks and endures through "tiny displacements" over time. Yet his spaces of the otherwise also come into existence in connection to the war on drugs and its deadly effects—if not inside it, then in clearings along its edges. Like the sudden surge of care and concern inaugurated by the work of disaster, the potential for the emergence of an otherwise is often found in relation to the threat of death. However, it is not only through future-oriented projects but also in the present moment of being together that we can glimpse an otherwise—if only for a fleeting moment. As Phul Kumari said to Bina as they sat facing the end of care together, "When you talk, I feel that I have everyone. . . . I feel like my heart has broadened with joy. . . . When you leave, it is again the same loneliness."

After the earthquakes, there was a beginning and an end to care, which did not neatly align with the temporality of suffering for clients. This was patchwork care, in the same way people in Kathmandu patched up the cracks in their concrete homes with putty and plaster, without rebuilding the structural damage beneath. But the counselors were not entirely limited by the logic of humanitarian care within which they found themselves. In spite of the troubled and time-limited mode of humanitarian intervention, moments of kindness and gentleness between counselors and clients were still possible. Writing of the anthropologist William Rivers who was tasked with the "regeneration" of traumatized soldiers during World War I, Dufourmantelle notes that "Rivers proposed a listening that recreated the reliability of a human bond based on compassion. What he offered them was neither redemption nor a possible escape, but words that would come to give shelter."[51] In the therapeutic encounters between counselors and clients, gentleness manifested in a certain form of listening and being-with that created a temporary shelter, not of corrugated metal, but of words and gestures.

The temporary shelter of counseling is similar to what Sarah Willen has described as "inhabitable spaces of welcome" in her work on the everyday lived experience of illegality. Spaces of welcome, Willen argues, are a "small zone of familiarity, comfort, meaning, and safety in the shadow of laws, policies, and practices explicitly designed to make people—in this case unauthorized migrants—feel unwelcome."[52] Such spaces create openings for people to sustain their own ethical commitments and existential imperatives in a world defined by surveillance, abjection, and extreme constraints on agency. For the undocumented woman that Willen describes, her inhabitable space of welcome manifested in the form of a relationship that inspired her to face the uncertainty of her immigration status and the existential threats it generated. In the aftermath of the earthquakes, counseling sessions served as temporary shelters and "inhabitable spaces of welcome" where long-suffering people sometimes found momentary respite. As Ganga Maya said when Bina asked how she was doing, "You came, so now my heart-mind is a little refreshed [sital]." In Nepali, sital means "shade" or "coolness," and is often used in reference to taking shelter or rest in the gentle shade beneath a tree.[53] Through the course of a given counseling session, care might be extended through touch or a certain turn of phrase, through the use of kinship terms, through the delivery of medication, through a guided breathing session, or simply through walking a great distance to listen to the suffering of another and share the emotional burden of their pain. Yet just as quickly, a moment of connection between counselor and client could dissolve into disconnection, a touch could be withdrawn, a judgment made, a face might turn away.

The psychoanalyst Daniel Stern has argued that throughout the course of therapy, there are moments in the "here and now" of the session in which something unique happens between the therapist and the patient that can change a life. These affectively charged "now-moments" often involve the threat of a rupture in the therapeutic relationship, leading to a crisis that demands an immediate resolution. However, like all crises, such now-moments also contain a "small window of becoming and opportunity" that has transformative potential, a "moment of meeting."[54] Moments of meeting cannot be trained but involve context-specific, improvised responses on the part of the therapist.[55] Stern classifies such moments as a "micro-*kairos*," in reference to the ancient Greek concept of kairos, a critical moment that requires action. One path of resolution to the anxiety-provoking kairos of the now-moment is a moment of meeting between therapist and client, an intersubjective interaction that resolves the crisis and strengthens the therapeutic alliance. If the anxiety-laden, affectively charged now-moment is met by a successful moment of meeting, the results can be powerful. As Stern argues, now-moments and moments of meeting generate "a new experience that does not repair the past by filling in a deficit, but rather creates a new experience that can be carried forward and built upon in the future."[56] Stern's concept of micro-kairos reminds us that even a transient experience of gentleness might be transformative.

The possibility for an otherwise to emerge is always already there as a potentiality in the intersubjective space between us. We can find it in moments of gentleness and hope that instill small changes in the present and continue to live in memory, no matter how transient or precarious the conditions of their creation. As Dufourmantelle argues, gentleness is "a force of secret life-giving transformation, linked to potentiality."[57] We glimpse the *intersubjective otherwise* when Kiran imagines with Indira that his appetite has returned and he feels fresh, when Vishal tells Bina again and again that she has given him hope that he will be cured, or when Phul Kumari feels her heart broaden with joy as she sits with Bina, imagining she is surrounded by a family who loves her. The intersubjective otherwise is a moment of affective and emotional contact that creates a shelter, a new experience, or an imaginative potentiality that can renew life in the face of despair. As Indira said when reflecting on her work as a psychosocial counselor, "I think that if we can help them, even a little bit, even for a few moments, then we can give new life."

Attending to small moments of gentleness, of hope, and imagination—what Veena Das has described as "the small quotidian acts that stand up to the horrific"—in the midst of humanitarian care does not excuse a form of intervention that perpetuates violence, nor does it suggest that economic sources of suffering will be solved by individual counseling sessions, or that happiness is simply a matter of personal choice.[58] Instead, it asks the reader to consider the complexity of the ethics of care as it is lived between people. As Michael Lempert has noted, when examined at the level of intersubjective interaction, it is clear that most "ethical events" are precarious accomplishments.[59] The intersubjective otherwise is a similarly fragile achievement and, as we can see when Bina's session with Ganga Maya veered off into a normative exercise focused on the need to "choose" happiness, sometimes was barely present at all. In the encounters between counselors and clients, we find moments of hope and gentleness within individual-focused interventions that risk medicalizing and personalizing social and economic sources of despair. We find the brutality of short-term interventions that operate according to donor time and counselors who performed immense emotional labor to respond to the ethical demand of the Other in in the name of humanitarianism's impossible task. In Kathmandu during a supervisor training, the capacity to "stay in emotional contact" with a client, to hold eye contact, to mirror body language, and to embody empathy and emotional connectedness was celebrated by all as among the most important skills in the work of counseling. While the counselor's ability to be in "emotional contact" was a key element that could allow the intersubjective otherwise to emerge, from a critical phenomenological perspective we can also see it as the embodiment of a global humanitarian politics of care at the most intimate level of emotional and affective experience. When examined from the perspective of intersubjective interaction, humanitarian care is both violent and gentle.

One might be tempted to dismiss the intersubjective otherwise as a fantasy or a temporary flight from reality. However, the experience of gentleness or the invitation to imagine that life could be otherwise should not be underestimated. To create spaces in which hope is possible can be the first step in personal and collective transformation. As Mattingly has shown in her work on "therapeutic emplotment" and the role of hope in the therapeutic encounter, the ability to imagine a future is a crucial element in the process of healing.[60] Therapeutic encounters are "stories-in-the-making" where patients and therapists co-construct new understandings of self, illness, and one's relation to the future and the world.[61] To attend to small moments of gentleness, hope, and imagination in the midst of a therapeutic encounter is to question ontologies of scale that assume world building only occurs through the organization of alternative social and political projects and not in the ordinary ethics of everyday interactions and gestures of care.[62] The intersubjective otherwise is not the grand plan of building back better but the small mark left on a single life that has been touched by the kindness and concern of another. The question is how we might intentionally cultivate otherwise encounters that do not depend on threats of annihilation and temporalities of crisis to bring them into being. As Bina reminds us, "the ghosts close by are more useful than distant gods," for they are always already with us. To build back otherwise beyond the temporality of crisis is to find a way to sustain an ethics of gentleness, with each other and the world, that may be generated by the work of disaster but is not dependent on it.

Repair

In the village in Khotang, days after the rupture of the earthquakes, there was a sense that to dwell too much on tension was dangerous. Tension was a disease that could lead to death. It was something to be hidden away. Confronted with the instability of the land beneath them, people spoke about the uncertainty of death as destiny, as part of their fate that was already written (*lekheko*). Some turned to alcohol, others to ritual to hold themselves and their homes together. The radio was kept on throughout the day and into the night in a continuous stream of information. From its broadcasts, we learned that the ancient temples of Kathmandu had been destroyed, and listened to bittersweet songs of mourning play over and over again. Listeners called in from all over the country to share their perspectives on the disaster and their feelings of fear, worry, and dizziness (*ringata lagyo*). Broadcasters informed their listeners that tension was something that should be shared not hidden and that a disease called depression could be treated with medication and by sharing the worries one held in the heart-mind.

In Kathmandu, international humanitarians and journalists declared that the earthquakes had created a "mental health crisis" that would require psychosocial counseling and psychiatric medication at a scale never before seen in Nepal. Their claims of crisis justified the expansion of new forms of care and therapeutics in a region with a long history of shamanic and ritual healing for psychospiritual distress. Counselors were trained and dispatched into the still trembling hills. When they arrived in the earthquake-affected villages, they introduced the concepts of mental health and counseling and then invited people to join their sessions. They explained that sharing one's worries and talking about loss could bring relief to the heart-mind and that this intangible relief was what they had to offer. In a context where concealing negative emotion was highly valued and talking about grief was discouraged, psychosocial counseling created a space for a different kind of expression. As the earth continued to tremble with repeated aftershocks, counseling sessions and circles became temporary shelters for hoping, grieving, and imagining new ways of living and relating to loss.

In the months that followed, counselors soon discovered trajectories of psychic affliction that did not neatly align with the temporality of the disaster. As they traversed the fourteen earthquake-affected districts, counselors met people suffering from highly stigmatized, previously invisible forms of social and psychic affliction that far predated the earthquakes. Viewed through the frame of crisis, chronic suffering had suddenly become worthy of humanitarian care. Yet this concern would last only as long as the region was deemed a disaster zone. Faced with the inevitable end of care, counselors struggled to respond to the ethical demands of clients who asked for more treatment and medication when none could be promised.

Yet within the troubled and time-bound humanitarian response, there were two faces of transient care. On one side were the structural limitations of predetermined temporalities of suffering and victimhood; on the other were new ways of living and being together made possible by the disaster and its conceptualization as a "mental health crisis." To insist on the simultaneity of both limits and possibilities is to engage in a reparative reading of humanitarian care that holds open the potential to be surprised.[1] As Sedgwick writes, hope is "among the energies by which the reparatively positioned reader tries to organize the fragments and part-objects she encounters."[2] The physical and existential challenges of working in the disaster zone where counselors faced risk to provide care exposed the inequalities embedded in the humanitarian project but also served to facilitate solidarity with clients that lent meaning to the work. Brief encounters between counselors and clients revealed the violence of transient care, as well as momentary possibilities for an *intersubjective otherwise* to emerge. As Félix Guattari has argued in his work on therapy as a tool for desubjectivation, sometimes interruptions that force deviation from normal paths and recurrent mental loops can lead to new ways of being and living together.[3] If unexpected acts of kindness, understanding, and gentleness between strangers in the aftermath of disaster can introduce moments of hesitancy, they may similarly disrupt habits and create new ways of being and perceiving the world.[4]

Critiques of humanitarian reason have long focused on how humanitarian care is a form of violence incapable of recognizing those who cannot properly embody the figure of the suffering subject.[5] When victimhood is a requirement for care, subjects are reduced to one-dimensional beings that must conform to the expectations of humanitarians. In requiring specific forms of suffering in order to become deserving care, the complexity of a person is erased. Drawing on the work of Levinas, Fassin has argued that "ultimately, what is lacking in humanitarian government is perhaps that, beyond life as sacred and suffering as value, it fails to recognize the Other as a 'face' . . . this face 'present in its refusal to be contained,' this face that resists any attempt to possess it even in the name of good."[6] For Levinas, to "see the face" of the Other is an ethical act in which a person is able to appear in all their singularity, in an expansiveness beyond any label that might reduce them to a type such as "the earthquake victim" or "the victim of trauma."[7] As opposed to humanitarian reason that seeks to intervene on behalf of predefined figures of suffering, a Levinasian concept of ethics entails a responsibility to care for the Other in their radical otherness—an otherness that will always evade attempts to fully grasp, understand, or know it.

It is precisely here that the story of humanitarian care in Nepal complicates long-standing critiques of humanitarianism in surprising ways. For unlike many places, in Nepal care was tied not to a specific performance of victimhood but to one's location within the earthquake-affected territory. As counselors met clients whose suffering overflowed humanitarian frames, they listened to their stories and responded to the ethical demand of the Other, in spite of the painful limitations they faced within the program's design. In the therapeutic encounters between clients and counselors that were inaugurated by the work of disaster, humanitarian reason could not destroy an ethics of care and responsibility toward the Other. Clients were not required to perform a story of destitution and injury of a certain type to receive support. Instead, counselors made space for clients to speak of the complexity of their biographical life, "the life through which they could, independently, give a meaning to their own existence."[8] When examined at the level of intersubjective interaction, we find that even within biopolitical projects of humanitarian intervention, sometimes there may be possibilities for care that is attuned to "the face" of the Other.[9]

Since Sedgwick's formulation, reparative reading has been met with a number of critiques. Some have argued that by embracing a reparative approach, one turns away from critical research concerned with exposing injustice, violence, and harm. By emphasizing practices of survival and hope that may offer a glimpse of the otherwise within the horrors of the present, it may be more difficult to envision a completely different world that is not grounded within the violent infrastructures of capitalism, colonialism, and empire.[10] As Patricia Stuelke writes, the "celebration of survival strategies and coping mechanisms as beautiful seeds of that which might one day save the world—can sometimes seem to stave off the difficult work of imagining possible worlds that break definitively with this one."[11] Yet a turn toward repair does not necessarily have to be a turn away from critique. This book has tried to examine both the violence and gentleness of humanitarianism in the aftermath of disaster and consider how both may coexist simultaneously.[12]

Monsoon Rains

In July 2019, the monsoon came late to Nepal. Farmers waited and prayed for rain as they watched their crops dry up and die. Then when the rain came, it came in an endless deluge, washing away the young growth and the earth as well. The unusually heavy rains caused landslides across the districts of eastern Nepal, killing a number of people, yet never rising to the status of an event. Three years had passed since the end of the postearthquake intervention, and I had returned with Bina to a rural village where she had provided psychosocial counseling. In the village, we stayed in the home of Sita, a former CPSW in the project. New "earthquake houses" were everywhere, built with USD 3,000 of government reconstruction grants and following the state-approved architectural plans. The small buildings were strange structures that bore no resemblance to traditional Nepali homes. Sita's family used what they referred to as their "earthquake house" (*bhukampa ghar*) only for sleeping and during the day continued to inhabit the bottom floor of their cracked mud home, where they cooked and ate together around the mud hearth. Earthquake houses might be constructed of durable rebar, cement blocks, and sheets of iron roofing, but they were not places for dwelling.[13]

Like many staff on the project, Sita had been temporarily provided a salary through the work of disaster. Since the project had phased out, her family no longer had a source of income. A year after the earthquakes, her husband quit his job in Kathmandu after struggling with unspecified body pain. Despite spending money on treatment from both doctors and *dhamis*, he had not seen improvement and no physical ailment had been identified. Sita watched her husband and observed his behavior with concern. "Psychosis *hunchha*? [Could it be psychosis?]," she wondered aloud. Sita had learned about psychiatric diagnoses and treatments through her work as a postdisaster CPSW, yet her husband remained hesitant to seek a psychiatric evaluation because of the stigma it continued to carry.

"We must listen to Sita's problems," Bina told me that morning with resolve. Even though Bina was no longer a counselor, since the time of the earthquakes, this form of listening had become part of her way of being-in-the-world. As we traveled over the same misty mountain trails that we had walked together years earlier, people appeared asking if they could share with her the worries they held in their heart-minds. "Damn child! I'm so happy to see you again! [*Hatteri babu! Malai khushi lagyo pheri bhetna lai!*]," an elderly woman called out to Bina. How different the woman looked since we had seen her last; she was now dressed in a bright green *lungi* and matching necklace of glass beads, her face glowing with a bright smile. The last time we met, she was sheltering in a makeshift tent made from discarded USAID tarps, considering the possibility of undergoing surgery for heart palpitations. After talking with Bina, her palpitations mysteriously disappeared. At the village health post, a nurse thanked Bina for helping her mother-in-law after the earthquakes and mentioned that since the disaster, elderly women had been stopping by to ask for medicine for *manko kura khelne* (things playing in the heart-mind). Both counselors and clients were changed by the work of disaster and the novel treatments and forms of care it had inaugurated. Throughout the disaster zone, there was an increased awareness of the concepts of mental health and counseling, as well as use of psychiatric drugs. Even after care had dried up and programs had ended, many people who had been prescribed medication through the humanitarian psychosocial intervention chose to continue their treatment on their own.

Arun was a young Tamang man who had received psychosocial counseling from Bina during the postearthquake program. As had been the case years earlier, he was still suffering from *chhopne* and taking medicine for epilepsy. *Chhopne*, a Nepali term that means "to cover" or "to be taken over," was colloquially used to describe symptoms such as fainting, shaking, and loss of consciousness, especially during states of spirit possession.[14] When we first met Arun in 2015, he had spoken about the painful stigma of his symptoms, explaining that people in the village avoided him because they were afraid his affliction was contagious. That day Arun had shown us a fresh wound on his leg from falling during a sudden attack of *chhopne* while taking his goats to graze in the steep terrain. Years later, like many others seen in the humanitarian intervention, Arun continued to take the medication that he had discovered through the work of disaster. Even though epilepsy medication was included on the Free Drugs List, Arun paid for his treatment himself. In order to buy the medicine, he had to travel from his village to the district headquarters, an endeavor that cost him over NPR 3000 (USD 30) per month.[15] Sita prepared a lunch of rice, dal, and vegetables and invited Arun to stay and eat inside her cracked mud house with us. After finishing his food, he took his medicine, swallowing his pills reluctantly and without water. One of the pills dropped on the ground, and he kicked it toward the door, where it dissolved in a puddle that had pooled on the mud floor. Even when treatment is within reach, one can feel ambivalence and frustration about a medication that must be taken forever in order to manage symptoms that cannot be cured.

In the village, it rained incessantly for three days. I had never seen so much rain. This rain was different from the usual monsoon showers, not fat drops but thin, coming down in sheets without end. Day and night, day and night, the rain rang on the corrugated metal roof of Sita's earthquake house. At midnight, lightning cracked, and the electrical outlet exploded. I could hear tumbling rocks and debris rolling down the hills around us. I had imagined that disaster was something in the past, but now the land around us was crumbling, dissolving, and washing away. The unusual rains foretold a new weather future in Nepal, in which each year would bring a monsoon, more and more unpredictable. Later I learned that forty-three people died in landslides. The double image of land and pills dissolving in endless rain illustrates the challenge of living with chronic ruptures of disaster—both personal and planetary—beyond the temporality of crisis.

The politics of attention in global health today has shown that crisis is a requirement for care. Situations must be transformed into objects of attention before they can become worthy of care, leading to the creation of new economies of crisis. When crisis opens the door to care, sometimes a disaster may be a boon. After the massive mobilization around mental health that was set into motion by the earthquakes and their humanitarian response, it was surreal to be in a similar situation years later that seemed to inspire little attention beyond local news reports. This time there was no rush to aid Nepal; no foreign journalists reporting on risks of PTSD; no training and dispatching of counselors; no walking along mountain paths shaken by aftershocks; no counseling sessions done on thatched mats, under tin shelters, and in fields; no medicine handed out for free; no meetings to imagine what the future of the mental health system might be. There were only sheets of rain, falling endlessly down as the earth slowly dissolved.

As we live through an era marked by environmental catastrophe and war, mental health has become one of the most pressing issues of our time. The management of mental health has become the new terrain of biopolitics today, evidenced by the growing concern of governments worldwide in the aftermath of COVID-19. As scholars we must remain cautious of declarations of crisis that justify interventions into the psychic life of a population, for psychotherapeutic modalities can easily be harnessed in the service of capital to promote increased productivity and social control. Yet this is only one of many possibilities. Therapeutic encounters can also be sites of understanding, imagination, hope, critique, and personal and social transformation.

In anthropology, there have been polarizing debates about the project of global mental health that seeks to promote mental health treatments at a global scale. Some scholars have argued that global mental health is a form of medical imperialism that seeks to eradicate local practices of healing and medicalize social suffering with pharmaceutical drugs.[16] Others, in support of global mental health, see access to psychiatry and counseling as a human right.[17] This book has moved beyond these debates to show what happens when mental health becomes a momentary object of attention in the aftermath of a disaster, and the consequences of transient care. To do so required following what was generated by the disaster and its conceptualization as a crisis for mental health, and the acts of violence and gentleness that were inaugurated as a result.[18]

Possibilities of Repair

In Melanie Klein's psychoanalytic theory of reparation, the child's urge to repair the damage it has done to its objects is ultimately grounded in the child's imagination, not in the reality of the Other's experience of harm.[19] Thinking with Klein, Carolyn Laubender warns that there are "ethico-political dangers in reparative endeavors, which name the object and narrate its injury according to the parameters of one's own self."[20] This basic idea can be extended to the entire project of MHPSS in Nepal, which both defined the problem (trauma and PTSD caused by the event of an earthquake) and introduced the solution (brief psychosocial interventions) in its own terms. As I was walking with my host Chandra along a village path in Khotang in the early days after the earthquakes, he suggested that the arrival of foreign humanitarians in Nepal may be about their desire for "prestige." That is, interventions done in the name of others ultimately reflects the reparative fantasies of humanitarians as opposed the desires and needs of the people they seek to help. As Lauren Berlant warns, "how would we know when the 'repair' we intend is not another form of narcissism?"[21]

From my unanticipated position in the midst of an unfolding disaster, I sought to make sense of the problematization of mental health that the earthquakes had set into motion. As I tracked the work of disaster across various sites and scales, I explored how the material disruption of the earth and its conceptualization as a crisis for mental health shaped and constrained possibilities for repair. Using critical phenomenology as method, I explored how a rupture was objectified through processes of collective intentionality, demanding certain modes of treatment, response, and intervention, and the historical dynamics of power that determined whose concepts became dominant in this process. For example, aware of the problem of sustainability of treatment after humanitarian intervention, in the UN mental health subcluster humanitarians reported on their postdisaster programs and articulated plans for building back better—constructing Nepal's mental health system in the midst of the emergency. Guided by the WHO's recommendations, this vision of "the better" involved increasing access to pharmaceuticals as opposed to developing services for the abandoned mentally ill or other modalities of care. While the disaster created a brief opening to imagine Nepal's mental health future, ultimately ideas of "the better" to be built were directed by the WHO's priorities, not Nepali visions. Even if psychotropic medications can be efficacious, the idea of the better as access to psychiatric drugs is also another instantiation of the magic bullet approach in global health that continues to prioritize individual-focused, technical fixes to complex social and relational problems.[22]

The humanitarian psychosocial intervention was also marked by an absence of engagement with religion and Nepal's many traditional practices of healing. While traveling through the rural villages of the disaster zone, I recall encountering a woman as she walked up the stone steps of a temple to make an offering. She turned to me and said, "All of our homes were destroyed but the *mandir* [the temple] is still standing. This is the place where God stays." Yet despite the power of religion and ritual healing as a widespread source of strength and solace, such topics rarely came up in conversations between clients and counselors. For unlike religious and shamanic explanations for suffering, psychosocial counseling emphasized the role of individual agency. As Michelle, the foreign psychologist in the NGO explained to a room of Nepali supervisors, through counseling people become conscious "That the hand is my hand, not the hand of God. That it is my decision at every step. Every second is a decision." In Nepal, the postdisaster expansion of psychiatry and counseling thus marked a shift toward the secularization of treatment for psychospiritual affliction.

Since 2015, mental health governance in Nepal has continued to expand. In 2017, the government drafted a new National Mental Health Policy to ensure all citizens the right to mental health care. While the policy was not adopted, protections for people with mental and psychosocial disabilities were included in the Act Relating to Rights of Persons with Disabilities, which was passed the same year. In 2020, the government drafted the National Mental Health Strategy and Action Plan, which outlined plans to include mental health treatment in primary health care, create easier access to psychiatry and counseling services, and increase service user involvement in mental health advocacy.[23] Alongside policies and plans, over the past decade, increasing numbers of government health workers have been trained in psychiatric diagnosis and counseling and placed in district hospitals and health posts across the country.

While anthropologists have tended to locate the repair of broken worlds in practices of ritual, relationality, and ways of being-with others in quotidian scenes of the everyday, in the aftermath of disaster, we find the actions imagined to facilitate repair to be widely variable.[24] Throughout this book, each chapter illuminated a tension between humanitarian imaginaries and local dreams and practices of repair. In the sphere of governance, humanitarian repair focused on increasing access to pharmaceutical drugs and training community mental health workers as opposed to local activist calls to create social and institutional support for the abandoned mentally ill. In the space of the counseling session, humanitarians imagined repair to be accomplished through a form of listening and absorbing of negative emotion that could provide a temporary shelter, while local practices and religious rituals of repair focused on severing attachments and releasing the spirits of the dead so they might transform into their next incarnation. In the embodied work of counseling, humanitarians assumed that repair required access to special protections for foreign humanitarian workers while for local counselors this work required shared exposure to risk. In the temporality of the humanitarian "project form," repair was an endpoint that could ultimately be reached and measured, as opposed to an ongoing, possibly endless process.[25]

In phenomenology, groundlessness is used metaphorically to speak about a nonconceptual starting point or clearing from which to think. It is through the ungrounding or the "defrosting" of concepts that we can create openings for new possibilities to emerge.[26] In the context of an earthquake, this ungrounding is not only a metaphor but is also material and embodied. In the Madhyamaka tradition of Buddhist metaphysics, groundlessness is synonymous with *sunyata*, the realization of emptiness and dependent arising of all things.[27] Emptiness is a notoriously slippery idea, especially in the English language, where it is associated with nothingness or absence. Yet *sunyata* is not nothingness but quite the opposite—it is the realization that all things arise codependently with the concepts that bring them forth.

In the notion of dependent arising, we find a way to understand disaster as a force that both destroys and creates new possibilities for natality. As the ancient Indian philosopher Nagarjuna once wrote, "there is no destruction without becoming."[28] Every rupture, earthly or human, is also an opportunity for repair. The work of disaster allows us to follow the process of destruction and becoming, rupture and repair, in all its contingency, as it is emerging, assembling, and crystalizing through the concepts that shape perception and guide response. To approach the study of disaster from a critical phenomenological perspective introduces a different tempo into claims of crisis, one slow enough to identify brief openings where things might have been otherwise—a different vision of the better, a different endpoint of care, a different modality of treatment, a different response, a different practice of repair.

Acknowledgments

I am profoundly grateful to the many people who have supported this work. While some I can thank by name, others, especially those whose stories I write about in this book, must remain anonymous.

At Sarah Lawrence College, Bob Desjarlais introduced me to anthropology and taught me countless lessons about the strange beauty of ethnographic writing. His mentorship and intellectual generosity set me on the path that has made everything else possible. At UCLA, Jason Throop's rigorous seminars on phenomenology and intersubjectivity were rivaled only by his Levinasian ethics of care for his students. Sherry Ortner offered wise feedback and brilliant insights that have helped keep this work critically grounded. Doug Hollan's psychoanalytic anthropology of dreams and early mentorship continue to shape my scholarship in important ways. Nancy Levine was an extraordinary guide through the anthropology of Nepal. At the University of Virginia, Jarrett Zigon's generous support created an unparalleled opportunity to immerse myself in theories of biopolitics, moral experience, and critical phenomenology. Todd Meyers has been a mentor from afar, providing guidance and encouragement at key moments in the life of this manuscript.

In Nepal, I could not have found my way without the Lama family. Thank you to Binod, Kanchi Omu, and Tenzin Lama for welcoming me back to Kathmandu year after year and to Sangye, Karma, and Dawa Lama, who received me in their home in Jackson Heights, Queens, so many years ago. Thank you to the Oli family for hospitality in the Dang-Deukari valley and to the Shrestha family, who hosted me in the village in Khotang and cared for me during and after the earthquakes. My work on mental health in Nepal could not have been possible without the support of many colleagues in Kathmandu over the years. Thank you Phanindra Adhikari, Kedar Marahatta, Yashoda Oli, Rabi

Shakya, and Nawaraj Upadhaya, for teaching me so much. Most of all, I owe an infinite debt of gratitude to Pashupati Mahat, Karuna Kunwar, Laxshmi Tamang, and everyone at CMC–Nepal for making this research possible, and to Barbara Weyerman for guidance, encouragement, and friendship. My fellow anthropologists in Nepal have been excellent comrades over the years— thank you Dannah Dennis, Michelle Grocke, Ashley Hagaman, Drew Haxby, Austin Lord, Sujit Shrestha, and especially my *sathi*, Amy Johnson, for your friendship. Erica Adhikary and her team provided meticulous transcription and translation work. Thank you to my teachers Shambhu Oja, Amlesh Bajracharya, and Sunita Limbu for sharing the beautiful gift that is the Nepali language.

In Paris, a number of colleagues shaped this work in formative ways. At the Centre for Research on Medicine, Science, Health, Mental Health, and Society (CERMES3), Anne Lovell, Claudia Lang, Ursula Read, Andy McDowell, and the many speakers in the Global Health seminar series transformed my thinking about global mental health. At Nanterre, Anne de Salles and Marie Lecomte-Tilouine provided feedback on an early chapter that contained the seeds of this book. During a truly inspirational semester as a visiting professor at the Centre d'anthropologie culturelle (CANTHEL) at Université Paris Cité, collaboration with Serena Bindi helped me to deepen my thinking on the anthropology of grief and loss in the Himalayas. At the University of Notre Dame, colleagues in the Department of Anthropology and beyond have welcomed me into their intellectual community. I am especially grateful for the mentorship and support I've received from Chris Ball, Susan Blum, Cat Bolton, Alex Chavez, Meredith Chessin, Tarryn Chun, Lee Gettler, Donna Glowaki, Michel Hockx, Julia Kowalski, Ian Kuijt, Rahul Oka, Mark Schurr, and Vania Smith-Oka.

I am indebted to many other colleagues who have provided feedback, guidance, advice, and inspiration over the years, especially Mara Buchbinder, Devin Flaherty, Alexa Hagerty, Jan Hauck, Sandra Hyde, Erik Linstrum, Alexandra Lippman, Chris Nelson, Dave Novak, Elinor Ochs, Seth Palmer, Claire Payton, Sarah Pinto, Janak Rai, Liz Roberts, China Scherz, Lotte Segal, Sara Shneiderman, Chris Stephan, Lisa Stevenson, and Sylvia Tidey. Conversations with Samuele Collu helped me rethink the meaning of psychic life. Sienna Craig offered incredible feedback and encouragement at key moments in the writing of this manuscript. Biella Coleman's wise advice on all things anthropological continues to be a treasure. Camille Frazier not only read and commented on many drafts of this project over the years but has been a steadfast friend through thick and thin. Jake Harris's excellent copyediting skills helped sharpen the manuscript in its final stages. I'm especially grateful to my students at the University of Virginia, the University of Notre Dame, and Martin Chautari in Kathmandu, who have taught me so much.

Chapters of this book have greatly benefited from audience feedback during invited talks in the Division of Social & Transcultural Psychiatry at McGill University; the Department of Comparative Human Development at the University of Chicago; CERMES3 in Paris; CANTHEL at Université Paris Cité; the Centre d'etudes Himalayenne at EHESS; the Department of Anthropology at the Chinese University of Hong Kong; Martin Chautari in Kathmandu; and the Team Phenomenology Working Group at the University of California, Los Angeles.

I am forever grateful to the incredible team at the University of Chicago Press and others who have supported the publication of this book. Dylan Montanari swiftly led this manuscript though the review process and provided invaluable editorial guidance and advice along the way. Fabiola Enríquez Flores's editorial support has been equally essential. Kate Blackmer lent her exceptional cartographic skills to design the map for this book. Many thanks to David Luljak for indexing. I would also like to express sincere gratitude to my two reviewers, whose insights have helped improve this manuscript in countless ways. I am especially grateful to Holli Bryan, whose editorial wisdom and close reading helped sharpen the book's arguments early on.

Funding for the research and writing of this book was made possible in part through the generous support of the Wenner Gren Foundation, the UCLA Graduate Division, and the Institute for Scholarship in the Liberal Arts, College of Arts and Letters, University of Notre Dame. Thank you to Dhana Lama, executive director of United Mission to Nepal, for permission to reproduce images from the Archives of the United Mission to Nepal, held in the Special Collections at Yale Divinity School, and to Umesh Shrestha for allowing me to include a photograph of his painting *Under the Himalaya: Experience of Students* in this book. Portions of the introduction, chapter 1, and chapter 5 appeared in the previously published article "The Work of Disaster: Building Back Otherwise in Post-Earthquake Nepal," *Cultural Anthropology* 35, no. 2 (2020): 237–63.

To my brilliant friends who are a wellspring of creative inspiration: Tanya, Isis, Lindsay, Willa, Eugenie, Kyle, Leila, Lauren, Alejandro, Sarah, Ary, Erin, Sam, Lizzie, Camille, Alexandra, Amy, Danni, Hadas, and Kitta. To my extended family, stretched across multiple continents and planes of existence: Linda, Gala, Naomi, Samuel, my Grandmothers Joyce and Rosalie, and my

Brazilian family: Regina, Uiraja, Rosa, Stella, Leo, Nathalia, Luana, Maria Antonia, Carlos, and Isabel. To my parents, Brian and Allegra, for love and generosity and for creating space for me to write during long visits to California. Thank you most of all to Felipe, who has read far too many drafts and has remained a constant source of love and support as we've traveled along our itinerant anthropological paths. Without you none of this would be possible.

Notes

Prologue

1. All personal names used in the ethnography are pseudonyms.

2. Devkota 1980, 125–26.

Introduction

1. Seale-Feldman 2019.

2. For a description of the *Bhandai-Sundai* program, see United Nations Children's Fund 2016b, 5–6.

3. As Bruno Latour (2004, 246) writes, "give me one matter of concern and I will show you the whole earth and heavens that have to be gathered to hold it in place." Latour argues that to renew the practice of critique, we must shift from deconstructing "facts" toward following the assembly of "matters of concern."

4. Seale-Feldman and Upadhaya 2015.

5. United Nations Children's Fund 2016a.

6. Bennett 2015.

7. Like the international media and humanitarian focus on PTSD among earthquake victims in Nepal, in the context of the nuclear disaster in Fukushima, Morimoto (2024, 13) notes that "radiation, the contaminated environment, and its potential detrimental health effects became the dominant, expected, and selectively curated story."

8. For ethnographies of shamanic healing, Sowa Rigpa (Tibetan medicine), and Ayurveda in Nepal, see Desjarlais 1992; Craig 2012; Cameron 2019.

9. The literal translation of *chinta basne* is "worry sitting." In Nepali, *chinta* means "worry, anxiety, or concern"; however, the word holds different meanings in psychiatric and shamanic contexts (Schmidt 1994, 193).

10. As Frantz Fanon (1965, 96) has argued in his essay on the creation of Free Radio Algeria in colonial Algeria, the radio is a powerful "means of perception" that can radically transform "the very world of perception."

11. Nichter 1981; Seale-Feldman 2022b.

12. For a discussion of psychiatry and epistemic violence in Nepal, see Seale-Feldman 2022b.

13. Kunreuther 2014.

14. Rai, Gurung, and Gautam 2021.

15. Acland 2002; Seale-Feldman 2020a.

16. Upadhaya et al. 2014.

17. Foucault 1978; Povinelli 2011; Fassin 2012.

18. Foucault 1978.

19. Foucault 2003.

20. For Martin Heidegger, the compound expression "being-in-the-world" is a way to describe the state of Being for humans (Dasein). "Being-in-the-world" illustrates the idea that humans are not separate from their environment but are fully immersed in and constituted by the world in which they exist. In this way, for Heidegger, the world in which one lives cannot be disentangled from the being that one is. The related concept of "being-with" [*mitsein*] speaks to the idea that the world in which humans exist is a common world that is shared and experienced with others. When Heidegger writes about "being-with-others" he describes the various ways humans care for, concern themselves with, or disregard other people. See Heidegger 2010.

21. Seale-Feldman 2020b.

22. Here I use the term *ground* loosely to refer to the physical earth and the lifeworld— what Ted Toadvine (2020, 238) has described as the "ontological foundation of experiential meaning"—as well as the conceptual ground from which we think.

23. Moran 2000, 6.

24. Desjarlais 1992; Csordas 1994; Mattingly 1998; Throop 2010b; Desjarlais and Throop 2011.

25. As Thomas Csordas (1990, 9) writes, "the goal of a phenomenological anthropology of perception is to capture that moment of transcendence in which perception begins, and, in the midst of arbitrariness, constitutes and is constituted by culture."

26. Desjarlais and Throop 2011, 88. Dermot Moran (2000, 151) describes the practice of "bracketing" as a "redirection of attention."

27. Fanon 2008.

28. Desjarlais and Throop 2011, 95.

29. For examples of critical phenomenology, see Desjarlais 1997; Ahmed 2006; Fanon 2008; Guenther 2013; Al-Saji 2014; Salamon 2018; Mattingly 2019; Zigon 2019; Guenther 2021.

30. Adams et al. 2019, 1389.

31. Kalofonos 2010; Livingston 2012; Benton 2015.

32. Moran (2000, 231) writes that in phenomenology, intentionality is about "'directedness,' how we orient ourselves towards things." However, as Sara Ahmed (2006) reminds us, phenomenologists must also critically examine the way the ability to orient our attention toward some things and not others is always grounded in a *particular* body.

33. Mattingly 2019; Seale-Feldman 2019; Zigon 2019.

34. Desjarlais 1997, 24.

35. Mattingly 2019; Zigon 2019. Desjarlais' (1994) early work on the concept of "experience" demonstrates a similar approach that uses phenomenology as a tool for concept critique.

36. Zigon 2019, 3.

37. Hoffman and Oliver-Smith 2002.

38. Kreps 1995; Oliver-Smith 1996; Hoffman 1999; Oliver-Smith and Hoffman 2002.

39. N. Klein 2007; Gunewardena and Schuller 2008; Adams 2013; Choi 2015.

40. Lovell 2011.

41. Barrios 2017, 157.

42. Fortun 2001; Petryna 2003; Bond 2013; Tironi 2014.

43. Petryna 2022.

44. Oliver-Smith and Hoffman 2002, 6.

45. In his study of frame analysis, Erving Goffman (1974, 24) argued that "we tend to perceive events in terms of primary frameworks, and the type of framework we employ provides a way of describing the event to which it is applied."

46. Goffman 1974, 21.

47. In her essay on thinking in dark times, Hannah Arendt writes that concepts, clichés, stock phrases, and conventional modes of expression place limits on things; concepts are "like a frozen thought which thinking must unfreeze, defrost as it were, whenever it wants to find out its original meaning" (Arendt 1971, 431, cited in Mattingly 2019). Capturing the moral urgency of this project, Arendt (1971, 446) argues that thinking, as she defines it, may guard against evil and "indeed may prevent catastrophes."

48. Butler 2016, xiii.

49. Povinelli 2011. For a discussion of the social construction of crisis as a question of problematization, see Fassin 2021, 268.

50. Speech made during the televised "International Conference on Nepal's Reconstruction: Towards a Resilient Nepal 2015." See Koirala 2015.

51. Seddon, Gurung, and Adhikari 1998; Graner 2009; World Bank 2016.

52. Seddon, Gurung, and Adhikari 1998.

53. Jackson 2015.

54. Manyena 2006; Barrios 2016.

55. The concept of "resilience" in disaster management finds its origins in physics and ecological theory, where it was used to describe the qualities that enable a material that has been exposed to stress to return to a state of equilibrium and the ability of a system to absorb an external disturbance without changing its structure. See Holling 1973.

56. UNISDR 2005.

57. Barrios 2016.

58. Associated Press 2017.

59. Shneiderman et al. 2023, 503.

60. Tamang 2015.

61. Tamang 2015.

62. Jha 2014; Kunreuther 2014; Snellinger 2018.

63. Consider, for example, the casual and derogatory use of the word "sherpa" in English to refer to someone who willingly carries heavy loads. Sherpa people are an ethnic group indigenous to the Mount Everest region of Nepal, who have historically served as guides and porters on the mountaineering expeditions of privileged Europeans. See Ortner 1999.

64. Regmi 1978.

65. A. Adhikari 2014, 18.

66. Rana 2013, 73–74.

67. Abramowitz 2014, 93.

68. Abramowitz 2014.

69. Schmidt 1994, 506.

70. Foucault 1978; 2003.

71. Prince et al. 2007.

72. McHugh 1989; Desjarlais 1992; Parish 1994; Maskarinec 1995. For a review of this literature, see Seale-Feldman 2022a.

73. Kohrt and Harper 2008; Kohrt and Hruschka 2010.

74. Kohrt and Harper 2008.

75. Seale-Feldman 2020a.

76. The postdisaster transformation of mental health care is not unique to Nepal. For a discussion of humanitarian psychiatry and the development of novel mental health interventions after the 1999 earthquake in Turkey, see Dole 2020; 2023.

77. Bemme and D'souza 2014; Mills 2014.

78. Kleinman 2009; Bemme and D'souza 2014.

79. For critiques of psychosocial interventions as "medical imperialism" and the "globalization of the American psyche," see Watters 2010; Summerfield 2013.

80. For a haunting discussion of ethnographic disquiet, see Meyers 2022.

81. Günel, Varma, and Watanabe 2020; Malinowski 2002.

82. Winnicott 2005.

83. Ahmed 2006, 38.

84. Lassiter 2005.

85. Nepal is a diverse country of many different languages, religions, castes, and ethnic groups. The largest caste/ethnic group is comprised of high caste Hindus (27.7% of the population). Rai and Tamang are two indigenous groups which make up 2.2% and 5.6 % of the population, respectively. See Government of Nepal, National Statistics Office 2023, 32.

86. Harrison 2011.

87. Haraway 1988; Ahmed 2006.

88. Ortner 2016.

89. Robbins 2013.

90. Sedgwick 2003.

91. As Eve Sedgwick (2003, 141) writes, "I'm a lot less worried about being pathologized by my therapist than about my vanishing mental health coverage—and that's given the great good luck of having health insurance at all."

92. Ticktin 2011; Fassin 2012; Fassin and Pandolfi 2013.

93. Robert Desjarlais and C. Jason Throop (2011, 88) define intersubjectivity as "the existential organization, recognition, and constitution of relations between subjects."

94. As Heidegger writes, there are multiple modes of being-with-others: "Being for-, against-, or without-one-another, passing-one-another-by, not-mattering-to-one-another—are possible ways of concern. And precisely the last-named modes of deficiency and indifference characterize everyday and average being-with-one-another." See Heidegger 2010, 118.

95. Former US President Bill Clinton first introduced the "build back better" concept to disaster recovery in response to the 2004 Indian Ocean Tsunami when he was the United Nation's secretary-general's special envoy for tsunami recovery. Since then, build back better discourse has become widespread, with recent examples being US President Joe Biden's postpandemic "Build Back Better Framework."

96. For work on "therapeutic citizenship," see Pupavac 2001; Nguyen 2010.

97. Ingold 2000; 2010.

98. Povinelli 2011; Hardt and Negri 2013; Stevenson 2014; Murphy 2017; Zigon 2019.

Chapter One

1. International Medical Corps (IMC) 2015.

2. Koselleck 2006.

3. Koselleck 2006, 358.

4. Koselleck 2006, 361.

5. Brown 2009; Fassin 2021.

6. Vigh 2008.

7. Masco 2017, S66.

8. Roitman 2014, 94.

9. Stockton 2015.

10. Luitel et al. 2015.

11. World Health Organization 2013.

12. World Health Organization 2013, 3.

13. N. Klein 2007; Simpson 2014.

14. Seale-Feldman 2020a.

15. Roitman 2014; Fassin 2021.

16. Latour 2004, 246.

17. Austin 1962. As Fassin (2021, 272) notes on the naming of crisis, "the fact of not only labeling it but also interpreting it gives the power to transform the representation of the world and act in consequence according to one's interests or the interests of the group with whom one is allied. Those who are granted such authority define the problems, decide the stakes, and determine the solutions."

18. Mead 1954; Linstrum 2016, 189.

19. Vaughan 1992.

20. Vaughan 1992, 107.

21. Mead 1954.

22. Mead 1954, 8.

23. Mead 1954, 9.

24. WHO Expert Committee on Mental Health 1975.

25. WHO Expert Committee on Mental Health 1975, 7.

26. WHO Expert Committee on Mental Health 1975, 7.

27. WHO Expert Committee on Mental Health 1975, 8.

28. WHO Expert Committee on Mental Health 1975, 10.

29. WHO Expert Committee on Mental Health 1975, 23.

30. WHO Expert Committee on Mental Health 1975, 7.

31. Sartorius 1983, 1.

32. Foyle 1987; World Health Organization 1978.

33. Hickingbotham and Wright n.d.

34. Hickingbotham and Wright n.d.

35. Foyle 1987; United Mission to Nepal n.d.; United Mission to Nepal 1988.

36. WHO Expert Committee on Mental Health 1975, 10.

37. WHO Expert Committee on Mental Health 1975, 11.

38. Critiques of "irrational" interventions will appear again in the MGMH in the 2000s. But as China Mills (2014, 3) asks, "Who decides what constitutes irrationality? The MGMH frames distress as an illness like any other, calling for global equity in access to psychiatric medication. However there is a growing body of research from the global North that documents the harmful effects of long-term use of psychiatric medication and questions the use of psychiatric models."

39. Hickingbotham 1985.

40. Wright 1986.

41. For contemporary examples of the similar use of metrics in global mental health, see Bemme and D'souza 2014.

42. D. M. Shrestha, Pach, and Rimal 1983. For a description of UMN's Mental Health Project, see Acland 2002.

43. Acland 2002; Luitel et al. 2015.

44. Cohen, Kleinman, and Saraceno 2002.

45. A. Adhikari 2014.

46. Pettigrew 2013, 16.

47. Pettigrew 2013; Thapa 2011.

48. Thapa 2011; Weyerman 2010.

49. Abramowitz 2009; James 2010a.

50. "Minors" refer to children who were born after May 25, 1988, and recruited to fight in Maoist battalions. "Late Recruits" refers to combatants recruited by Maoists after the ceasefire agreement on May 25, 2006. See Subedi 2014.

51. Summerfield 1999.

52. Fassin and Rechtman 2009.

53. World Bank 2022.

54. Pattison 2013; 2014.

55. J. Adhikari and Hobley 2015.

56. In rural villages and urban towns, clandestine lovers no longer exchanged handwritten letters but met on Facebook, where they nurtured secret affairs. For an ethnography documenting changing attitudes toward love in Nepal in the era prior to digital technology, see Ahearn 2001.

57. For example, a study of the impact of migration on women in eastern Nepal found that while remittances increased household well-being, many people also reported an increase in family breakdown and elopement in families with husbands working abroad (J. Adhikari and Hobley 2015, 18). For a discussion of the relationship between remittances and love in Nepal, see Zharkevich 2019.

58. As a study of well-being among former "child soldiers" in Nepal argues, while psychosocial interventions framed ex–child soldiers as passive victims, for some people, including youth, participation in armed insurgency was an expression of political solidarity and source of community and personal well-being (Medeiros et al. 2019).

59. World Bank 1993.

60. Desjarlais et al. 1996.

61. The new framing of mental health in terms of economic loss indicated the extent to which neoliberal market ideologies had penetrated the field of global health (Packard 2016, 285).

62. Prince et al. 2007.

63. Prince et al. 2007, 859.

64. Prince et al. 2007, 860.

65. Prince et al. 2007, 859.

66. Bemme and D'souza 2014.

67. Bemme and D'souza 2014.

68. For anthropological studies of the field of global mental health, see Bemme and D'souza 2014; Lovell, Read, and Lang 2019.

69. World Bank and World Health Organization 2016.

70. World Bank and World Health Organization 2016.

71. Foucault 2003, 243–44; Murphy 2017.

72. Seale-Feldman 2020a.

73. Murphy 2017, 78. For a recent example of cutting-edge experimentation, see van Heerden et al.'s (2024) description of the implementation of an mHealth (mobile health) intervention that incorporates smartphones and wearable devices to improve psychosocial interventions for mothers with depression in Nepal.

74. See McHugh 1989; Desjarlais 1992; Parish 1994; Maskarinec 1995.

75. See Kohrt and Harper 2008; Kohrt and Hruschka 2010. Following Brandon Kohrt and DJ Hrushka's (2010) model, these interventions would ideally take place alongside other forms of biomedical, community, and traditional healing and would promote referral across modalities.

76. See Kohrt and Harper 2008.

77. Harper 2014, 84–86.

78. In Nepal, such dynamics of knowledge/power are not unique to the domain of mental health. As Stacy Pigg (2001) has observed in the case of HIV/AIDS awareness campaigns in the 1990s, global health programs in Nepal had to first introduce new forms of knowledge about the disease and the body before they could convince the population to fight an anticipated epidemic that remained largely invisible.

79. For a description of the "historical a priori," see Foucault 1972, 127. For an argument that a critical practice of phenomenology should engage with Foucauldian methods of genealogy, problematization, and archaeology when studying a particular lifeworld, see Guenther 2021.

80. Dunn 2012, 6.

81. Key issues driving the protests included the new constitution's demarcation of federal provinces, laws regarding proportional representation for minorities in parliament, and the revision of the citizenship law to restrict citizenship by descent to children born of Nepali fathers only, all of which were interpreted as systemic acts of discrimination designed to limit the legal rights and representation of Madhesi people. As a minority group that frequently intermarries across the Nepal-India border, Madhesi activists saw the revision of the citizenship law as direct evidence of discrimination by high-caste Hindu ruling elites from the hills. See Strasheim 2018.

82. This had a silencing effect on some of the Nepali NGO staff, who appeared less confident speaking formally in English than in Nepali, yet did not ask for help in translation.

83. Inter-Agency Standing Committee (IASC) 2007.

84. Abramowitz and Kleinman 2008, 219.

85. Abramowitz and Kleinman 2008, 220.

86. United Nations Children's Fund 2016a.

87. Although regular meetings between Nepali mental health NGOs had been attempted in the past, such as the Kathmandu Psychosocial Forum (KFP), according to NGO staff, competition between organizations over status and donor funding made their sustainability impossible.

88. Calhoun 2010; Ticktin 2011; Redfield 2012; Packard 2016.

89. Calhoun 2010, 39; Ticktin 2014, 282.

90. Redfield 2012, 374.

91. For work on humanitarian afterlives, see McKay 2012.

92. Varma 2016a.

93. Zigon 2019.

94. Stockton 2015.

95. Chase et al. 2018.

96. For a description of the original four figures of biopolitics, see Foucault 1978.

97. For work on the challenge of thinking in dark times, see Arendt 1971; Brown 2009. As Elaine Scarry (2011, 13) writes, "the implicit claim of emergency is that all procedures and all thinking must cease because the emergency requires that 1) an action must be taken, and 2) the action must be taken relatively quickly."

Chapter Two

1. For work on land, belonging, and identity in Nepal, see Shneiderman 2015.

2. Ninglekhu 2017.

3. "GI Sheets" refers to sheets of corrugated galvanized iron roofing.

4. Pupavac 2001; Abramowitz 2009; James 2010a.

5. Young 1997; Summerfield 1999; Fassin and Rechtman 2009.

6. Summerfield 1999; Fassin 2008.

7. Fassin 2008.

8. Fassin 2008, 538.

9. James 2010b.

10. For discussions of biological and therapeutic citizenship, see Petryna 2003; Nguyen 2005; James 2010b.

11. Apte 1957, 1594.

12. Obeyesekere 1985; S. Lewis 2020.

13. What Desjarlais (1992, 142) has noted in the case of Hyolmo Buddhists in Nepal is applicable throughout the Himalayan region—that is, there is great value placed on "the ability to "hold" one's heart-mind—to "hide" one's thoughts within the body and not let on, when faced with grief, pain, or anger, that one is hurting."

14. For a discussion of collective practices of "memory work" among members of the Langtang community in the aftermath of the Nepal earthquakes, see Lord and Bradley 2021.

15. Summerfield 1999, 1455,

16. Devereux 1951; Kleinman 1977. For a description of ethnopsychiatry and the integration of the patient's cultural etiologies in the therapeutic space, see Nathan and Stengers 2018.

17. For a discussion of the limits of the use of the concept of culture in ethnopsychiatry, see Giordano 2014. For a searing analysis of the negative psychological effects of cultural values of racism, see Fanon 2008.

18. In What Is Philosophy? Gilles Deleuze and Félix Guattari (1994, 95) argue that philosophy is the creation of concepts carried out in relation to territory and the earth. They write, "Philosophy is a geophilosophy in precisely the same way history is a geohistory." Geophilosophy is the point of departure through which to explore the relation between philosophy and geography, and to set into motion the deterritorialization of thought by questioning the dominance of Western philosophy.

19. Arendt 1971; 2018; Mattingly 2019; Zigon 2019.

20. Arendt 1971, 434.

21. Mattingly 2019, 416.

22. Summerfield 1999; Abramowitz and Kleinman 2008.

23. Inter-Agency Standing Committee (IASC) 2007.

24. Goldmann and Galea 2014, 177.

25. Inter-Agency Standing Committee (IASC) 2007, 119.

26. Parry 1995, 155.

27. Desjarlais 1992, 142.

28. Pattison 2014. For a discussion of the relationship between labor migration and psychological distress in Nepal, see Khadka 2020.

29. For work on affective atmospheres, the circulation of intensities, and public feeling, see Anderson 2009; Stewart 2011.

30. For work on emotional labor and the management of outward expressions of negative emotion in diverse cultural contexts, see Hochschild 1983; Wikan 1990.

31. Parry 1995; Desjarlais 2016.

32. Parry 1995, 152.

33. Parry 1995, 155; Das 2007.

34. Parry 1995, 190.

35. Das 2007.

36. Parry 1995, 158.

37. Seale-Feldman 2019.

38. Eck 1999, 343.

39. Conze 2001.

40. The idea of *sunyata* or codependent arising can be visualized through the allegory of the god Indra's net. As Elmar Weinmayr, John Krummel, and Douglas Berger (2005, 245) describe it, "Into each knot of this net a gem is sewn. Since every gem is clear, that is, 'empty' or 'nothing,' all other gems are reflected in it, as it is also reflected in every other gem. Reality is this 'inexhaustible, infinite mirroring,' a coherence of effects in which everything is connected with everything else."

41. Turner 1965, 429.

42. Turner 1965, 574.

43. Turner 1965, 313.

44. Turner 1965, 612.

45. For example, "the worker bee is familiar with the blossoms it frequents, along with their color and scent, but it does not know the stamens of these blossoms *as* stamens, it knows nothing about the roots of the plant and it cannot know anything about the number of stamens or leaves. As against this, the world of man is a rich one, greater in range, far more extensive in its penetrability, constantly extendable not only in its range (we can always bring more and more beings into consideration) but also in respect to the manner in which we can penetrate ever more deeply in this penetrability. Consequently we can characterize the relation man possesses to the world by referring to the extendibility of everything that he relates to. This is why we speak of man as world-forming" (Heidegger 1995, 193).

46. Heidegger 1995, 177.

47. As Heidegger (1995, 195–96) writes, "The stone is without world. The stone is lying on the path, for example. We can say that the stone is exerting a certain pressure upon the surface of the earth. It is 'touching' the earth. But what we call 'touching' here is not a form of touching at all in the stronger sense of the word. It is not at all like *that* relationship which the lizard has to the stone on which it lies basking in the sun. And the touching implied in both these cases is above all not the same as *that* touch which we experience when we rest our hand upon the head

of another human being . . . the earth is *not given* for the stone as an underlying support which bears it, let alone given as earth . . . the stone lies on the path. If we throw it into the meadow then it will lie wherever it falls."

48. Turner 1965, 584.

49. Eck 1999, 374.

50. Eck 1999, 325.

51. Desjarlais 2016, 68.

52. As Desjarlais (2016, 69) writes, "The texts sound prayers, mete out instructions, and describe the look of deities. They urge their readers to act in certain ways, contemplate certain visions, and avoid some options in death while attending to those that will lead to either liberation or a good rebirth into a human body."

53. Hacking 1986; S. Lewis 2013; Obeyesekere 1985.

54. Bista 2008, 4.

55. For a discussion of the work of Dor Bahadur Bista and his critique of caste hierarchy in Nepal, see: J. Fisher 1997; Dennis 2020; Seale-Feldman and Romero 2020; Shakya 2020.

56. As Sara Lewis (2020, 53) writes, for the Tibetan Buddhist refugees with whom she worked "techniques such as thinking of all the others in the world who are experiencing similar (or worse) problems and wishing for happiness for all sentient beings are considered very skillful ways of working with distress."

57. As Savannah Shange (2019, 12) writes on social apocalypse and the ongoing life of settler colonialism, "for Black and indigenous people in the Americas, the apocalypse came and never left."

58. For work on ethics and responsivity, see Levinas 1985; Zigon 2007; Wentzer 2017.

59. Goldmann and Galea 2014, 170.

60. Goldmann and Galea 2014, 175.

61. For a discussion of the value of sociality and the pathology of isolation and solitude in the Newari community of Nepal, see Parish 1994.

62. In rural areas, women are disproportionately exposed to indoor air pollution such as smoke from burning wood and other combustibles in open hearths for cooking. Cardiovascular problems are the leading cause of death in Nepal, accounting for 25 percent of all deaths in 2015 (Aryal et al. 2020).

63. Bachelard 1988, 10.

64. For a discussion of Tibetan Buddhist elders' interpretations of the 2015 earthquakes as a sign of environmental exploitation and social, moral, and religious decline, see Childs et al. 2021.

65. Garfield 1995.

66. Obeyesekere 1985, 140.

67. Obeyesekere 1985, 147.

68. Mattingly 2019.

Chapter Three

1. Lord 2016.

2. A Village Development Committee (VDC) is a subunit of a district. This term was used until 2017 when VDCs were dissolved and replaced by *gaupalika*, rural municipalities.

3. Gibson 1966, 127.

4. Shneiderman 2014.

5. J. Lee and Ingold 2006, 79.

6. J. Lee and Ingold 2006.

7. For a nuanced discussion of the limits of homologous experiences as the basis for empathic insight and understanding, see Throop 2010a.

8. De Leon 2015.

9. Ingold 2010, S121.

10. Across his work, Tim Ingold explores human-environmental relationships by bringing together the anti-Cartesian phenomenology of Merleau-Ponty and Heidegger alongside Gibson's ecological psychology. This synthesis serves as the basis of Ingold's (2000, 171) anthropological approach, which takes the "agent-in-an-environment" as its point of departure and seeks to study "such processes as thinking, perceiving, remembering and learning . . . within the ecological contexts of people's interrelations with their environments."

11. As Sigmund Freud (2010, 5) writes, "Now let us, by a flight of imagination, suppose that Rome is not a human habitation but a psychical entity with a similarly long and copious past. An entity, that is to say, in which nothing that has once come into existence will have passed away and all the earlier phases of development continue to exist alongside the latest one . . . where the Coliseum now stands we could at the same time admire Nero's vanished Golden House."

12. Debord 2006.

13. Fassin 2010.

14. OED Online 2023.

15. Durkheim 1984.

16. Kropotkin 2006, xvi.

17. Spade 2020.

18. As Desjarlais and Throop (2011, 89) write in their review of the phenomenological anthropology and the concept of embodiment, the body is understood as "a locus from which our experience of the world is arrayed," it is the entity "by which, and through which, we actively experience the world." For foundational work on embodiment in anthropology, see Csordas 1990.

19. Khatri, Mishra, and Khanal 2017.

20. Djukanovic and Mach 1975; Packard 2016, 243.

21. Packard 2016, 242.

22. Sidel 1972.

23. The "accompaniment model" was inspired in part by liberation theology, the radical Latin American Catholic tradition dedicated to serving the poor so they might liberate themselves from historical structures of injustice. For a discussion of the intersection of liberation theology and public health, see Farmer 2014.

24. As Nancy Scheper-Hughes put it in an interview, adopting and adapting the sentiment of the work to anthropology, to be a "barefoot anthropologist" is "to do anthropology with our feet on the ground. You're grounded, you're really there. This doesn't mean that you're not theoretical but it's theory in action." See Brice 2017. For Scheper-Hughes, the idea of a "barefoot anthropology" informed her notion of "militant anthropology" in which she argued that responding to the call of the Other is the foundation for a universal ethics. For a description of "militant anthropology," see Scheper-Hughes 1995.

25. Following the global economic recession and emergence of HIV in the 1980s, investment in primary healthcare was soon displaced once again by a focus on disease eradication programs. For a detailed discussion of the challenges of implementing the Alma-Ata vision of

primary healthcare, see Packard 2016, 259. For an analysis of Nepal's early community health programs see Justice 1986.

26. World Health Organization 2008b.

27. World Health Organization 2008b, 1.

28. World Health Organization 2008a; Kohrt and Mendenhall 2016, 25.

29. Appel, Anand, and Gupta 2018, 6.

30. Larkin 2013.

31. Harvey and Knox 2012.

32. Pigg 1992; Dennis 2017; Rankin et al. 2017.

33. Schmidt 1994, 441.

34. Fassin 2010.

35. IOM 2023.

36. International Humanitarian Partnership 2019.

37. Spade 2020, 7.

38. Dean Spade (2020, 62) argues that in the charity model of disaster response, "people come looking for a job, wanting to climb a hierarchy, build a career or become 'important'" as opposed to those working in a mode of mutual aid who volunteer to help others because they are passionate about social justice and care for the community.

39. Berlant 2011.

40. Moral experience is a way of getting to the phenomenology of ethics and morality—that is, the way a wide range of experiences and ways of being-in-the-world can become ethical experiences for different people at different times. In contrast to approaches to morality focused on ethical self-cultivation, neo-Aristotelian virtue ethics concerned with the good, or approaches influenced by ordinary language philosophy, a phenomenological approach to moral experience opens up space for the exploration of moral sentiments. Based on this approach, scholars have explored a range of experiences that fall outside those generally assumed to delineate "moral and ethical domains" such that gesture, mood, anxiety, hope, or even the illicit might emerge as expressions of the ethical. Here any action or emotion has the potential to become a moral experience, depending on its singular meaning for a particular person. Likewise, the same experience might be a moral experience for one person but not another. For an introduction to the anthropology of "moral experience," see Zigon and Throop 2014. For approaches to morality focused on ethical self-cultivation, see Foucault 1997; Mahmood 2005. For an example of anthropological applications of neo-Aristotelian virtue ethics concerned with "the good," see Mattingly 2014. For approaches to the study of the anthropology of ethics and morality influenced by ordinary language philosophy, see Lambek 2010; Das 2012.

41. Freud 1958; Ogden 1989; Langs 2005.

42. Nepali paper (*lokta* paper) is a handcrafted, artisanal, fibrous paper made from the bark of the Daphne shrub. The paper is thick and highly durable.

43. For an analysis of *jham-jham*, somatization, and depression in rural Nepal, see Kohrt et al. 2005.

44. In Nepal, control of emotion is highly valued, especially among women. See Parish 1994.

45. A *cholo* is a women's blouse, often worn with a *sari*. A *lungi* is a skirt fashioned out of a single, wrapped piece of cloth.

46. "Walking affirms, suspects, tries out, transgresses, respects . . . the trajectories it 'speaks,'" writes Certeau (2011, 99).

47. Certeau 2011, 101.

Chapter Four

1. For an introduction to the concept of code-switching, see Gardner-Chloros 2009.

2. Words in italics were said in English, all other words were originally said in Nepali.

3. Strathern 2000.

4. Throop 2010b, 3.

5. Callon 1998.

6. Callon 1998, 247.

7. Levi-Strauss 1963; Csordas 1988; Csordas and Kleinman 1996; Craig 2012.

8. Young 1976.

9. Waldram 2000.

10. R. Scott 2014, 1.

11. Daston and Galison 2007.

12. Daston and Galison 2007, 17. However, as Donna Haraway (1988) reminds us, it is ultimately impossible to achieve a purely objective view from nowhere. Despite how hard one may strive for total objectivity, all knowledge is situated in a particular body.

13. Redfield 2013, 15.

14. Prince et al. 2007; Bemme and D'souza 2014; Packard 2016, 285.

15. Abramowitz and Kleinman 2008.

16. As global mental health practitioner Wietse Tol and colleagues (2014, 349) write of the challenges of RCTs in humanitarian settings, "it would be unethical not to conduct research and evaluations on MHPSS interventions in emergencies, given the need for more evidence in this field; while it would also be unethical to conduct such research without benefit to beneficiaries."

17. Dajani et al. 2018.

18. Biruk 2012; Adams 2016.

19. Singal, Higgins, and Waljee 2014.

20. In the field of humanitarianism money flows much faster than in the field of development. As one development worker I spoke with in Nepal put it, the speed of humanitarianism is so accelerated that "one million, one page" is their mode of budget justification.

21. In their work on the rise of evidence-based medicine, Stefan Timmermans and Marc Berg (2003, 8) note that "the notion that predictability, accountability, and objectivity will follow uniformity belongs to the Enlightenment master narratives promising progress through increased rationality and control."

22. Adams 2016, 11.

23. Engle Merry 2016, 1.

24. J. W. Scott 1991; Desjarlais 1994; Throop 2003; 2010b.

25. For example, in 2020 six Dalit boys were killed in Rukum district by members of a high-caste community after one of the boys visited the home of his high-caste girlfriend. See R. Adhikari 2020.

26. Varma 2016b.

27. Ahearn 2001.

28. Although Ram does not mention the caste of the girl, this clandestine relationship may have been an inter-caste affair, which might explain the extreme nature of his paranoia. In Nepal and India, Dalit men are frequently threatened and murdered by mobs of high-caste men for being in romantic relationships with high-caste women.

29. Ram's encounter with Christianity was likely facilitated by others in the Dalit community. Although proselytizing is illegal in Nepal, Christianity is rapidly growing especially among

Dalit communities. Many Dalit people find the inclusivity and nondiscrimination of Christianity appealing, and see conversion to Christianity as not only a source of welfare support but also offering an experience of freedom and liberation from the caste system that is embedded in Hinduism (Pariyar et al. 2021).

30. Harper 2014.

31. As Latour (1986, 16) vividly writes, "Bleeding and screaming rats are quickly dispatched. What is extracted from them is a tiny set of figures."

32. Here I follow Sienna Craig (2012, 5), who offers the term *social ecologies* as a way of understanding medical pluralism that captures the "interrelationships among environmental, socioeconomic, biological, political, and cosmological sources of, or explanations for, health problems."

33. Pigg 1996; Varma 2020.

34. Csordas and Kleinman 1996, 20.

35. Govindrajan 2015; 2018.

36. The Free Drugs List is a list of essential medicines to be provided to all citizens of Nepal free of cost. As of the fiscal year of 2020–21 (2075–76 Bikram Sambat) the list included seventy medicines, seventeen of which are used in the treatment of mental illness. See Government of Nepal 2020; Singh et al. 2017.

37. World Health Organization 2008a; World Health Organization and United Nations High Commissioner for Refugees 2015.

38. Aviv 2019.

39. Callon 1998.

40. Young 1976.

41. Callon 1998.

42. Freud 1917.

43. "Prolonged grief disorder" is defined as the persistent and pervasive longing for and preoccupation with the deceased in which bereavement exceeds cultural norms. See Killikelly and Maercker 2018.

44. Freud 2003.

45. Craig 2012, 7.

46. Breslau 2000, 185; Fassin 2012.

47. Breslau 2000, 183.

48. Ticktin 2011; Fassin 2012; R. Scott 2014.

49. Nguyen 2010.

50. Husserl 1970; Daston and Galison 2007.

51. Throop 2003; Adams 2016.

52. Roberts 2021, 356.

Chapter Five

1. See Bruslé 2009; Pattison 2013.

2. World Bank 2022.

3. Pattison 2013.

4. Government of Nepal 2022, 108–11.

5. Pattison 2014.

6. Government of Nepal 2022, 108.

7. Government of Nepal 2022, 111.

8. Pattison and Acharya 2023.

9. Ticktin 2011.

10. See Ticktin 2011; 2017.

11. See Ticktin 2006; James 2010.

12. Ticktin 2011; Redfield 2013.

13. Agamben 1998, 133.

14. Foucault 1978; 2003; Stevenson 2012; 2014; Garcia 2014; Zigon 2019.

15. Levinas 1998; Stevenson 2014; Zigon 2019.

16. Stevenson 2012, 578 .

17. Garcia 2014; Zigon 2019.

18. Cassin et al. 2014, 125.

19. Cassin et al. 2014, 125.

20. B. Fisher and Tronto 1990, 40.

21. Tronto 1998, 16–17.

22. Schmidt 1994, 303.

23. Perpich 2008.

24. As Levinas (1969, 215) writes, "to hear [the Other's] destitution which cries out for justice . . . is to posit oneself as responsible . . ."

25. Dufourmantelle 2018, 26.

26. Turner 1965, 206.

27. Kohrt and Jallah 2016.

28. Harper, Rawal, and Subedi 2011, 6.

29. For a discussion of the intersection of eventfulness, slow violence, and precarity see Allison 2013; Raschig 2017; Ahmann 2018. For literature on "slow disasters," particularly in relation to toxic exposure, see Fortun 2001; Nixon 2011; Liboiron, Tironi, and Calvillo 2018.

30. P. M. Shrestha 2023.

31. Hardt and Negri 2000, 18.

32. Hagaman, Maharjan, and Kohrt 2016.

33. Anthropological research on suicide in Nepal has found that incidents are commonly preceded by abuse, interpersonal conflict, migration, and family history of suicidal behavior. While suicides among women were often connected to physical and emotional abuse as well as shame due to loss of *ijjat* (honor), suicides among men were frequently related to alcohol abuse and the inability to live up to social expectations. See Hagaman et al. 2018.

34. Turin 2002.

35. See Freud 1989.

36. For Melanie Klein (1975, 313) reparation is a means through which the subject can repair the negative effects that her (real or imagined) acts of destruction have had on the people she loves.

37. Laplanche and Pontalis 1973, 388.

38. M. Klein 1975, 312.

39. M. Klein 1975, 312.

40. In a sense, counselors helped to "emplot" their clients so they could begin to visualize alternate futures (Mattingly 1994).

41. The miracle question intervention is a central technique in solutions-focused therapy, a therapeutic approach designed to help clients identify their goals and what they need to do to attain them. See Shazer 1985.

42. Strong and Pyle 2009, 329.

43. Steinbrecher, Jordan, and Turns 2021.

44. For work on debriefing theory in disaster psychiatry, see Breslau 2000. For an example of a postdisaster intervention focused on debriefing in Turkey, see Dole 2020.

45. Al-Saji 2014.

46. For a discussion of "dark anthropology," see Ortner 2016. For an outline of "otherwise anthropology," see McTighe and Raschig 2019.

47. For Elizabeth Povinelli (2011), examples of "alternative social projects" range from an Indigenous-led augmented-reality GPS mapping project to the underground practice of União do Vegetal, a Brazilian ayahuasca religion that was criminalized in the US until 2006.

48. Povinelli 2011, 129.

49. Zigon 2019, 158.

50. Zigon 2019.

51. Dufourmantelle 2018, 77.

52. Willen 2014, 86.

53. In her definition of *sital*, Ruth Laila Schmidt (1994, 594) offers the following example to demonstrate common use: "the porters are sitting in the shade [*sital*] of a tree and resting."

54. Stern 2004, 269.

55. Stern 2004.

56. Stern 2004, 167.

57. Dufourmantelle 2018, 6.

58. As Veena Das (2015, 70) writes, ordinary ethics "describes one modality of being in the world in relation to . . . malignancies; as an anthropologist I feel that making the effort to describe what such an ethics entails, how the small quotidian acts stand up to the horrific, is one way I can keep fidelity with the people I have worked with."

59. Lempert 2013, 371.

60. Mattingly 1994.

61. As Cheryl Mattingly (1994, 817) writes, "to see myself as a story, or a series of stories, is to see my life in time as stretching out toward possibilities (both hopeful and fearful) which I have some influence in bringing about."

62. As Das (2012, 145) writes, "it seems that the 'ordinary ethics' evident in such gestures have the potential to generate an eventual everyday from the ruins of the actual everyday by putting together the rubbles and ruins and learning to live in that very space of devastation once again." For a discussion of the "pragmatics of scale" that attends to "the social circumstances, dynamics, and consequences of scale-making as social practice and project," see E. S. Carr and Lempert 2016, 9. For a discussion of the "everydayness" of world building, see Zigon 2019.

Conclusion

1. Sedgwick 2003, 130.

2. Sedgwick 2003, 146. At the same time, attending to the *intersubjective otherwise*, to small moments of kindness, gentleness, hope, imagination, and acts of solidarity as they arise in the midst of humanitarianism, carries risks. In this ethnographic attentiveness there is a danger of softening the force of vitally necessary critiques of a regime of care that perpetuates structural violence. There is also the possibility that one may be projecting one's own desire for the good in the midst of crushing despair. As Lauren Berlant (2011, 122) writes, in projects of reparative

NOTES TO PAGES 132-139

reading there is a risk of "misrecognition," that is, "the psychic process by which fantasy calibrates what we encounter so that we can imagine that some thing or someone can fulfil our desire." Or, as Robyn Wiegman (2014, 19) puts it, reparative readings may ultimately be about "finding interpretations that can sustain us." These warnings remind us that we must not be naïve in our engagement with reparative readings.

3. In *Chaosmosis*, Félix Guattari sees psychotherapy as a tool for desubjectification—that is, a space where the subject can loosen itself free from capitalist desires and transform into new ways of being. Here Guattari (1995, 120) poses the question: "How do we change mentalities, how do we reinvent social practices that would give back to humanity—if we ever had it—not only for its own survival, but equally for the future of all life on the planet, for animal and vegetable species, likewise for incorporeal species such as music, the arts, cinema, the relation with time, love and compassion for others, the feeling of fusion at the heart of the cosmos?" Guattari argues that new forms of subjectivity can be produced through a vast range of social, aesthetic, and self-practices, including but not limited to film, literature, institutional psychotherapy, psychoanalysis, poetry, experimental pedagogies, architecture, and even urban planning. See also Guattari 2000, 68.

4. Al-Saji 2014.

5. Ticktin 2011; Fassin 2012.

6. Fassin 2012, 254.

7. As Throop (2010b, 271) writes, "what escapes typification, what resists a present-at-hand rendering of being as a type of category, quality, or thing, is precisely what Levinas terms 'the face.' In his words, the face refers to 'the way in which the other presents himself, *exceeding the idea of the other in me.'* "

8. Fassin 2012, 254.

9. For work on attuned care versus the anonymity of biopolitical care, see Stevenson 2014; Zigon 2019.

10. Stuelke 2021.

11. Stuelke 2021, 17.

12. As Peter Redfield (2024, 517) has noted in his reflections on the limits of humanitarian reason, "writing critically about humanitarianism at a moment when hospitals are again bombed freely—without even the pretense of an apology—comes with a particular pathos."

13. Heidegger 1993; Shneiderman et al. 2023.

14. Pach, Rimal, and Shrestha 2002; Seale-Feldman 2019.

15. NPR 3,000 was a considerable sum of money, especially for someone living in a rural village without a salaried job.

16. Summerfield 2013. For an overview of this debate, see Bemme and D'souza 2014.

17. Patel et al. 2018.

18. As Latour (2004) has argued, instead of deconstructing "matters of fact" (such as the fact of a mental health crisis), a more generous mode of critique involves following "matters of concern" and the gathering—of people, ideas, technologies, geology—that brings them into being.

19. Acts of repair are based on what the child imagines the Other needs, not on what the Other has themselves experienced or requested. See, M. Klein 1975.

20. Laubender 2019, 53.

21. Berlant 2011, 124.

22. On magic bullet approaches in global health, see Biehl and Petryna 2013; Packard 2016.

23. WHO Special Initiative for Mental Health 2021.

24. As Das (2015, 116) writes, "it is in the everyday that we might find the work of repair that is constantly engaged whether through creation of ritual spaces, or through silent unremarkable acts of caring or of absorbing the poisonous knowledge that large and small events secrete into our lives." See also Cousins 2023; J. S. Lewis 2024; Thomas 2024.

25. Graan 2022.

26. Arendt 1971; Mattingly 2019; Zigon 2019.

27. Garfield 1995, 87–99.

28. Garfield 1995, 56.

Bibliography

Abramowitz, Sharon. 2009. "Psychosocial Liberia: Managing Suffering in Post-Conflict Life." PhD diss., Harvard University.

Abramowitz, Sharon. 2014. *Searching for Normal in the Wake of the Liberian War.* University of Pennsylvania Press.

Abramowitz, Sharon, and Arthur Kleinman. 2008. "Humanitarian Intervention and Cultural Translation: A Review of the IASC Guidelines on Mental Health and Psychosocial Support in Emergency Settings." *Intervention* 6 (3/4): 219–27.

Acland, Sarah. 2002. "Mental Health Services in Primary Care: The Case of Nepal." In *World Mental Health Casebook: Social and Mental Health Programs in Low-Income Countries,* edited by Alex Cohen, Arthur Kleinman, and Benedetto Saraceno. Kluwer Academic/Plenum.

Adams, Vincanne. 2013. *Markets of Sorrow, Labors of Faith: New Orleans in the Wake of Katrina.* Duke University Press.

Adams, Vincanne. 2016. Introduction to *Metrics: What Counts in Global Health.* Edited by Vincanne Adams. Duke University Press.

Adams, Vincanne, Dominique Behague, Carlo Caduff, Ilana Löwy, and Francisco Ortega. 2019. "Re-Imagining Global Heath through Social Medicine." *Global Public Health: An International Journal for Research, Policy and Practice* 14 (10): 1383–1400.

Adhikari, Aditya. 2014. *The Bullet and the Ballot Box: The Story of Nepal's Maoist Revolution.* Verso.

Adhikari, Jagannath, and Mary Hobley. 2015. "'Everyone Is Leaving. Who Will Sow Our Fields?' The Livelihood Effects on Women of Male Migration from Khotang and Udaypur Districts, Nepal, to the Gulf Countries and Malaysia." *HIMALAYA, The Journal of the Association for Nepal and Himalayan Studies* 35 (1): 11–23.

Adhikari, Rojita. 2020. "Nepal to Investigate Dalit Killings Following Arranged Marriage Dispute." *The Guardian,* June 13, 2020, sec. Global development. https://www.theguardian.com/global-development/2020/jun/13/nepal-to-investigate-dalit-killings-following-arranged-marriage-dispute.

Agamben, Giorgio. 1998. *Homo Sacer: Sovereign Power and Bare Life.* Stanford University Press.

Ahearn, Laura M. 2001. *Invitations to Love: Literacy, Love Letters, & Social Change in Nepal.* University of Michigan Press.

Ahmann, Chloe. 2018. "'It's Exhausting to Create an Event Out of Nothing': Slow Violence and the Manipulation of Time." *Cultural Anthropology* 33 (1): 142–71.

Ahmed, Sara. 2006. *Queer Phenomenology: Orientations, Objects, Others.* Duke University Press.

Allison, Anne. 2013. *Precarious Japan.* Duke University Press.

Al-Saji, Alia. 2014. "A Phenomenology of Hesitation: Interrupting Racializing Habits of Seeing." In *Living Alterities: Phenomenology, Embodiment, and Race,* edited by Emily Lee. State University of New York Press.

Anderson, Ben. 2009. "Affective Atmospheres." *Emotion, Space and Society* 2:77–81.

Appel, Hannah, Nikhil Anand, and Akhil Gupta. 2018. "Temporality, Politics, and the Promise of Infrastructure." In *The Promise of Infrastrucutre,* edited by Nikhil Anand, Akhil Gupta, and Hannah Appel. Duke University Press.

Apte, Vaman Shivaram. 1957. *Revised and Enlarged Edition of Prin. V. S. Apte's The Practical Sanskrit-English Dictionary.* Prasad Prakashan.

Arendt, Hannah. 1971. "Thinking and Moral Considerations: A Lecture." *Social Research* 38 (3): 417–46.

Arendt, Hannah. 2018. *Thinking Without a Banister: Essays in Understanding 1953–1975.* Edited by Jerome Kohn. Schocken Books.

Aryal, Anu, David Citrin, Scott Halliday, Anirudh Kumar, Prajwol Nepal, Archana Shrestha, Rachel Nugent, and Dan Schwarz. 2020. "Estimated Cost for Cardiovascular Disease Risk-Based Management at a Primary Healthcare Center in Nepal." *Global Health Research and Policy* 5 (2).

Associated Press. 2017. "Tired of the Cold Wait, Nepal Quake Survivors Rebuild." January 4, 2017. https://apnews.com/article/2d453dedd5c344beb38a9b6aa3e53237.

Austin, J.L. 1962. *How to Do Things with Words.* Harvard University Press.

Aviv, Rachel. 2019. "Bitter Pill: The Challenge of Going off Psychiatric Drugs." *The New Yorker,* 2019. https://www.newyorker.com/magazine/2019/04/08/the-challenge-of-going-off-psychiatric-drugs.

Bachelard, Gaston. 1988. *Water and Dreams: An Essay on the Imagination of Matter.* Translated by Edith Farrell. Dallas Institute Publications.

Barrios, Roberto. 2016. "Resilience: A Commentary from the Vantage Point of Anthropology." *Annals of Anthropological Practice* 40 (1): 28–38.

Barrios, Roberto. 2017. "What Does the Catastrophe Reveal for Whom? The Anthropology of Crises and Disasters at the Onset of the Anthropocene." *Annual Review of Anthropology* 46:151–66.

Bemme, Doerte, and Nicole A. D'souza. 2014. "Global Mental Health and Its Discontents: An Inquiry into the Making of Global and Local Scale." *Transcultural Psychiatry* 51 (6): 850–74.

Bennett, Claire. 2015. "The Nepal Earthquakes Have Unleashed a Mental Health Disaster." *The Guardian,* May 15, 2015, sec. Opinion.

Benton, Adia. 2015. *HIV Exceptionalism: Development through Disease in Sierra Leone.* University of Minnesota Press.

Berlant, Lauren. 2011. *Cruel Optimism.* Duke University Press.

Biehl, João, and Adriana Petryna, eds. 2013. *When People Come First: Critical Studies in Global Health.* Princeton University Press.

Biruk, Crystal. 2012. "Seeing Like a Research Project: Producing 'High Quality Data' in AIDS Research in Malawi." *Medical Anthropology* 31 (4): 347–66.

Bista, Dor Bahadur. 2008. *Fatalism and Development: Nepal's Struggle for Modernization*. Orient Longman.

Bond, David. 2013. "Governing Disaster: The Political Life of the Environment during the BP Oil Spill." *Cultural Anthropology* 28 (4): 694–715.

Breslau, Joshua. 2000. "Globalizing Disaster Trauma: Psychiatry, Science, and Culture after the Kobe Earthquake." *Ethos* 28 (2): 174–97.

Brice, Anne. 2017. "Celebrating 'Barefoot Anthropology'—a Q&A with Nancy Scheper-Hughes." *Berkeley News* (blog), April 28, 2017. https://news.berkeley.edu/2017/04/28/celebrating -barefoot-anthropology-nancy-scheper-hughes/.

Brown, Wendy. 2009. "Untimeliness and Punctuality: Critical Theory in Dark Times." In *Edgework: Critical Essays on Knowledge and Politics*. Princeton University Press.

Bruslé, Tristan. 2009. "Who's in a Labour Camp? A Socio-Economic Analysis of Nepalese Migrants in Qatar." *European Bulletin of Himalayan Research* 35–36:154–73.

Butler, Judith. 2016. *Frames of War: When Is Life Grievable?* Verso.

Calhoun, Craig. 2010. "The Idea of Emergency: Humanitarian Action and Global (Dis)Order." In *Contemporary States of Emergency: The Politics of Military and Humanitarian Interventions*. Zone Books.

Callon, Michel. 1998. "An Essay on Framing and Overflowing: Economic Externalities Revisited by Sociology." *Sociological Review* 46 (1): 244–69.

Cameron, Mary. 2019. *Three Fruits: Nepali Ayurvedic Doctors on Health, Nature, and Social Change*. Lexington Books.

Carr, E. Summerson, and Michael Lempert. 2016. "Introduction: Pragmatics of Scale." In *Scale: Discourse and Dimensions of Social Life*, edited by E. Summerson Carr and Michael Lempert. University of California Press.

Cassin, Barbara, Emily Apter, Jacques Lezra, and Michael Wood, eds. 2014. *Dictionary of Untranslatables: A Philosophical Lexicon*. Translated by Steven Rendall, Christian Hubert, Jeffrey Mehlman, Nathanael Stein, and Michael Syrotinski. Princeton University Press.

Certeau, Michel de. 2011. *The Practice of Everyday Life*. University of California Press.

Chase, Liana, Kedar Marhatta, Kripa Sidgel, Sujan Shrestha, Kamal Gautman, Nagendra P. Luitel, Bhogendra Raj Dotel, and Ruben Samuel. 2018. "Building Back Better? Taking Stock of the Post-Earthquake Mental Health and Psychosocial Response in Nepal." *International Journal of Mental Health Systems* 12 (44).

Childs, Geoff, Sienna Craig, Christina Juenger, and Kristine Hildebrandt. 2021. "This Is the End: Earthquake Narratives and Buddhist Prophesies of Decline." *HIMALAYA, The Journal of the Association for Nepal and Himalayan Studies* 40 (2): 32–49.

Choi, Vivian. 2015. "Anticipatory States: Tsunami, War, and Insecurity in Sri Lanka." *Cultural Anthropology* 30 (2): 286–309.

Cohen, Alex, Arthur Kleinman, and Benedetto Saraceno, eds. 2002. *World Mental Health Casebook: Social and Mental Health Programs in Low-Income Countries*. Kluwer Academic/Plenum Publishers.

Conze, Edward, trans. 2001. *Buddhist Wisdom: The Diamond Sutra and the Heart Sutra*. Vintage Books.

Cousins, Thomas. 2023. *The Work of Repair: Capacity After Colonialism in the Timber Plantations of South Africa*. Fordham University Press.

Craig, Sienna. 2012. *Healing Elements: Efficacy and the Social Ecologies of Tibetan Medicine*. University of California Press.

Csordas, Thomas. 1988. "Elements of Charismatic Persuasion and Healing." *Medical Anthropology Quarterly* 2 (2): 121–42.

Csordas, Thomas. 1990. "Embodiment as a Paradigm for Anthropology." *Ethos* 18 (1): 5–47.

Csordas, Thomas. 1994. *The Sacred Self: A Cultural Phenomenology of Charismatic Healing.* University of California Press.

Csordas, Thomas, and Arthur Kleinman. 1996. "The Therapeutic Process." In *Handbook of Medical Anthropology: Contemporary Theory and Method.* Greenwood Press.

Dajani, Rana, Kristin Hadfield, Stan van Uum, Michael Greff, and Catherine Panter-Brick. 2018. "Hair Cortisol Concentrations in War-Affected Adolescents: A Prospective Intervention Trial." *Psychoneuroendocrinology* 89:138–46.

Das, Veena. 2007. "Three Portraits of Grief and Mourning." In *Life and Words.* University of California Press.

Das, Veena. 2012. "Ordinary Ethics." In *A Companion to Moral Anthropology.* Wiley-Blackwell.

Das, Veena. 2015. "What Does Ordinary Ethics Look Like?" In *Four Lectures on Ethics: Anthropological Perspectives*, by Michael Lambek, Veena Das, Didier Fassin, and Webb Keane. HAU Books.

Daston, Lorraine, and Peter Galison. 2007. *Objectivity.* Zone Books.

De Leon, Jason. 2015. *The Land of Open Graves: Living and Dying on the Migrant Trail.* University of California Press.

Debord, Guy. 2006. "Introduction to a Critique of Urban Geography." In *Situationist International Anthology*, translated by Ken Knabb. Bureau of Public Secrets.

Deleuze, Gilles, and Félix Guattari. 1994. *What Is Philosophy?* Translated by Hugh Tomlinson and Graham Burchell. Columbia University Press.

Dennis, Dannah. 2017. "On the Road to Nowhere: Stalled Politics and Urban Infrastructure in Kathmandu." *HIMALAYA, The Journal of the Association for Nepal and Himalayan Studies* 37 (1): 98–106.

Dennis, Dannah. 2020. "Theorizing Privilege with Dor Bahadur Bista." *Fieldsites* (blog), December 10, 2020. https://culanth.org/fieldsights/theorizing-privilege-with-dor-bahadur-bista.

Desjarlais, Robert. 1992. *Body and Emotion: The Aesthetics of Illness and Healing in the Nepal Himalayas.* University of Pennsylvania Press.

Desjarlais, Robert. 1994. "Struggling Along: The Possibilities for Experience among the Homeless Mentally Ill." *American Anthropologist* 96 (4): 886–901.

Desjarlais, Robert. 1997. *Shelter Blues: Sanity and Selfhood Among the Homeless.* University of Pennsylvania Press.

Desjarlais, Robert. 2016. *Subject to Death: Life and Loss in a Buddhist World.* University of Chicago Press.

Desjarlais, Robert, Leon Eisenberg, Byron Good, and Arthur Kleinman. 1996. *World Mental Health: Problems and Priorities in Low-Income Countries.* Oxford University Press.

Desjarlais, Robert, and C. Jason Throop. 2011. "Phenomenological Approaches in Anthropology." *Annual Review of Anthropology* 40:87–102.

Devereux, George. 1951. *Reality and Dream: Psychotherapy of a Plains Indian.* International Universities Press.

Devkota, Laxmi Prasad. 1980. *Nepali Visions, Nepali Dreams: The Poetry of Laxmi Prasad Devkota.* Translated by David Rubin. Columbia University Press.

Djukanovic, V., and E. P. Mach, eds. 1975. *Alternative Approaches to Meeting Basic Health Needs in Developing Countries.* WHO.

Dole, Christopher. 2020. "Experiments in Scale: Humanitarian Psychiatry in Post-Disaster Turkey." *Medical Anthropology* 39 (5): 398–412.

Dole, Christopher. 2023. "Psychiatry, Disaster, Security: Mediterranean Assemblages." *Culture, Medicine and Psychiatry* 47:62–81.

Dufourmantelle, Anne. 2018. *Power of Gentleness: Meditations on the Risk of Living*. Translated by Katherine Payne and Vincent Sallé. Fordham University Press.

Dunn, Elizabeth Cullen. 2012. "The Chaos of Humanitarian Aid: Adhocracy in the Republic of Georgia." *Humanity: An International Journal of Human Rights, Humanitarianism, and Development* 3 (1): 1–23.

Durkheim, Emile. 1984. *The Division of Labor in Society*. Free Press.

Eck, Diana. 1999. *Banaras: City of Light*. Columbia University Press.

Engle Merry, Sally. 2016. *The Seductions of Quantification: Measuring Human Rights, Gender Violence, and Sex Trafficking*. University of Chicago Press.

Fanon, Frantz. 1965. "This Is the Voice of Algeria." In *A Dying Colonialism*, translated by Haakon Chevalier. Grove Press.

Fanon, Frantz. 2008. *Black Skin, White Masks*. Translated by Richard Philcox. Grove Press.

Farmer, Paul. 2014. "Sacred Medicine: How Liberation Theology Can Inform Public Health." *Sojourners*, January 2014. https://sojo.net/magazine/january-2014/sacred-medicine.

Fassin, Didier. 2008. "The Humanitarian Politics of Testimony: Subjectification through Trauma in the Israeli-Palestinian Conflict." *Cultural Anthropology* 23 (3): 531–58.

Fassin, Didier. 2010. "Noli Me Tangere: The Moral Untouchability of Humanitarianism." In *Forces of Compassion: Humanitarianism Between Ethics and Politics*. School for Advanced Research Press.

Fassin, Didier. 2012. *Humanitarian Reason: A Moral History of the Present*. University of California Press.

Fassin, Didier. 2021. "Crisis." In *Words and Worlds: A Lexicon for Dark Times*, edited by Veena Das and Didier Fassin, 261–76. Duke University Press.

Fassin, Didier, and Mariella Pandolfi, eds. 2013. *Contemporary States of Emergency: The Politics of Military and Humanitarian Interventions*. Zone Books.

Fassin, Didier, and Richard Rechtman. 2009. *The Empire of Trauma: An Inquiry into the Condition of Victimhood*. Princeton University Press.

Fisher, Berenice, and Joan Tronto. 1990. "Towards a Feminist Theory of Care." In *Circles of Care*, edited by E. Abel and M. Nelson. State University of New York Press.

Fisher, James. 1997. "An Interview with Dor Bahadur Bista." *HIMALAYA, The Journal of the Association for Nepal and Himalayan Studies* 17 (1): 25–32.

Fortun, Kim. 2001. *Advocacy After Bhopal: Environmentalism, Disaster, New Global Orders*. University of Chicago Press.

Foucault, Michel. 1972. *The Archaeology of Knowledge and the Discourse on Language*. Translated by A.M. Sheridan Smith. Pantheon Books.

Foucault, Michel. 1978. "Right of Death and Power Over Life." In *The History of Sexuality, Vol. 1: An Introduction*, translated by Robert Hurley, 137–48. Pantheon Books.

Foucault, Michel. 1997. "The Ethics of the Concern for Self as a Practice of Freedom." In *Ethics: Subjectivity and Truth*, edited by Paul Rabinow, translated by Robert Hurley and others. New Press.

Foucault, Michel. 2003. *"Society Must Be Defended" Lectures at the Collège de France, 1975–76*. Translated by David Macey. Picador.

Foyle, Marjory. 1987. "Report on Visit to Nepal." H-03.04.01/0032, Box 80, Folder 8–9. Archives of United Mission to Nepal, Record Group No. 212, Special Collections, Yale Divinity School Library, New Haven, CT.

Freud, Sigmund. 1917. "Mourning and Melancholia." In *The Standard Edition of the Complete Psychological Works of Sigmund Freud, Volume XIV (1914–1916): On the History of the Psycho-Analytic Movement, Papers on Metapsychology and Other Works*, translated by James Strachey, 237–58. Hogarth Press.

Freud, Sigmund. 1958. "On Beginning the Treatment (Further Recommendations on the Technique of Psycho-Analysis)." In *The Standard Edition of the Complete Psychological Works of Sigmund Freud, Volume XII (1911–1913): The Case of Schreber, Papers on Technique and Other Works*, translated by James Strachey, 123–44. Hogarth Press.

Freud, Sigmund. 1989. "Observations on Transference-Love." In *The Freud Reader*, edited by Peter Gay. W. W. Norton.

Freud, Sigmund. 2003. "Letter from Freud to Ludwig Binswanger, April 11, 1929." In *The Sigmund Freud-Ludwig Binswanger Correspondence, 1908–1938*, edited by Gerhard Fichtner, translated by A. J. Pomerans. Other Press.

Freud, Sigmund. 2010. *Civilization and Its Discontents*. W. W. Norton.

Garcia, Angela. 2014. "The Promise: On Morality of the Marginal and the Illicit." *Ethos* 42 (1): 51–64.

Gardner-Chloros, Penelope. 2009. *Code-Switching*. Cambridge University Press.

Garfield, Jay, trans. 1995. *The Fundamental Wisdom of the Middle Way: Nagarjuna's Mulamadhyamakakarika*. Oxford University Press.

Gibson, James. 1966. *The Ecological Approach to Visual Perception*. Houghton Mifflin.

Giordano, Cristiana. 2014. *Migrants in Translation: Caring and the Logics of Difference in Contemporary Italy*. University of California Press.

Goffman, Erving. 1974. *Frame Analysis: An Essay on the Organization of Experience*. Northeastern University Press.

Goldmann, Emily, and Sandro Galea. 2014. "Mental Health Consequences of Disasters." *Annual Review of Public Health* 35:169–83.

Government of Nepal. 2020. "Revised List of Free Essential Medicines to Be Purchased for the Fiscal Year 2075/76." http://dohs.gov.np/wp-content/uploads/2018/08/Free_Drugs_List.pdf (accessed December 10, 2023).

Government of Nepal. 2022. "Nepal Labour Migration Report 2022." Government of Nepal–Ministry of Labour, Employment, and Social Security.

Government of Nepal, National Statistics Office. 2023. "Nepal Population and Housing Census 2021: National Report on Caste/Ethnicity, Language & Religion." https://censusnepal.cbs .gov.np/results/cast-ethnicity.

Govindrajan, Radhika. 2015. "'The Goat That Died for Family': Animal Sacrifice and Interspecies Kinship in India's Central Himalayas." *American Ethnologist* 42 (3): 504–19.

Govindrajan, Radhika. 2018. *Animal Intimacies: Interspecies Relatedness in India's Central Himalayas*. University of Chicago Press.

Graan, Andrew. 2022. "What Was the Project? Thoughts on Genre and the Project Form." *Journal of Cultural Economy* 15 (6): 735–52.

Graner, Elvira. 2009. "Leaving Hills and Plains, Migration and Remittances in Nepal." *European Bulletin of Himalayan Research* 35–36:24–42.

Guattari, Félix. 1995. *Chaosmosis: An Ethico-Aesthetic Paradigm*. Translated by Paul Bains and Julian Pefanis. Indiana University Press.

Guattari, Félix. 2000. *The Three Ecologies*. Translated by Ian Pindar and Paul Sutton. Athlone Press.

Guenther, Lisa. 2013. *Solitary Confinement: Social Death and Its Afterlives*. University of Minnesota Press.

Guenther, Lisa. 2021. "Six Senses of Critique for Critical Phenomenology." *Puncta: Journal of Critical Phenomenology* 4 (2): 5–23.

Günel, Gökçe, Saiba Varma, and Chika Watanabe. 2020. "A Manifesto for Patchwork Ethnography." *Fieldsights* (blog), June 9, 2020. https://culanth.org/fieldsights/a-manifesto-for-patchwork-ethnography.

Gunewardena, Nandini, and Mark Schuller, eds. 2008. *Capitalizing on Catastrophe: Neoliberal Strategies in Disaster Reconstruction*. AltaMira Press.

Hacking, Ian. 1986. "Making Up People." In *Reconstructing Individualism: Autonomy, Individuality, and the Self in Western Thought*, edited by Thomas C. Heller, Morton Sosna, and David E. Wellbery, 161–71. Stanford University Press.

Hagaman, Ashley, Seema Khadka, Amber Wutich, Shyam Lohani, and Brandon Kohrt. 2018. "Suicide in Nepal: Qualitative Findings from a Modified Caseseries Psychological Autopsy Investigation of Suicide Deaths." *Culture, Medicine and Psychiatry* 42 (3): 704–34.

Hagaman, Ashley, Uden Maharjan, and Brandon Kohrt. 2016. "Suicide Surveillance and Health Systems in Nepal: A Qualitative and Social Network Analysis." *International Journal of Mental Health Systems* 10 (46).

Haraway, Donna. 1988. "Situated Knowledges: The Science Question in Feminism and the Privilege of Partial Perspective." *Feminist Studies* 14 (3): 575–99.

Hardt, Michael, and Antonio Negri. 2000. *Empire*. Harvard University Press.

Hardt, Michael, and Antonio Negri. 2013. "Biopolitical Production." In *Biopolitics: A Reader*, edited by Timothy Campbell and Adam Sitze. Duke University Press.

Harper, Ian. 2014. *Development and Public Health in the Himalaya: Reflections on Healing in Contemporary Nepal*. Routledge.

Harper, Ian, Nabin Rawal, and Madhusudan Subedi. 2011. "Disputing Distribution: Ethics and Pharmaceutical Regulations in Nepal." *Studies in Nepali History and Society* 16 (1): 1–40.

Harrison, Faye. 2011. "Ethnography as Politics." In *Decolonizing Anthropology: Moving Further Toward an Anthropology for Liberation*, edited by Faye Harrison, 3rd ed. American Anthropological Association.

Harvey, Penny, and Hannah Knox. 2012. "The Enchantments of Infrastructure." *Mobilities* 7 (4): 521–36.

Heerden, Alastair van, Anubhuti Poudyal, Ashley Hagaman, Sujen Man Maharjan, Prabin Byanjankar, Dörte Bemme, Ada Thapa, and Brandon A. Kohrt. 2024. "Integration of Passive Sensing Technology to Enhance Delivery of Psychological Interventions for Mothers with Depression: The StandStrong Study." *Scientific Reports* 14 (1): 13535. https://doi.org/10.1038/s41598-024-63232-3.

Heidegger, Martin. 1993. "Building Dwelling Thinking." In *Basic Writings*, edited by David Farrell Krell. HarperCollins.

Heidegger, Martin. 1995. *The Fundamental Concepts of Metaphysics: World, Finitude, Solitude*. Translated by William McNeill and Nicholas Walker. Indiana University Press.

Heidegger, Martin. 2010. *Being and Time*. Translated by Joan Stambaugh. State University of New York Press.

Hickingbotham, David. 1985. "Pilot Community Mental Health Program." H-03.04.01/0011, Box 80, Folder 8–9. Archives of United Mission to Nepal, Record Group No. 212, Special Collections, Yale Divinity School Library, New Haven, CT.

Hickingbotham, David, and Christine Wright. n.d. "Training in Psychiatry for Community Health Workers in Nepal." H-03.04.01/0021, Box 80, Folder 8–9. Archives of United Mission to Nepal, Record Group No. 212, Special Collections, Yale Divinity School Library, New Haven, CT.

Hochschild, Arlie Russell. 1983. *The Managed Heart: Commercialization of Human Feeling.* University of California Press.

Hoffman, Susanna. 1999. "After Atlas Shrugged: Cultural Change or Persistence after a Disaster." In *The Angry Earth: Disaster in Anthropological Perspective*, edited by Anthony Oliver-Smith and Susanna Hoffman. Routledge.

Hoffman, Susanna, and Anthony Oliver-Smith, eds. 2002. *Catastrophe and Culture: The Anthropology of Disaster.* School for Advanced Research Press.

Holling, Crawford. 1973. "Resilience and Stability of Ecological Systems." *Annual Review of Ecology and Systematics* 4:1–23.

Husserl, Edmund. 1970. *The Crisis of European Sciences and Transcendental Phenomenology.* Translated by David Carr. Northwestern University Press.

Ingold, Tim. 2000. *The Perception of the Environment: Essays on Livelihood, Dwelling and Skill.* Routledge.

Ingold, Tim. 2010. "Footprints Through the Weather-World: Walking, Breathing, Knowing." *Journal of the Royal Anthropological Institute* 16 (s1): S121–39.

Inter-Agency Standing Committee (IASC). 2007. "IASC Guidelines on Mental Health and Psychosocial Support in Emergency Settings." IASC.

International Humanitarian Partnership (IHP). 2019. "Support Modules Catalogue." https://emergencymanual.iom.int/sites/g/files/tmzbdl1956/files/2023-05/92802_ihp_support_module_catalogue_jun19_1.pdf.

International Medical Corps (IMC). 2015. "International Medical Corps 2015 Annual Report." Los Angeles: International Medical Corps.

IOM. 2023. "Humanitarian Hubs | Emergency Manual." Humanitarian Hubs. May 22, 2023. https://emergencymanual.iom.int/humanitarian-hubs.

Jackson, Ruth. 2015. "Rebuilding a More Resilient Nepal: Key Recommendations for Reconstruction and Recovery." Oxfam International.

James, Erica Caple. 2010a. *Democratic Insecurities: Violence, Trauma, and Intervention in Haiti.* University of California Press.

James, Erica Caple. 2010b. "Ruptures, Rights, and Repair: The Political Economy of Trauma in Haiti." *Social Science & Medicine* 70:106–13.

Jha, Prashant. 2014. *Battles of the New Republic: A Contemporary History of Nepal.* Aleph Book Company.

Justice, Judith. 1986. *Policies, Plans, and People: Foreign Aid and Health Development.* University of California Press.

Kalofonos, Ippolytos Andreas. 2010. "'All I Eat Is ARVs': The Paradox of AIDS Treatment Interventions in Central Mozambique." *Medical Anthropology Quarterly* 24 (3): 363–80.

Khadka, Upasana. 2020. "In the Minds of Nepal's Migrant Workers: There Is a Mental Health Cost to the Country's Foreign Remittance-Dependent Economy." *Nepali Times*,

October 10, 2020. https://www.nepalitimes.com/here-now/in-the-minds-of-nepals-migrant -workers/.

Khatri, Resham Bahadur, Shiva Raj Mishra, and Vishnu Khanal. 2017. "Female Community Health Volunteers in Community-Based Health Programs of Nepal: Future Perspective." *Frontiers in Public Health* 5.

Killikelly, Clare, and Andreas Maercker. 2018. "Prolonged Grief Disorder for ICD-11: The Primacy of Clinical Utility and International Applicability." *European Journal of Psychotraumatology* 8, no. S6: 1476441.

Klein, Melanie. 1975. *Love, Guilt and Reparation and Other Works 1921–1945*. Free Press.

Klein, Naomi. 2007. *The Shock Doctrine: The Rise of Disaster Capitalism*. Picador.

Kleinman, Arthur. 1977. "Depression, Somatization and the 'New Cross-Cultural Psychiatry.'" *Social Science & Medicine* 11:3–10.

Kleinman, Arthur. 2009. "Global Mental Health: A Failure of Humanity." *The Lancet* 374 9690: 603–4.

Kohrt, Brandon, Richard Kunz, Jennifer Baldwin, Naba Koirala, Vidya Sharma, and Mahendra Nepal. 2005. "'Somatization' and 'Comorbidity': A Study of Jhum-Jhum and Depression in Rural Nepal." *Ethos* 33 (1): 125–47.

Kohrt, Brandon, and Ian Harper. 2008. "Navigating Diagnoses: Understanding Mind-Body Relations, Mental Health, and Stigma in Nepal." *Culture, Medicine and Psychiatry* 32:462–91.

Kohrt, Brandon, and D. J. Hruschka. 2010. "Nepali Concepts of Psychological Trauma: The Role of Idioms of Distress, Ethnopsychology and Ethnophysiology in Alleviating Suffering and Preventing Stigma." *Culture, Medicine and Psychiatry* 34 (2): 322–52.

Kohrt, Brandon, and Bill Jallah. 2016. "People, Praxis, and Power in Global Mental Health: Anthropology and the Experience Gap." In *Global Mental Health: Anthropological Perspectives*, edited by Brandon Kohrt and Emily Mendenhall, 259–76. Routledge.

Kohrt, Brandon, and Emily Mendenhall, eds. 2016. *Global Mental Health: Anthropological Perspectives*. Routledge.

Koirala, Bishweshwar Prasad. 2015. "Inaugural Address by PM Koirala at International Conference on Nepal's Reconstruction." *Nepal Foreign Affairs*, June 25, 2015. https://nepalforeign affairs.com/inaugural-address-by-pm-koirala-at-international-conference-on-nepals -reconstruction/.

Koselleck, Reinhart. 2006. "Crisis." *Journal of the History of Ideas* 67 (2): 357–400.

Kreps, Gary. 1995. "Disaster as Systemic Event and Social Catalyst: A Clarification of Subject Matter." *International Journal of Mass Emergencies and Disasters* 13 (3): 255–84.

Kropotkin, Peter. 2006. *Mutual Aid: A Factor of Evolution*. Dover.

Kunreuther, Laura. 2014. *Voicing Subjects: Public Intimacy and Mediation in Kathmandu*. University of California Press.

Lambek, Michael. 2010. Introduction to *Ordinary Ethics: Anthropology, Language, and Action*, edited by Michael Lambek. Fordham University Press.

Langs, Robert. 2005. "The Initial Contact with the Patient." In *The Technique of Psychoanlaytic Psychotherapy*, by Robert Langs. Rowman & Littlefield.

Laplanche, J., and J.-B. Pontalis. 1973. *The Language of Psychoanalysis*. Translated by Donald Nicholson-Smith. W. W. Norton.

Larkin, Brian. 2013. "The Politics and Poetics of Infrastructure." *Annual Review of Anthropology* 42:327–43.

Lassiter, Luke Eric. 2005. *The Chicago Guide to Collaborative Ethnography*. University of Chicago Press.

Latour, Bruno. 1986. "Visualisation and Cognition: Drawing Things Together." *Knowledge and Society: Studies in the Sociology of Culture Past and Present* 6:1–40.

Latour, Bruno. 2004. "Why Has Critique Run Out of Steam? From Matters of Fact to Matters of Concern." *Critical Inquiry* 30:225–48.

Laubender, Carolyn. 2019. "Beyond Repair: Interpretation, Reparation, and Melanie Klein's Clinical Play-Technique." *Studies in Gender and Sexuality* 20 (1): 51–67.

Lee, Joe, and Tim Ingold. 2006. "Fieldwork on Foot: Perceiving, Routing, Socializing." In *Locating the Field: Space, Place and Context in Anthropology*, edited by Simon Coleman and Peter Collins, 67–85. Berg.

Lempert, Michael. 2013. "No Ordinary Ethics." *Anthropological Theory* 13 (4): 370–93.

Levinas, Emmanuel. 1969. *Totality and Infinity: An Essay on Exteriority*. Translated by Alphonso Lingis. Duquense University Press.

Levinas, Emmanuel. 1985. *Ethics and Infinity*. Duquense University Press.

Levinas, Emmanuel. 1998. *Entre Nous: Thinking-Of-The-Other*. Columbia University Press.

Levi-Strauss, Claude. 1963. "The Effectiveness of Symbols." In *Structural Anthropology*. Basic Books.

Lewis, Jovan Scott. 2024. "Black Life Beyond Injury: Relational Repair and the Reparative Conjuncture." *Political Geography* 108: 102963.

Lewis, Sara. 2013. "Trauma and the Making of Flexible Minds in the Tibetan Exile Community." *Ethos* 41 (3): 313–36.

Lewis, Sara. 2020. *Spacious Minds: Trauma and Resilience in Tibetan Buddhism*. Cornell University Press.

Liboiron, Max, Manuel Tironi, and Nerea Calvillo. 2018. "Toxic Politics: Acting in a Permanently Polluted World." *Social Studies of Science* 48 (3): 331–49.

Linstrum, Erik. 2016. *Ruling Minds: Psychology in the British Empire*. Harvard University Press.

Livingston, Julie. 2012. *Improvising Medicine: An African Oncology Ward in an Emerging Cancer Epidemic*. Duke University Press.

Lord, Austin. 2016. "Citizens of a Hydropower Nation: Territory and Agency at the Frontiers of Hydropower Development in Nepal." *Economic Anthropology* 3:145–60.

Lord, Austin, and Jennifer Bradley. 2021. "Gathering Absences and Presences: Memory Work, Photographs, and Affective Recovery in the Langtang Valley." In *Epicentre to Aftermath: Rebuilding and Remembering in the Wake of Nepal's Earthquakes*, edited by Michael Hutt, Mark Liechty, and Stefanie Lotter. Cambridge University Press.

Lovell, Anne. 2011. "Debating Life After Disaster: Charity Hospital Babies and Bioscientific Futures in Post-Katrina New Orleans." *Medical Anthropology Quarterly* 25 (2): 254–77.

Lovell, Anne, Ursula Read, and Claudia Lang. 2019. "Genealogies and Anthropologies of Global Mental Health." *Culture, Medicine and Psychiatry* 43:519–47.

Luitel, Nagendra P., Mark J. D. Jordans, Anup Adhikari, Nawaraj Upadhaya, Charlotte Hanlon, Crick Lund, and Ivan H. Komproe. 2015. "Mental Health Care in Nepal: Current Situation and Challenges for Development of a District Mental Health Care Plan." *Conflict and Health* 9 (3).

Mahmood, Saba. 2005. *Politics of Piety: The Islamic Revival and the Feminist Subject*. Princeton University Press.

Manyena, Siambabala Bernard. 2006. "The Concept of Resilience Revisited." *Disasters* 30 (4): 434–50.

Masco, Joseph. 2017. "The Crisis in Crisis." *Current Anthropology* 58:S65–76.

Maskarinec, Gregory. 1995. *The Rulings of the Night: An Ethnography of Nepalese Shaman Oral Texts.* University of Wisconsin Press.

Mattingly, Cheryl. 1994. "The Concept of Therapeutic 'Emplotment.'" *Social Science & Medicine* 38 (6): 811–22.

Mattingly, Cheryl. 1998. *Healing Dramas and Clinical Plots: The Narrative Structure of Experience.* Cambridge University Press.

Mattingly, Cheryl. 2014. *Moral Laboratories: Family Peril and the Struggle for the Good Life.* University of California Press.

Mattingly, Cheryl. 2019. "Defrosting Concepts, Destabilizing Doxa: Critical Phenomenology and the Perplexing Particular." *Anthropological Theory* 19 (4): 415–39.

McKay, Ramah. 2012. "Afterlives: Humanitarian Histories and Critical Subjects in Mozambique." *Cultural Anthropology* 27 (2): 286–308.

McHugh, Ernestine. 1989. "Concepts of the Person Among the Gurungs of Nepal." *American Ethnologist* 16 (1): 75–86.

McTighe, Laura, and Megan Raschig. 2019. "Introduction: An Otherwise Anthropology." *Fieldsights* (blog), July 31, 2019. https://culanth.org/fieldsights/introduction-an-otherwise-anthropology.

Mead, Margaret, ed. 1954. *Cultural Patterns and Technical Change. A Manual Prepared by the World Federation for Mental Health.* UNESCO.

Medeiros, Emilie, Prabin Nanicha Shrestha, Himal Gaire, and David M. R. Orr. 2019. "Life After Armed Group Involvement in Nepal: A Clinical Ethnography of Psychosocial Well-Being of Former 'Child Soldiers' over Time." *Transcultural Psychiatry* 57 (1): 183–96.

Meyers, Todd. 2022. *All That Was Not Her.* Duke University Press.

Mills, China. 2014. *Decolonizing Global Mental Health: The Psychiatrization of the Majority of the World.* Routledge.

Moran, Dermot. 2000. *Introduction to Phenomenology.* Routledge.

Morimoto, Ryo. 2023. *Nuclear Ghost: Atomic Livelihoods in Fukushima's Gray Zone.* University of California Press.

Murphy, Michelle. 2017. *The Economization of Life.* Duke University Press.

Nathan, Tobie, and Isabelle Stengers. 2018. *Doctors and Healers.* Polity Press.

Nguyen, Vinh-Kim. 2005. "Antiretroviral Globalism, Biopolitics, and Therapeutic Citizenship." In *Gobal Assemblages: Technology, Politics, and Ethics as Anthropological Problems*, edited by Ahiwa Ong and Stephen J. Collier. Blackwell.

Nguyen, Vinh-Kim. 2010. *The Republic of Therapy: Triage and Sovereignty in West Africa's Time of Aids.* Duke University Press.

Nichter, Mark. 1981. "Idioms of Distress: Alternatives in the Expression of Psychological Distress: A Case Study from South India." *Culture, Medicine and Psychiatry* 5:379–408.

Ninglekhu, Sabin. 2017. "'Inauthentic' Sukumbasi: The Politics of Aesthetics and Urgency in Kathmandu." *HIMALAYA, The Journal of the Association for Nepal and Himalayan Studies* 37 (1): 72–83.

Nixon, Rob. 2011. *Slow Violence and the Environmentalism of the Poor.* Harvard University Press.

Obeyesekere, Gananath. 1985. "Depression, Buddhism, and the Work of Culture in Sri Lanka." In *Culture and Depression: Studies in the Anthropology and Cross-Cultural Psychiatry of Affect and Disorder*, edited by Arthur Kleinman and Byron Good. University of California Press.

OED Online. 2023. "Solidarity, n." Oxford University Press. https://www.oed.com/dictionary /solidarity_n (accessed June 3, 2023).

Ogden, Thomas. 1989. "The Initial Analytic Meeting." In *The Primitive Edge of Experience*, by Thomas Ogden. Jason Aronson.

Oliver-Smith, Anthony. 1996. "Anthropological Research on Hazards and Disasters." *Annual Review of Anthropology* 25:303–28.

Oliver-Smith, Anthony, and Susanna Hoffman. 2002. "Introduction: Why Anthropologists Should Study Disasters." In *Catastrophe and Culture: The Anthropology of Disaster*, edited by Susanna Hoffman and Anthony Oliver-Smith. School of American Research Press.

Ortner, Sherry. 1999. *Life and Death on Mount Everest: Sherpas and Himalayan Mountaineering*. Princeton University Press.

Ortner, Sherry. 2016. "Dark Anthropology and Its Others: Theory Since the Eighties." *HAU: Journal of Ethnographic Theory* 6 (1): 47–73.

Pach, Alfred, Krishna Prasad Rimal, and Dhruba Man Shrestha. 2002. "Chhopuwa, Distress, and Gender in a Hindu Village of Nepal." *Himalaya, The Journal of the Association for Nepal and Himalayan Studies* 22 (1): 40–47.

Packard, Randall M. 2016. *A History of Global Health: Interventions into the Lives of Other Peoples*. Johns Hopkins University Press.

Parish, Steven M. 1994. *Moral Knowing in a Hindu Sacred City: An Exploration of Mind, Emotion, and Self*. Columbia University Press.

Pariyar, Bishnu, Sushma Chhinal, Shyamu Thapa Magar, and Rozy Bisunke. 2021. "Pedalling Out of Sociocultural Precariousness: Religious Conversions Amongst the Hindu Dalits to Christianity in Nepal." *Religions* 12:856.

Parry, Jonathan. 1995. *Death in Banaras*. Cambridge University Press.

Patel, Vikram, Shekhar Saxena, Crick Lund, Graham Thornicroft, Florence Baingana, Paul Bolton, Dan Chisholm, et al. 2018. "The Lancet Commission on Global Mental Health and Sustainable Development." *Lancet* 392 (10157): 1553–98.

Pattison, Pete. 2013. "Revealed: Qatar's World Cup 'Slaves.'" *The Guardian*, September 25, 2013. http://www.theguardian.com/world/2013/sep/25/revealed-qatars-world-cup-slaves.

Pattison, Pete. 2014. "Sudden Death." *Nepali Times*, August 15, 2014, sec. Nation. http://archive .nepalitimes.com/article/nation/death-of-nepali-migrant-workers-in-qatar,1592.

Pattison, Pete, and Pramod Acharya. 2023. "Families Mourn 'Devastating' Suicide Rates Among Nepal's Migrant Workers." *The Guardian*, April 2, 2023. https://www.theguardian.com /global-development/2023/apr/06/families-mourn-devastating-suicide-rates-among-nepals -migrant-workers.

Perpich, Diane. 2008. *The Ethics of Emmanuel Levinas*. Stanford University Press.

Petryna, Adriana. 2003. *Life Exposed: Biological Citizens after Chernobyl*. Princeton University Press.

Petryna, Adriana. 2022. *Horizon Work: At the Edges of Knowledge in the Age of Runaway Climate Change*. Princeton University Press.

Pettigrew, Judith. 2013. *Maoists at the Hearth: Everyday Life in Nepal's Civil War*. University of Pennsylvania Press.

Pigg, Stacy. 1992. "Inventing Social Categories through Place: Social Representations and Development in Nepal." *Comparative Studies in Society and History* 34 (3): 491–513.

Pigg, Stacy. 1996. "The Credible and the Credulous: The Question of 'Villagers' Beliefs' in Nepal." *Cultural Anthropology* 11 (2): 160–201.

Pigg, Stacy. 2001. "Languages of Sex and AIDS in Nepal: Notes on the Social Production of Commensurability." *Cultural Anthropology* 16 (4): 481–541.

Povinelli, Elizabeth. 2011. *Economies of Abandonment: Social Belonging and Endurance in Late Liberalism.* Duke University Press.

Prince, Martin, Vikram Patel, Shekhar Saxena, Mario Maj, Joanna Maselko, Michael R. Phillips, and Atif Rahman. 2007. "No Health without Mental Health." *Lancet* 370:859–77.

Pupavac, Vanessa. 2001. "Therapeutic Governance: Psycho-Social Intervention and Trauma Risk Management." *Disasters* 25 (4): 358–72.

Rai, Yugesh, Deoman Gurung, and Kamal Gautam. 2021. "Insight and Challenges: Mental Health Services in Nepal." *BJPsych International* 18 (2): 1–3.

Rana, Brahma Shumsher Jung Bahadur. 2013. *The Great Earthquake in Nepal (1934 A.D.).* Translated by Kedar Lall. Ratna Pustak Bhandar.

Rankin, Katharine, Tulasi Sigdel, Lagan Rai, Shyam Kunwar, and Pushpa Hamal. 2017. "Political Economies and Political Rationalities of Road Building in Nepal." *Studies in Nepali History and Society* 22 (1).

Raschig, Megan. 2017. "Triggering Change: Police Homicides, Community Healing, and the Emergent Eventfulness of the New Civil Rights." *Cultural Anthropology* 32 (3): 399–423.

Redfield, Peter. 2012. "The Unbearable Lightness of Ex-Pats: Double Binds of Humanitarian Mobility." *Cultural Anthropology* 27 (2): 358–82.

Redfield, Peter. 2013. *Life in Crisis: The Ethical Journey of Doctors Without Borders.* University of California Press.

Redfield, Peter. 2024. "On the Humanitarian Horizon." *American Ethnologist* 51:516–18.

Regmi, Mahesh C. 1978. *Thatched Huts and Stucco Palaces: Peasants and Landlords in Nineteenth Century Nepal.* Vikas.

Robbins, Joel. 2013. "Beyond the Suffering Subject: Toward an Anthropology of the Good." *Journal of the Royal Anthropological Institute* 19 (3): 447–62.

Roberts, Elizabeth. 2021. "Making Better Numbers Through Bioethnographic Collaboration." *American Anthropologist* 123 (2): 355–69.

Roitman, Janet. 2014. *Anti-Crisis.* Duke University Press.

Salamon, Gayle. 2018. *The Life and Death of Latisha King: A Critical Phenomenology of Transphobia.* New York University Press.

Sartorius, Norman. 1983. "Mental Health in the Early 1980s: Some Perspectives." *Bulletin of the World Health Organization* 61 (1): 1–6.

Scarry, Elaine. 2011. *Thinking in Emergency.* W. W. Norton.

Scheper-Hughes, Nancy. 1995. "The Primacy of the Ethical: Propositions for a Militant Anthropology." *Current Anthropology* 36 (3): 409–40.

Schmidt, Ruth Laila. 1994. *A Practical Dictionary of Modern Nepali.* Ratna Sagar.

Scott, Joan W. 1991. "The Evidence of Experience." *Critical Inquiry,* no. 17: 773–97.

Scott, Rachel. 2014. "Imagining More Effective Humanitarian Aid: A Donor Perspective." OECD Development Co-Cooperation Working Paper 18. Organisation for Economic Co-operation and Development (OECD).

Seale-Feldman, Aidan. 2019. "Relational Affliction: Reconceptualizing 'Mass Hysteria.'" *Ethos* 47 (3): 307–25.

Seale-Feldman, Aidan. 2020a. "Historicizing the Emergence of Global Mental Health in Nepal (1950–2019)." *HIMALAYA, The Journal of the Association for Nepal and Himalayan Studies* 39 (2): 29–43.

Seale-Feldman, Aidan. 2020b. "The Work of Disaster: Building Back Otherwise in Post-Earthquake Nepal." *Cultural Anthropology* 35 (2): 237–63.

Seale-Feldman, Aidan. 2022a. "The Place of Nepal in Psychological Anthropology." In *Nepalese Psychology: Volume One*, edited by Yubaraj Adhikari, Sujan Shrestha, and Kripa Sigdel. Evincepub.

Seale-Feldman, Aidan. 2022b. "The Possibility of Translation: Turning Ghosts into Psychosomatic Disorders in Nepal." *South Asia: Journal of South Asian Studies* 45 (1): 130–45.

Seale-Feldman, Aidan, and Andrés Romero. 2020. "Castaway Man." *Fieldsites* (blog), December 10, 2020. https://culanth.org/fieldsights/series/castaway-man?token=Bi0NbxYkhLe6-dGS yeJQjGBMZu0u_4kk.

Seale-Feldman, Aidan, and Nawaraj Upadhaya. 2015. "Mental Health after the Earthquake: Building Nepal's Mental Health System in Times of Emergency." *Fieldsights* (blog), October 14, 2015. https://culanth.org/fieldsights/mental-health-after-the-earthquake-building -nepals-mental-health-system-in-times-of-emergency.

Seddon, David, Ganesh Gurung, and Jagannath Adhikari. 1998. "Foreign Labour Migration and the Remittance Economy of Nepal." *HIMALAYA, The Journal of the Association for Nepal and Himalayan Studies* 18 (2): 3–10.

Sedgwick, Eve Kosofsky. 2003. "Paranoid Reading and Reparative Reading, Or, You're So Paranoid, You Probably Think This Essay Is About You." In *Touching Feeling: Affect, Pedagogy, Performativity*. Duke University Press.

Shakya, Mallika. 2020. "Anthropology in the Margins." *Fieldsites* (blog), December 10, 2020. https://culanth.org/fieldsights/vanished-searching-for-a-missing-anthropologist.

Shange, Savannah. 2019. *Progressive Dystopia: Abolition, Antiblackness, + Schooling in San Francisco*. Duke University Press.

Shazer, Steve de. 1985. *Keys to Solution in Brief Therapy*. W. W. Norton.

Shneiderman, Sara. 2014. "Remoteness as a Relational Category, Remote and Edgy: New Takes on Old Anthropological Themes." Edited by Erik Harms, Shafqat Hussain, and Sara Schneiderman. *HAU: Journal of Ethnographic Theory* 4 (1): 361–81.

Shneiderman, Sara. 2015. *Rituals of Ethnicity: Thangmi Identities Between Nepal and India*. University of Pennsylvania Press.

Shneiderman, Sara, Bina Khapunghang Limbu, Jeevan Baniya, Manoj Suji, Nabin Rawal, Prakash Chandra Subedi, and Cameron David Warner. 2023. "House, Household, and Home: Revisiting Anthropological and Policy Frameworks through Postearthquake Reconstruction Experiences in Nepal." *Current Anthropology* 64 (5): 498–527.

Shrestha, D. M., Alfred Pach, and K. P. Rimal. 1983. "A Social and Psychiatric Study of Mental Illness in Nepal." United Nations Children's Fund.

Shrestha, Prithvi Man. 2023. "Nepal Among the Lowest in South Asia in HDI." *Kathmandu Post*, November 7, 2023, sec. National. https://kathmandupost.com/national/2023/11/07 /nepal-among-the-lowest-in-south-asia-in-hdi.

Sidel, Victor. 1972. "The Barefoot Doctors of the People's Republic of China." *New England Journal of Medicine* 286 (24): 1292–1300.

Simpson, Edward. 2014. *The Political Biography of an Earthquake: Aftermath and Amnesia in Gujarat, India.* Oxford University Press.

Singal, Amit G., Peter D. R. Higgins, and Akbar K. Waljee. 2014. "A Primer on Effectiveness and Efficacy Trials." *Clinical and Translational Gastroenterology* 5 (1): e45.

Singh, Devika, Alia Cynthia Gonzales Luz, Waranya Rattanavipapong, and Yot Teerawattananon. 2017. "Designing the Free Drugs List in Nepal." *Medical Decision Making Policy & Practice* 2 (1): 1–9.

Snellinger, Amanda. 2018. *Making New Nepal: From Student Activism to Mainstream Politics.* University of Washington Press.

Spade, Dean. 2020. *Mutual Aid: Building Solidarity During This Crisis (and the Next).* Verso.

Steinbrecher, Elijah, Sara Smock Jordan, and Brie Turns. 2021. "Providing Immediate Hope to Survivors of Natural Disasters: A Miracle Question Intervention." *American Journal of Family Therapy* 49 (2): 204–19.

Stern, Daniel. 2004. *The Present Moment in Psychotherapy and Everyday Life.* W. W. Norton.

Stevenson, Lisa. 2012. "The Psychic Life of Biopolitics: Survival, Cooperation, and Inuit Community." *American Ethnologist* 39 (3): 592–613.

Stevenson, Lisa. 2014. *Life Beside Itself: Imagining Care in the Canadian Arctic.* University of California Press.

Stewart, Kathleen. 2011. "Atmospheric Attunements." *Environment and Planning D: Society and Space* 29 (3): 445–53.

Stockton, Nick. 2015. "Let's Stop Nepal's Mental Health Crisis Before It Happens." *WIRED*, 2015. https://www.wired.com/2015/05/lets-stop-nepals-mental-health-crisis-happens/.

Strasheim, Julia. 2018. "No 'End of the Peace Process': Federalism and Ethnic Violence in Nepal." *Cooperation and Conflict* 54 (1): 83–98.

Strathern, Marilyn. 2000. *Audit Cultures: Anthropological Studies in Accountability, Ethics and the Academy.* Routledge.

Strong, Tom, and Nathan Pyle. 2009. "Constructing a Conversational 'Miracle': Examining the 'Miracle Question' as It Is Used in Therapeutic Dialogue." *Journal of Constructivist Psychology* 22 (4): 328–53.

Stuelke, Patricia. 2021. *The Ruse of Repair: US Neoliberal Empire and the Turn from Critique.* Duke University Press.

Subedi, D. B. 2014. "Discontents and Resistance of 'Unverified' Ex-Combatants and Challenges to Their Rehabilitation in Nepal." *Agrarian South: Journal of Political Economy* 3 (2): 203–37.

Summerfield, Derek. 1999. "A Critique of Seven Assumptions Behind Psychological Trauma Programs in War-Affected Areas." *Social Science & Medicine* 48:1449–62.

Summerfield, Derek. 2013. "'Global Mental Health' Is an Oxymoron and Medical Imperialism." *BMJ* 346:f3509.

Tamang, Siera. 2015. "Dangers of Resilience." *Kathmandu Post*, May 25, 2015, sec. Opinion. https://kathmandupost.com/opinion/2015/05/25/dangers-of-resilience.

Thapa, Manjushree. 2011. *The Lives We Have Lost: Essays and Opinions on Nepal.* Penguin Books.

Thomas, Deborah. 2024. "Refusal (and Repair)." *Annual Review of Anthropology* 53:93–109.

Throop, C. Jason. 2003. "Articulating Experience." *Anthropological Theory* 3 (2): 219–41.

Throop, C. Jason. 2010a. "Latitudes of Loss: On the Vicissitudes of Empathy." *American Ethnologist* 37 (4): 771–82.

Throop, C. Jason. 2010b. *Suffering and Sentiment: Exploring the Vicissitudes of Experience and Pain in Yap*. University of California Press.

Ticktin, Miriam. 2011. *Casualties of Care: Immigration and the Politics of Humanitarianism in France*. University of California Press.

Ticktin, Miriam. 2014. "Transnational Humanitarianism." *Annual Review of Anthropology* 43:273–89.

Ticktin, Miriam. 2017. "A World Without Innocence." *American Ethnologist* 44 (4): 577–90.

Timmermans, Stefan, and Marc Berg. 2003. *The Gold Standard: The Challenge of Evidence-Based Medicine and Standardization in Health Care*. Temple University Press.

Tironi, Manuel. 2014. "Atmospheres of Indagation: Disasters and the Politics of Excessiveness." *Sociological Review* 62 (S1): 114–34.

Toadvine, Ted. 2020. "Geomateriality." In *50 Concepts for a Critical Phenomenology*, edited by Gail Weiss, Ann Murphy, and Gayle Salamon, 237–45. Northwestern University Press.

Tol, Wietse A., Pierre Bastin, Mark J. D. Jordans, Harry Minas, Renato Souza, Inka Weissbecker, and Mark Van Ommeren. 2014. "Mental Health and Psychosocial Support in Humanitarian Settings." In *Global Mental Health: Principles and Practice*, edited by Vikram Patel. Oxford University Press.

Tronto, Joan. 1998. "An Ethic of Care." *Generations: Journal of the American Society on Aging* 22 (3): 15–20.

Turin, Mark. 2002. "Call Me Uncle: An Outsider's Experience of Nepali Kinship." *Contributions to Nepalese Studies* 28 (2): 277–83.

Turner, Ralph. 1965. *A Comparative and Etymological Dictionary of the Nepali Language*. Routledge & Kegan Paul.

UNISDR. 2005. "Hyogo Framework for Action 2005–2015: Building the Resilience of Nations and Communities to Disasters." United Nations. https://www.unisdr.org/2005/wcdr/inter gover/official-doc/L-docs/Hyogo-framework-for-action-english.pdf.

United Nations Children's Fund. 2016a. "Child Protection Sub Cluster 5W Update." https://www .humanitarianresponse.info/en/operations/nepal/document/5w-update-6-sep-0 (accessed February 2, 2019).

United Nations Children's Fund. 2016b. "UNICEF Nepal C4D Response Earthquake 2015." Pulchowk, Lalitpur, Nepal: United Nations Childrens Fund (UNICEF) Nepal Country Office. https://www.unicef.org/nepal/media/2756/file/UNICEF%20Nepal%20C4D%20response %20earthquake%202015.pdf.

United Mission to Nepal. 1988. "Samudayika Swastha Karyakartako Laagi Tayar Pariyeko Manasik Swastha Pustika: Manasik Swastha Karyakram." H-03.04.01/0039, Box 160, Folder 3. Archives of United Mission to Nepal, Record Group No. 212, Special Collections, Yale Divinity School Library, New Haven, CT.

United Mission to Nepal. n.d. "Features of Mental Disorders." H-03.04.01/0027, Box 80, Folder 8–9. Archives of United Mission to Nepal, Record Group No. 212, Special Collections, Yale Divinity School Library, New Haven, CT.

Upadhaya, Nawaraj, Nagendra P. Luitel, Suraj Koirala, Ramesh P. Adhikari, Dristy Gurung, Pragya Shrestha, Wietse Tol, Brandon Kohrt, and Mark Jordans. 2014. "The Role of Mental Health and Psychosocial Support Nongovernmental Organisations: Reflections from Post Conflict Nepal." *Intervention* 12 (1): 113–28.

Varma, Saiba. 2016a. "Disappearing the Asylum: Modernizing Psychiatry and Generating Manpower in India." *Transcultural Psychiatry* 53 (6): 783–803.

Varma, Saiba. 2016b. "Love in the Time of Occupation: Reveries, Longing, and Intoxication in Kashmir." *American Ethnologist* 43 (1): 50–62.

Varma, Saiba. 2020. *The Occupied Clinic: Militarism and Care in Kashmir*. Duke University Press.

Vaughan, Megan. 1992. *Curing Their Ills: Colonial Power and African Illness*. Stanford University Press.

Vigh, Henrik. 2008. "Crisis and Chronicity: Anthropological Perspectives on Continuous Conflict and Decline." *Ethnos* 73 (1): 5–24.

Waldram, James. 2000. "The Efficacy of Traditional Medicine: Current Theoretical and Methodological Issues." *Medical Anthropology Quarterly* 14 (4): 603–25.

Watters, Ethan. 2010. *Crazy Like Us: The Globalization of the American Psyche*. Free Press.

Weinmayr, Elmar, John W. M. Krummel, and Douglas Berger. 2005. "Thinking in Translation: Nishida Kitaro and Martin Heidegger." *Philosophy East and West* 55 (2): 232–56.

Wentzer, Thomas Schwartz. 2017. "Human, the Responding Being: Considerations Towards a Philosophical Anthropology of Responsiveness." In *Moral Engines: Exploring the Ethical Drives in Human Life*, edited by Cheryl Mattingly, Rasmus Dyring, Maria Louw, and Thomas Schwarz Wentzer. Berghahn Books.

Weyerman, Barbara. 2010. *Close Encounters: Stories from the Frontline of Human Rights Work in Nepal*. Himal Books.

WHO Expert Committee on Mental Health. 1975. "Organization of Mental Health Services in Developing Countries: Sixteenth Report of the WHO Expert Committee on Mental Health." World Health Organization Technical Report Series, no. 564. Meeting held October 22 to 28, 1974, Geneva, Switzerland. World Health Organization.

WHO Special Initiative for Mental Health. 2021. "Nepal: WHO Special Initiative for Mental Health Situational Assessment." World Health Organization. https://www.who.int/publications/m/item/nepal---who-special-initiative-for-mental-health.

Wiegman, Robyn. 2014. "The Times We're In: Queer Feminist Criticism and the Reparative 'Turn.'" *Feminist Theory* 15 (1): 4–25.

Wikan, Uni. 1990. *Managing Turbulent Hearts: A Balinese Formula for Living*. University of Chicago Press.

Willen, Sarah. 2014. "Plotting a Moral Trajectory, Sans Papiers: Outlaw Motherhood as Inhabitable Space of Welcome." *Ethos* 42 (1): 84–100.

Winnicott, D.W. 2005. "Transitional Objects and Transitional Phenomena." In *Playing and Reality*. Routledge.

World Bank. 1993. *World Development Report 1993: Investing in Health*. Oxford University Press.

World Bank. 2016. "Personal Remittances, Received (% of GDP)." DataBank World Development Indicators. https://data.worldbank.org/indicator/BX.TRF.PWKR.DT.GD.ZS?year_high_desc=true.

World Bank. 2022. "Personal Remittances, Received (% of GDP)." DataBank World Development Indicators. https://data.worldbank.org/indicator/BX.TRF.PWKR.DT.GD.ZS?end=2021&locations=NP&start=1993&year_high_desc=true.

World Bank and World Health Organization. 2016. "Out of the Shadows: Making Mental Health a Global Development Priority." https://documents1.worldbank.org/curated/en/270131468187759113/pdf/105052-WP-PUBLIC-wb-background-paper.pdf.

World Health Organization. 1978. "Alma-Ata Declaration." World Health Organization.

World Health Organization. 2008a. "mhGAP: Mental Health Gap Action Programme: Scaling up Care for Mental, Neurological, and Substance Use Disorders." World Health Organization.

World Health Organization. 2008b. "Task Shifting: Rational Redistribution of Tasks Among Health Workforce Teams: Global Recommendations and Guidelines." World Health Organization.

World Health Organization. 2013. "Building Back Better: Sustainable Mental Health Care After Emergencies." World Health Organization. https://www.who.int/publications/i/item/97 89241564571.

World Health Organization and United Nations High Commissioner for Refugees. 2015. "mhGAP Humanitarian Intervention Guide (mhGAP-HIG): Clinical Management of Mental, Neurological and Substance Use Conditions in Humanitarian Emergencies." Geneva: WHO. https://www.who.int/mental_health/publications/mhgap_hig/en/.

Wright, Christine. 1986. "Annual Report April 1985-April 1986." H-03.04.01/0015, Box 80, Folder 8–9. Archives of United Mission to Nepal, Record Group No. 212, Special Collections, Yale Divinity School Library, New Haven, CT.

Young, Allan. 1976. "Some Implications of Medical Beliefs and Practices for Social Anthropology." *American Anthropologist* 78:5–24.

Young, Allan. 1997. *The Harmony of Illusions: Inventing Post-Traumatic Stress Disorder*. Princeton University Press.

Zharkevich, Ina. 2019. "Money and Blood: Remittances as a Substance of Relatedness in Transnational Families in Nepal." *American Ethnologist* 121 (4): 884–96.

Zigon, Jarrett. 2007. "Moral Breakdown and the Ethical Demand: A Theoretical Framework for an Anthropology of Moralities." *Anthropological Theory* 7 (2): 131–50.

Zigon, Jarrett. 2019. *A War on People: Drug User Politics and a New Ethics of Community*. University of California Press.

Zigon, Jarrett, and Jason Throop. 2014. "Moral Experience: Introduction." *Ethos* 42 (1): 1–15.

Index

Page numbers in italics indicate figures.

abandoned mentally ill, 20, 28, 43–44, 138
Abramowitz, Sharon, 13, 41
accompaniment model, 69, 155n23
accountability, 91–92
Act Relating to Rights of Persons with Disabilities, 138
Adams, Vincanne, 92
African insanity, 26
alcohol, 110
Alma-Ata Declaration (1978), 28, 36, 69
Al-Saji, Alia, 125
anthropology: "barefoot" and "militant," 155n24; critiques of care regimes in, 113; critiques of humanitarianism in, 17, 19, 20, 22, 88–89, 91, 108; and the efficacy of therapeutic care, 89, 92, 108, 117; ethics of, 16, 18–19, 126, 160n58; and global mental health, 137; on mediating function of infrastructure, 70; and MHPSS, 14–15, 27, 38, 42; phenomenology applied in, 6, 8; and politics, 17–18; practice of, in disaster areas, 15–18; reparative turn in, 19; transformations in the field of, 18–19
anxiety. *See* depression/anxiety
Arendt, Hannah, 50, 147n47
Ayurvedic medicine, 3, 115

Bardo Thödol ("Liberation upon Hearing in the Between"), 59, 154n52
bare life, 112
barefoot doctors, 68–69
Barrois, Roberto, 8
Berg, Marc, 157n21
Berlant, Lauren, 137, 160n2
Bhandai-Sundai (talking-listening), 1, 3–4

Bhutanese refugees, 33
Biden, Joe, 148n95
Binswanger, Ludwig, 106
biomarkers, 91
biopolitics: and care, 113; critical phenomenology of, 7; defined, 5; disasters linked to exercise of, 4–5; life and death as concerns of, 5, 14; and mental health governance, 4, 14, 136; narratives justifying, 45
birth/rebirth, 20, 49, 53, 56–58, 62, 139
Bista, Dor Bahadur, 59
blockade, at Indian border, 1, 40, 64, 79, 114, 117
Bond, David, 9
Bradley, Jennifer, 49
Brahmanism, 59
Breslau, Joshua, 106
brief interventions. *See* transient care
Buddhism. *See* Tibetan Buddhism; Zen Buddhism
"building back better," 20, 24–25, 42–45, 129–30, 138. *See also* World Health Organization (WHO): *Building Back Better*
Butler, Judith, 9

Callon, Michel, 88, 107
care: definitions and practices of, 113–14, 127, 132–33; ethics of, 113, 128–29, 133; framing of subjects for, 111–12; gentleness manifested in, 19, 22, 108, 114–15, 126, 128–30, 132, 134; regimes of, 111–12; violence linked to, 113–14, 132–33. *See also* efficacy of humanitarian care; mental health and psychosocial support; transient care
caste, 18, 93, 157n25, 157n28
Centre for Mental Health and Counselling (CMC-Nepal), 16–17

Certeau, Michel de, 85
Chan, Margaret, 69
charity, 74, 156n38. *See also* humanitarianism
China, 68
Christianity, 94–95, 157n29. *See also* United Mission to Nepal
citizenship: rights associated with, 11–12; therapeutic, 20, 34, 45, 47–48, 107
clients: counselor interactions with, 19, 22, 46–47, 50, 52–56, 65, 81, 84, 93–106, 109, 115–16, 118–24, 126–29; medication compliance of, 94–97, 99–100, *101*, 103, 116, 135–36; perceptions of therapeutic efficacy, 87–88, 90–92, 96–97, 99, 104, 106, 108, 115; solidarity of counselors with, 21, 65, 74
climate, 74, 76
Clinton, Bill, 148n95
colonialism, 43
community health care, 68–69
community psychosocial workers (CPSWs), 64, 93, 118, 134. *See also* female community health volunteers
contentment. *See* happiness
counseling. *See* counselors; mental health and psychosocial support
counselors: backgrounds of, 17, 69, 80–81; client interactions with, 19, 22, 46–47, 50, 52–56, 65, 81, 84, 93–106, 115–16, 118–24, 126–29; embodied work of, 17, 21, 64–68, 74, 85; gender of, 68; importance of, 69–70; lodgings of, 51–52, 64, 72–73, 76, 80, 134; and methods of dealing with loss, 53, 61, 63; Nepali definitions of, 14, 38; personal growth of, through their training and practice, 81; physical environment faced by, 66, 70–74, *71*; on the radio, 1; solidarity of clients with, 21, 65, 74; training of, 5, 13, 17, 41, 53, 69, 82–83, 86–87, 90, 111, 120, 125, 129, 138; travel required to reach clients, 5, 17, 21, 46, 50, 64–67, 70–74, *71*, *75*, 76, 79–80
COVID-19, 136
CPSWs. *See* community psychosocial workers
Craig, Sienna, 106, 158n32
crisis: forms of response in, 74; humanitarian harnessing of, 24–25, 120, 136; meanings of, 24, 149n17; mental health framed as, 2–3, 5, 7, 9, 19–20, 23–26, 36–45, 59, 120, 131; in therapeutic relationships, 128. *See also* disasters
critical phenomenology, 6–8, 19, 21, 50, 63, 67, 85, 129, 137, 140, 156n40
Csordas, Thomas, 98, 146n25
culture. *See* work of culture

Dalit people, 93, 157n25, 157n28, 157n29
Das, Veena, 128, 160n58, 160n62, 162n24
Daston, Lorraine, 90

death: attitudes about, xiv, xvi, 49, 52–56, 61, 63, 104, 131; biopolitics and, 5; birth in relation to, v, 20, 49, 53, 56–59, 62, 139; good vs. bad, 55–56; of migrant workers, 35, 53, 110–11; rituals associated with, 55–56, 59, 63, 78
Debord, Guy, 66
debriefing, 51, 59, 125
deculturation, 26
deinstitutionalization, 44
DeLeon, Jason, 66
Deleuze, Gilles, 152n18
Department for International Development (United Kingdom), 37
depression/anxiety, xvii, 1, 15, 131. *See also* mental health/illness/affliction/distress; suffering
Desjarlais, Robert, 8, 52, 152n13, 154n52, 155n18
development. *See* international/foreign development
Devotka, Laxshmi Prasad, xvii
dhami-jakhri (shaman), 3, *30*, 38, 88, 119
Diagnostic and Statistical Manual (*DSM-III*), 59
disability-adjusted life years (DALYs), 36–37
disaster syndrome, 61
disasters: as a boon to societies, 2, 19, 24–26, 43, 45, 120, 136; embodiment of, 21; ethics and the experience of, 61, 62; importance of companionship after, 61; "mental health crisis" as concern after, 14, 25, 120; sociopolitical effects generated by, 4–6, 8–9. *See also* crisis; earthquakes (2015) in Nepal
Dolakha, Nepal, 17, 50, 57, 64, 70, 76–78, 109
donors: and accountability measures, 91–92; limitations placed by, on duration of services, 1, 4, 21–22, 24, 89, 112–13, 126–27, 129, 132; limitations placed by, on uses of funding, 44; narratives that appeal to, 25, 28, 34, 37; reports submitted to, 86–87, 92
dreams, 52, 82–83, 104–5
drugs. *See* psychiatric medication
Dufourmantelle, Anne, 115, 127, 128
dukha. See suffering
Dunn, Elizabeth Cullen, 39
Durkheim, Émile, 67

earthquake houses, 134
earthquakes (2015) in Nepal: author's experience of, xiii–xviii, 1, 15–19; demographics of victims of, 10; map of areas affected by, *viii*; MHPSS after, 2–3, 5, 7, 15–19, 22, 23, 25–26, 39–45, 131–32; outcomes of response to, 1, 11. *See also* disasters
Eck, Diana, 53
education, 47, 60, 69. *See also* psychoeducation
efficacy of humanitarian care: anthropology's study of, 89, 92, 108, 117; clients' perceptions of, 87–88, 90–92, 96–97, 99, 108, 115–17; counselors'

perceptions of, 87–88, 95; defining, 89; effectiveness compared to, 91–92; humanitarian conceptions/frames of, 21–22, 88–92, 97–98, 101, 106–8; indeterminacy of evidence for, 88, 92, 100, 107–8; measurement of, 87, 90–91, 96–98, 107–8; outcome-based assessment of, 98, 101

embodiment: in counselors' work, 17, 21, 64–68, 74, 85; of disaster, 21, 50, 62, 64–65; objectivity and, 157n12. See also walking

emptiness. See nothingness/emptiness

ethics and morality: anthropology and, 16, 18–19, 126, 160n58; of care, 113, 128–29, 133; of counseling sessions, 124–25; disaster and, 61, 62; lay medical care and, 68–69; ordinary, 129, 160n58, 160n62; and the Other, 114–15, 122, 124, 129, 133; phenomenological approach to, 156n40; precarity of, 129; and RCTs, 157n16; of transient psychosocial care, 15, 19, 22, 113; walking and, 78–79

ethnography. See anthropology

ethnopsychology and ethnopsychiatry, 38, 49

European Commission, 37

event, 9, 44, 89, 98, 107, 134, 137, 159n29

evidence-based approaches, 86–87, 91–92, 157n21

externalities, of therapeutic care, 88–89, 101, 107

Facebook, 23

Fanon, Frantz, 7, 145n10

Farmer, Paul, 69

Fassin, Didier, 34, 47, 133, 149n17

female community health volunteers (FCHVs), 13, 68

First People's Movement, 33

Fisher, Berenice, 113

foreign development. See international/foreign development

Forest Chairman (ban adhyaksa), 61

Fortun, Kim, 9

Foucault, Michel, 5, 19

frames/framing: of care in humanitarianism, 114; of disaster, 9, 63; of efficacy of humanitarianism, 21–22, 88–92, 97–98, 101, 106–8; limits and possibilities created by, 6, 8–9, 44; of mental health, 2–3, 5, 7, 9, 19–20, 23–26, 34, 36–45, 59, 120, 131, 135; neoliberal, 37, 91; overflows of, 22, 63, 88–89, 92, 98, 101, 103, 107–8, 133; phenomenological analysis of, 6–9, 63, 107–8, 139; of PTSD, 91; of victimhood, by humanitarianism, 1, 5, 21–22, 34, 35, 48, 88, 97, 100–101, 103, 132–33. See also objectifications

Freud, Sigmund, 66, 106, 155n11

Galison, Peter, 90

Gaurishankar, 52, 73, 76

gender. See women

gentleness, 19, 22, 108, 114–15, 126, 128–30, 132, 134

gestures, 8, 74, 108, 127

ghost and spirit possession, 3, 4, 15, 38, 135

Gibson, James, 65

global mental health: biopolitics and, 14; community-based care promoted for, 28, 31, 69–70; cultural factors considered in, 38; debates over, 15, 137; goal of, 14; history of, 26–32; movement for, 36–38; NGOs dedicated to, 4; rural services associated with, 4

goats, xv, 13, 99, 115

Goffman, Erving, 9, 147n45

government aid: Nepalis' hopes for, xvii, 11, 47, 57; provision of, xvii; responses to failures of, 11–12

Govindrajan, Radhika, 99

Grand Challenges Canada, 37

grief. See loss; mourning; suffering

groundlessness. See nothingness/emptiness

Guardian, The (newspaper), 111

Guattari, Félix, 132, 152n18, 161n3

Guidelines on Mental Health and Psychosocial Support in Emergency Settings, 41

Haiti, 69

Handicap International, 23, 39

happiness (sukha), 49, 57–58, 105, 120–22

Haraway, Donna, 157n12

Harrison, Faye, 17–18

Heart Sutra, 56

heart-mind. See man

Heidegger, Martin, 58, 146n20, 148n94, 153n45, 153n47

Hickingbotham, David, 31–32

Hinduism: aims of life in, 58; and caste, 17, 52, 59, 93; concept of the world in, 58–59, 62; critiques of, 59; and death, 52, 53, 55–58; liberation as goal of, 58; mourning in, xiii; Nepalese monarchy grounded in, 11, 40

HIV/AIDS, 7, 69

Hoffman, Susanna, 9

hope, 9, 11, 18, 21, 22, 61, 114, 115–16, 125–26, 129, 132–33. See also intersubjective otherwise; miracle question

humanitarian hubs, 72–74, 73, 82, 85

humanitarianism: business model of, 107; care as conceived/framed by, 114; crises/disasters as motivation for, 4, 24–25; critiques of, 17, 19, 20, 22, 43, 47, 88–89, 91, 97, 107, 108, 132–33, 137, 139; efficacy as conceived/framed by, 21–22, 88–92, 97–98, 101, 106–8; framing of victimhood in, 1, 5, 21–22, 34, 35, 48, 97, 100–101, 103, 111–12, 132–33; funding of, 157n20; inequalities in, 21, 67, 72–74, 83, 85, 90; and MHPSS, 2, 12, 15; organizations contributing to, 23; reparative turn in, 19, 132–33; temporality of, 22, 89, 98, 103, 106,

humanitarianism (*cont.*)
119, 122, 126, 130, 157n20; UN office for coordi-
nating, 39–40; violence of, 19, 22, 108, 112, 114,
116, 121, 124, 128–29, 132–34
Hyogo Framework for Action, 10
Hyolmo Buddhism, 59, 152n13

IASC. *See* United Nations: Inter-Agency Standing
Committee
impermanence, 49, 52, 58–59, 62
Ingold, Tim, 66, 155n10
INGOs. *See* international nongovernmental
organizations
intentionality, 6–7, 26, 137
International Classification of Diseases (ICD-11), 106
International Conference on Nepal's Reconstruc-
tion, 11
International Humanitarian Partnership (IHP), 73
International Medical Corps (IMC), 23
international nongovernmental organizations
(INGOs), 23, 40–41
International Organization of Migration (IOM), 39
international/foreign development: as cause of
mental illness, 26–28; government restrictions
on, 32; Maoist opposition to, 33; and MHPSS,
14, 33–34, 38–45
intersubjective otherwise, 22, 44, 124–30, 132–33,
140, 160n2. *See also* hope; miracle question;
Other, the
Inuit people, 113
IsraAID, 23, 39

jakhris. See *dhami-jakhri*
joy. *See* happiness

kairos (critical moment), 128
karma (fate), 47, 59
Kathmandu, Nepal, xiii, xiv, 2–5, 11, 13, 15–18, 23–
24, 32–33, 36, 39–41, 48, 50, 53, 58, 64–65, 76–78,
83–84, 86–87, 93–94, 97, 99–100, 104, 110–12,
117, 121, 125–26, 129, 131, 134
Khotang, Nepal, 1, 12, 68, 131, 137
kindness. *See* gentleness
kinship, 35, 122–23
Klein, Melanie, 19, 123, 137
Kleinman, Arthur, 41, 98
Kohrt, Brandon, 117, 151n75
Koirala, Sushil, 9, 11
Koselleck, Reinhard, 24
Kropotkin, Peter, 67

Lambo, T. A., 27–28
Lancet (journal), 36
landlessness, 46
landslides, 5, 10, 17, 21, 46, 49, 50, 52, 55, 60, 76,
134, 136

Latour, Bruno, 2, 25, 97, 145n3, 161n18
Laubender, Carolyn, 137
Lempert, Michael, 129
Levinas, Emmanuel, 114, 124, 133, 161n7
Lévi-Strauss, Claude, 89
Lewis, Sara, 59
liberation (*moksa*), 56–59, 62, 154n52
liberation theology, 155n23
Liberia, 117
listening, xviii, 15, 38, 106, 127, 134
Lord, Austin, 49
loss: and attitudes about the dead, 49, 52–53;
conceptualizations of, 20; counseling sessions
on, 46–50, 52–55, *54*, 57, 63; traditional ways of
dealing with, 49, 52–53

Madhesi people, 40, 151n81
magic, *30*, 94–97
Mahendra, King, 33
Malinowski, Bronisław, 16
man (heart-mind): care of, xvi, xviii, 47, 61, 131;
concealing contents of, 11, 13, 49, 152n13; defined, 13; pain in, 105, 122, 152n13; response of,
to earthquakes, 21; as seat of emotion and
desire, 38
manpower agents, 10, 35
Mao Zedong, 33, 68
Maoist insurgency. *See* People's War (1996–2006)
mass hysteria, 1, 120
mata (female shaman), 97
Mattingly, Cheryl, 8, 50, 129, 160n61
McTighe, Laura, 126
MDM. *See* Médicos del Mundo
Mead, Margaret, *Cultural Patterns and Technical
Change*, 26–27
Médecins Sans Frontières (MSF), 39, 43, 47, 51
medical pluralism, 97, 107, 138, 158n32
medication. *See* psychiatric medication
Médicos del Mundo (MDM), 23, 39
melancholia, 106
mental health and psychosocial support (MHPSS):
administration of, 14; anthropology and, 14–15,
27, 38, 42; benefits of, xvii–xviii; concept of the
psychosocial in, 12–13; controversies over, 15;
crises/disasters as opportunity for improvements in, 2, 19, 24–26, 43, 45, 120, 136; cultural
factors considered in, 49–50; depoliticization
accomplished through, 47–48; duration of
interventions/donor timelines for, 1, 4, 21–22,
24, 89, 112–13, 126–27, 129, 132; ethical nature
of, 124–25; explanations of, to Nepalis, 46–47;
externalities of, 88–89, 101, 107; funding of, 23;
gendering of, 68; goal of, 13; interagency coordination (and lack thereof) in, 41–43, 51;
international experts as promoters of, 14, 33–
34, 38–45; introduction of, in Nepal, 13–14;

knowledge vacuum for, 42; laypeople trained in, 14, 68–69; lead-up to counseling sessions, as factor in success of, 79; listening as key component of, xviii, 15, 38, 106, 127, 134; methods/ practices of, 13, 23–24, 51; neoliberal framing of, 37, 91; and the People's War, 13, 33–34; physical environment as factor in, 66, 70–74; private, 100; on the radio, 1–4, 131; rarity of, before 2015 earthquake response, 4, 12; training for, 3–5, 13–14, 16–17, 24, 28, 29, 30, 31, 34–35, 41, 82–83, 86–87, 100, 129, 138; UN guidelines on, 41. See also care; counselors; efficacy of humanitarian care; intersubjective otherwise; mental health/illness/affliction/distress; transient psychosocial care

mental health/illness/affliction/distress: abandonment of people with, 20, 28, 43–44, 138; development/modernization as causes of, 26–28; economic and social development affected by, 27–28, 34, 37; framing of, 2–3, 5, 7, 9, 19–20, 23–26, 34, 36–45, 59, 120, 135; as a human right, 15, 36–37; Nepalis' concealment of, 11–12, 20; Nepalis' postearthquake concern with, 2–5, 15–21, 23, 25–26, 39–45, 131–32; non-disaster-related causes of, 5, 22, 35, 89, 94, 97, 103, 107, 109–10, 112, 118–20, 122, 132; organizations' concern with, 2–3, 5; plurality of causes for, 97; stigma associated with, 14, 31, 37, 38, 42, 48, 65, 116, 117, 124, 132, 134, 135; traditional approaches to, 3, 12–15, 24, 31. See also depression/anxiety; global mental health; mental health and psychosocial support; post-traumatic stress disorder (PTSD); suffering; tension

Merry, Sally Engle, 92
MGMH. See Movement for Global Mental Health
MHPSS. See mental health and psychosocial support
migration, 10, 35, 53, 109–11
Mills, China, 149n38
Ministry for Women and Children, 39
Ministry of Health and Population, 39, 41
miracle question, 111, 115, 125, 159n41. See also intersubjective otherwise
modernization, 26
moksa. See liberation
monsoons, 13, 35, 50, 98, 134, 136
morality. See ethics and morality
Moran, Dermot, 146n32
Morimoto, Ryo, 145n7
mourning, xiii, 106, 131
Movement for Global Mental Health (MGMH), 14, 20, 149n38
MSF. See Médecins San Frontières
Murphy, Michelle, 37
mutual aid, 74, 156n38

Nagarjuna, v, 62, 139
nasako rog. See nerve illness
National Mental Health Policy, 32, 138
National Mental Health Strategy and Action Plan, 138
neoliberalism, 37, 91, 111
Nepal: caste discrimination in, 93, 157n25, 157n28; Christianity in, 157n29; Constituent Assembly, 40; constitution (2015) of, 40, 151n81; democracy in, 11, 33; demographics of, 148n85; economy of, 10, 35, 110; emotional expression in, 11, 49, 53–55, 105, 120–21, 131–32, 152n13; kinship in, 35, 122–23; mental health governance in, 2, 12–15, 20–21, 24, 32, 42–43, 68, 138–39; walking's cultural meanings in, 21, 65, 68. See also earthquakes (2015) in Nepal; rural areas
Nepal Labour Migration Report, 110–11
Nepal Police, 33
nerve illness (nasako rog), 38, 95
NGOs. See nongovernmental organizations
NIMHANS Bangalore, 28
nongovernmental organizations (NGOs), 3–5, 13, 15–18, 23–24, 32, 34, 36, 38–41, 43, 69, 77, 81, 83, 86–87, 91, 93–94, 99, 102, 103, 112–13, 115, 117, 119–20, 138
nothingness/emptiness (sunyata), 56–57, 139, 153n40

Obeyesekere, Gananath, 49, 62–63
objectifications, 6, 8–9, 24, 137. See also frames/ framing
objectivity, 90, 157n12
Okhaldhunga, Nepal, 17, 64, 70, 84
Oliver-Smith, Anthony, 9
ordinary ethics, 129, 160n58, 160n62
Ortner, Sherry, 18, 126
Other, the: biopolitical protection against, 5; care centered on, 113; ethical demand of, 114–15, 122, 124, 129, 133. See also intersubjective otherwise
otherwise. See intersubjective otherwise

pain. See suffering
Palestinians, 47–48
Parry, Jonathan, 52
Partners in Health, 69
People's War (1996–2006), 4, 11, 12, 13, 32–34, 77, 81
Petryna, Adriana, 8–9
phenomenology. See critical phenomenology
post-traumatic stress disorder (PTSD): assumption of, in disaster survivors, 3, 47, 59, 107; as defined in DSM-III, 59; depoliticization accomplished through diagnosis of, 47–48; framing of, by international organizations, 34; in victims of the People's War, 13, 33–34
Povinelli, Elizabeth, 9, 126
primary health care, 28, 36, 68–69

prolonged grief disorder, 106
psychiatric medication: availability of, 117; cessation of, 100, 112; client compliance with, 94–97, 99–100, *101*, 103, 116, 135–36; controversies over, 3, 15; criticisms of, 149n38; effectiveness of, 94–96, 99–100, 102–3, 115–17; free, 45, 48, 99–100, 112, 117–18, 135, 157n36; global mental health care and, 116; personal expenditures on, 99–100, 103, 118, 135; prescription of, 115, 119, 138
psychoeducation, 4, 13–14, 23, 42, 48
psychogeography, 66, 70–74
psychosocial support. *See* mental health and psychosocial support
PTSD. *See* post-traumatic stress disorder
pujas (ritual ceremonies), xv, 3, 96, 104
Pupavac, Vanessa, 47

radio, 131
Radio Nepal, xvi–xvii, 1
Ramechhap, Nepal, 17, 64, 70, 79–81
Rana, Brahma Shumsher Jung Bahadur, 12
randomized control trials (RCTs), 91–92, 108, 157n16
rape, 33
Raschig, Megan, 126
RCTs. *See* randomized control trials
Rechtman, Richard, 34
Red Cross, 51
Redfield, Peter, 43, 161n12
regimes of care, 111–12
religion, 138. *See also* Christianity; Hinduism; Tibetan Buddhism; Zen Buddhism
remittances, 10, 35, 110
repair: conceptualizations of, 12, 19, 20, 21, 25, 50, 62, 63, 85, 137, 139; critical attitude compatible with, 134; and Kleinian reparation, 19, 123, 127, 159n36; and the needs of the Other, 161n19; practices of, 19, 49, 128, 139, 140, 162n24; of worlds/nations, 34, 63, 113, 139
reparative approach, 19, 115, 132, 133, 137, 160n2
resilience, 9–12, 147n55
rights, 11–12, 15, 36–37, 111–12, 137, 138
Rivers, William, 127
Robbins, Joel, 18
Roberts, Elizabeth, 108
Roitman, Janet, 24
rural areas: earthquakes' effects in, 1, 10–11; living conditions in, 10; mental health programs in, 4; oppression and domination in, 12; romanticization of, 11–12

sadhus (ascetics), 58
samsara (world of suffering and illusion), 49, 56–59
Sartorius, Norman, 28
Scheper-Hughes, Nancy, 155n24
school. *See* education

Sedgwick, Eve Kosofsky, 19, 132, 133
shamans, 3, *30*, 38, 88, 97, 119
Sharma, Robin, xvii
Sherpa people, 147n63
Shneiderman, Sara, 65
solidarity: of counselors and clients, 21, 65, 74; in humanitarian community, 82–85; mutual aid as formation of, 74; obstacles to, in humanitarianism, 67; types of, 67
spaces of welcome, 127
Spade, Dean, 67, 74, 156n38
spirit possession. *See* ghost and spirit possession
Stern, Daniel, 127–28
Stevenson, Lisa, 113
Strathern, Marilyn, 87
Stuelke, Patricia, 133–34
suffering (*dukha*): concealment of, 11, 49, 53–55, 63, 105, 120–21, 131–32, 152n13; disturbance/interruption of, 125, 132; as essential part of life, 49, 55–58, 62, 105; ethics of transient care for, 19, 22, 132; ghosts' infliction of, 3, 56; giving meaning to, 49–50; non-disaster-related causes of, 5, 22, 35, 89, 103, 107, 109–10, 112, 114, 118–20, 122, 132; salience/making visible of, 1–7, 9, 120; technical approach to, 39. *See also* depression/anxiety; mental health/illness/affliction/distress
suicide, 103, 118, 121, 122, 159n33
sunyata. See nothingness/emptiness
Swiss Agency for Development and Cooperation, 23

Tamang, Siera, 11
task-shifting, 69, 88
tension, xiii–xiv, xvii–xviii, 131. *See also* depression/anxiety; mental health/illness/affliction/distress
therapeutic care. *See* care; efficacy of humanitarian care; mental health and psychosocial support
Throop, C. Jason, 88, 155n18, 161n7
Tibetan Buddhism: concept of the world in, 58–59, 62; and death, 52, 53, 55–59; liberation as goal of, 58–59
Tibetan medicine, 3
Ticktin, Miriam, 112
Timmermans, Stefan, 157n21
Tironi, Manuel, 9
Toadvine, Ted, 146n22
Tol, Wietse, 157n16
torture, 32–33
transient care: client interactions with, 109; consequences of, 1, 15, 89, 99–101; ethics of, 15, 19, 22, 113, 129, 132; limits and possibilities of, 5, 19, 22, 89, 97–98, 103, 112–18, 124, 126–27, 132
trauma. *See* post-traumatic stress disorder
Tribhuvan University, Kathmandu, Nepal, 121

Tronto, Joan, 113
Turin, Mark, 123

UMN. *See* United Mission to Nepal
UNESCO, 26
UNICEF, 1, 23
United Mission to Nepal (UMN), 4, 28–32, 38; training cards for, *29, 30*
United Nations: High Commissioner for Refugees, 33; Inter-Agency Standing Committee (IASC), 41, 51; Mental Health Sub-Cluster, 39, 41–44, 138; National Health Cluster, 39; Office for Disaster Risk Reduction, 10; Office for the Coordination of Humanitarian Affairs, 39–41; Psychosocial Working Group, 40, 42, 44
United States Agency for International Development (USAID), 135
UNM. *See* United Mission to Nepal

Vaughan, Megan, 26
victimhood, humanitarian conceptions/frames of, 1, 5, 21–22, 34, 35, 48, 88, 97, 100–101, 103, 111–12, 132–33
violence: of care regimes, 113–14, 132–33; of humanitarianism, 19, 22, 108, 114, 116, 121, 122, 124, 128–29, 132–34; women subject to, 103, 119, 121

Waldram, James, 89
walking, *71, 75*; cultural meanings of, 21, 65, 68, 72, 85; habit/lifestyle of, 70, 72; as a moral experience, 78–79; and psychogeography, 66–67; solidarity achieved through, 65–68; women and, 68
WFMH. *See* World Federation for Mental Health
WHO. *See* World Health Organization

Wiegman, Robyn, 161n2
Willen, Sarah, 127
WIRED (magazine), 24
witchcraft. *See* magic
women: as counselors, 68; in Nepali culture, 18, 68, 77–78; suicides of, 103, 108, 121, 122, 159n33; violence against, 103, 119, 121; and walking, 68
work of culture, 49, 52, 62–63
work of disaster: benefits for clients created by, 22, 43, 114, 118, 135; care and concern in, 113, 126, 130; counselors' role in, 22, 67, 133, 135; critical examination of, 9, 19–20, 26, 137, 139–40; defined, 6, 63; jobs created by, 134; material and psychological conditions of, 85; mental health framed by, 7, 15, 44; suffering made visible by, 89, 97, 100, 103, 120
world: Hindu/Buddhist concept of, 58–59, 62; phenomenological concept of, 58
World Bank, 36–37; *World Development Report*, 36
World Federation for Mental Health (WFMH), 26–27
World Health Organization (WHO), 20, 27–28, 32, 36–37, 41, 44, 68–69; *Building Back Better*, 24–25, 37, 44–45, 99, 118, 138; Global Burden of Disease Report, 36; Mental Health Gap Programme, 100
World Mental Health (book), 36
World Mental Health Casebook, 32
World War I, 127
Wright, Christine, 31, 32

Young, Allen, 89, 101

Zen Buddhism, 56
Zigon, Jarrett, 8, 126

www.ingramcontent.com/pod-product-compliance
Lightning Source LLC
Chambersburg PA
CBHW032137020426
42334CB00016B/1193